S0-AIZ-887

AMERICAN EDUCATION

Its Men

Ideas

and

Institutions

Democracy's College

The Land-Grant Movement in the Formative State

Earle D. Ross

ARNO PRESS & THE NEW YORK TIMES

*New York * 1969*

*

Library of Congress Catalog Card No. 74-89226

*

This edition is published by arrangement with
Iowa State University Press

*

Reprinted from a copy in
The New York State Library

*

Manufactured in the United States of America

Editorial Note

AMERICAN EDUCATION: *Its Men, Institutions and Ideas* presents selected works of thought and scholarship that have long been out of print or otherwise unavailable. Inevitably, such works will include particular ideas and doctrines that have been outmoded or superseded by more recent research. Nevertheless, all retain their place in the literature, having influenced educational thought and practice in their own time and having provided the basis for subsequent scholarship.

Lawrence A. Cremin
Teachers College

Democracy's College

The Land-Grant Movement in the Formative State

Democracy's College

THE LAND-GRANT MOVEMENT
IN THE FORMATIVE STAGE

By Earle D. Ross
DEPARTMENT OF HISTORY AND GOVERNMENT
IOWA STATE COLLEGE

Published in 1942, By
THE IOWA STATE COLLEGE PRESS
AMES, IOWA

PRINTED AT THE COLLEGIATE PRESS, INC.
IOWA STATE COLLEGE, AMES, IOWA, U.S.A.

TABLE OF CONTENTS

CHAPTER I

THE RISE OF AN AMERICAN SYSTEM OF EDUCATION

The land-grant college is a peculiarly American institution. It developed under native conditions and provided an essential element in the national educational system. For, as Paul Monroe has emphasized, with all the diversities in form and emphasis between states and localities, "there is a *system*" which in "the essential features of method, of curriculum, of organization, of purpose . . . can be identified as American, distinct from those of any other people."[1] The rise of such a system was one phase of an awakening nationalism.

It was in that formative half century during which national independence was consolidated through the building of a strong government and a thriving economy and was given assured expression in a native art and literature that there emerged this distinctive type of education—no less real because largely unconscious and unformulated. All these manifestations of latent nationality were so genuinely indigenous and practically purposed that systematic formulation was not required to justify them. With the nation actively and elaborately "on the make," doctrines were seldom promulgated except when needed to buttress and rationalize particular policies. Thus constitutional theories grew out of the attempted adjustment of the sectional balance of economic and social interests, diplomatic pronouncements were mainly concerned with specific controversies over colonization and trade, and the efforts of a nascent American school of economics to vindicate the pragmatic program of an American system of business were but an early attempt to make a workable application of the doctrine of national interest.

Analytical criticism of ideas and institutions was left to foreign observers. Though it reflected the American spirit and purpose no less truly, if more tardily and reservedly, than the homestead, the factory, the clipper, and the hustings, education certainly was not speculative; the immediate concerns—political participation, social uplift, and industrial efficiency—were too pressing to allow time for the consideration of origins and philosophies. American pedagogy was pragmatic long before the days of formalized pragmatism. Like other parts of the national establishment, the developing school system was a resultant of the free adaptation of European ideas and practices to the needs of an emerging society. The zeal with which Old World educational philosophies and practices were drawn upon was equalled only by the freedom with which they were modified and adjusted to conform to New World attitudes and purposes. The systems of Pestalozzi, Fellenberg, Herbart, and Froebel; monitorial and tutorial methods; object, shop, laboratory, and seminar—all might be transplanted enthusiastically, but invariably they took an unmistakable Yankee form and emphasis.

Despite a range of precedent embracing the whole experience of ancient, medieval, and modern teaching, a free and regionally varied experimentation, and the motivating forces of modern democracy and industrialism, American educational evolution has shown a degree of continuity that reflects a dominant and unifying motive. The determining influence has been that of popular determination and direction—a democratic system according to the expanding conceptions of that term. Such an aim has resulted in a progressive widening of opportunity, secular control on the basis of state initiative and federal aid, a liberal curriculum, vocational training, and an increasing concern over social welfare. While the emphasis has varied at different stages, these objectives have in some measure had a parallel development throughout, and all were definitely forecast by the forties.

The material basis for the establishment of such a democratic system lay in the peculiar national resource, the public domain. It was land, the main incentive in colonization, transoceanic and transcontinental, which provided down to the Civil War the financial resources necessary for public enterprises, "internal improvements" and education. In their origins all the branches of the American system of education from lowest to highest are "land-grant." In the colonial era the English practice of endowing educational and ecclesiastical establishments with land, the abundance of that form of property, and the scarcity of other capital funds made such gifts and rentals the chief basis for the support of educational as of most other public enterprises. Systems of land disposal in the various colonies exercised accordingly a determining influence upon the promotion of schools and colleges. There was a direct connection between the democratic land system of New England and the relative advancement of schools in that section.[2] The removal of tenure and settlement restrictions in the social reforms of the Revolution,[3] and the creation through that struggle of the first segment of the public domain had major significance for the future education of the nation. Most of the original states devoted the greater part of their own considerable domains to a common school fund and occasionally to aid for colleges. In its basic ordinance governing land disposal the Congress of the Confederation made somewhat generous provisions for education in the township reservations, not so much through benevolent foresight as from the pressure of learning-conscious prospective New England settlers. Likewise, in the contracts with the Ohio Company and the Miami proprietor, seminary or university grants were "wrung from the hands of an unwilling Congress."[4] Thus were established the precedents for the practice of the federal Congress in the successive state enabling acts of making regular provisions for schools and universities. Notwithstanding the generosity of these grants, Congress was besieged by the states from the twenties to the Civil War for additional special donations in aid of schools and colleges, but such supplications were rarely given any consideration.[5]

On a comparative basis the educational grants were easily justified,[6] but the record of the administration of these subsidies by the states was often one of resources tragically neglected or dissipated. Instead of the potentially princely endowments, comparative pittances were realized. Immediate pressure for funds, incompetence, regional competition, and flagrant corruption were responsible for long-time leases, short-sighted sales, poor investments, loss or diversion of funds. The system as a whole exhibits a horrible example in public finance.[7] The importance of the pre-Civil War grants lies therefore not so much in the permanent support provided as in their influence in furthering the movement for popular control and direction of the educational policies of the various states.

To the frontier influence there was added in the twenties and thirties that of the rising labor movement. Before the period of industrial specialization with its tendency toward fixation of status, labor leaders advocated general education as a means of social and political equality. Agitation for free schools was a natural phase of the leveling trend of the Jacksonian era;[8] there was an unanswerable and irresistible logic in universal education for manhood suffrage. It was inevitable, too, given the equalitarian appeal, that the popular system would extend beyond the elementary stage. The academy marked a widening of opportunity as well as a broadening of the range of studies over the old grammar school, and the American adaptation of the Fellenberg manual labor system provided, where tried, an institution still more democratic in extent and practical in content.[9] The full attainment of free education at the secondary level came, however, in the "free academy" or public high school which, from modest beginnings in the twenties, was steadily to grow in favor until it dominated both the finishing and college preparatory fields, although this function was to be relatively retarded and to leave for long a "missing link" between the elementary and higher levels.[10]

The same liberalizing influences tended toward the abolition of sex discriminations. The opportunity was improved strategically by the constructive champions of the cause—Emma Willard, Catherine Beecher, and Mary Lyon. In their epochal pronouncements and historic schools they gave marked impetus to the great objectives, old and new, of equal rights in secondary and higher education: religious nurture and character formation, scientific training for parenthood and household management, effective teacher training and placement, and the progressive opening of other vocations.[11] The case for the full inclusion of women in the American educational system was thus presented and on the way to definite realization by the forties, even though crusading Oberlin was the only college to venture the revolutionary trial of coeducation. The better seminaries, while modestly eschewing the conferring of degrees, provided the equivalent of the standard men's colleges, often with an extended program. The emphasis given to science and modern literature, regarded as more naturally appropriate to women's interests and capacities, influenced the transition from the classical dominance.[12]

In accord with American governmental principles and prejudices, a public school system including all classes and both sexes necessitated public control. In the colonies, as in the mother country, the typical educational project had been but an adjunct of established religion in aim, content, and direction. Against such general conformity the material trends of the eighteenth century opposed a secularizing influence that the evangelical zeal did not offset. Revolutionary theory in Europe and America was strongly hostile to religious establishment, and the dominant interest of the period was political. Variety of faiths, based upon national origins and sectarian division, made the constitutional provision for freedom of religion expedient as well as enlightened. The same influences operated in breaking surviving ecclesiastical control in the old states and preventing its establishment in the new, which had the added responsibility of training citizens for a political participation based on full manhood suffrage. While interested groups waged intermittent opposition, the battle for secular status was practically won by the fifties.[13]

Public responsibility for education presented the questions of the agency and method of control and the extent of provision. The New England township unit, perpetuated in the West by the early land grants, served passably only for a temporary stage of neighborhood development; it was a typically frontier system of policy determination that gave way gradually before the needs and interests of developing commonwealths. Educational supervision and standardization were to constitute one of the most vital issues in state administrative centralization. An essential phase of the educational awakening of the thirties lay in the beginnings of city and state supervision, but these efforts at administrative efficiency had long to contend against narrow prejudice and financial interest. State control came only with the acceptance of extended functions. Jefferson's inclusive design of a state supported and controlled system extending from the primary grades to the graduate school of a liberalized polytechnic university was very incompletely realized before the Civil War. In his own section the growth was from the top, with capstone universities founded before the understructure had been built.[14]

However premature their pretensions to full university status and to the direction of the state's education, these institutions were notable achievements in the development of popular education. They marked the goal to be attained in higher education and, illogical though it might be, the need for development at the lower levels to reach this highest goal. In two sections, through different combinations of influences and conditions, the state university found ready acceptance. In the South it was welcomed as a liberal protest against sectarian control and as a congenial recognition of the dignity and authority of the state. Georgia's was the earliest to be chartered, North Carolina's the first to provide instruction, and Virginia's, in organization and scope, by far the most significant.[15] The western type reflected equalitarian social ideals, land-grant foundation, and a widened program. It was an attempt to extend popular education to the highest levels and the widest ranges. The University of Michigan was the outstanding pioneer of the typical state university[16] which was to come to completed function by the addition of the technical content and inclusive appeal of the land-grant college, either in organic union or by complementary institutional establishment.

With many educational reformers in the formative as in the present period, the logical step to effective public education was a large, if not determining, degree of national activity. From the winning of independence there were proposals for the national establishment and control of education as a means of safeguarding the blessings of liberty and attaining the fuller realization of the great social ideals that had inspired the revolutionry movement on both sides of the water. To both Old and New World philosophers the infant republic offered the great opportunity for a conscious promotion of the instructional function for the attainment and direction of social progress. The nation itself, it was felt, was the only adequate and appropriate agency for this cultural indoctrination; the responsibility could not be left to the irregularity and inadequacy of regional determination. The movement thus combined social idealism with nationalistic enthusiasm and it was naively conscious and deliberate. The American Philosophical Society offered prizes for plans of national education, and broad-visioned social thinkers like Benjamin Rush, Robert Coram, DuPont de Nemours, and Noah Webster presented elaborate schemes on their own initiative.[17] Meanwhile, whatever the basis of control and direction, the textbook writers could do their bit to inculcate national consciousness and patriotic attitudes. Noah Webster and Jedidiah Morse provided readers, geographies, and histories characterized by native themes, ideas, and often prejudices, and Nicholas Pike even brought out a special arithmetic in the expectation that a "System might be calculated more suitable to our Meridian than those heretofore published."[18] Likewise, new colleges in astounding number were justified both as evidence of a native culture and as agencies for its extension and perpetuation.[19]

A still more specific proposal was that for a national university at the permanent seat of government. This had been the one educational question discussed in the constitutional convention and it was given enthusiastic support by a large number of representative leaders. With characteristic definiteness, while others talked, Washington projected the institution with a bequest. The endowment was lost—even from the record—and, while the project has had intermittent agitation down to the present, it has remained, like most of the other schemes of general national education, unrealized.[20]

In the twenties and thirties idealistic labor reformers like

Robert Owen, with the characteristic indifference of radical pressure groups to constitutional demarcations, advocated "national public schools," supported in part by congressional appropriations, as a means to immediate, standardized schooling opportunities for the masses.[21] Obviously, in a period in which the traditions of state rights and the practices of frontier individualism were so determining, there was lacking a sufficient sentiment of centralization and socialization to make possible federal initiative in educational policy involving the fixing of standards. The only nationally controlled institutions were the Military Academy, which—like military roads among internal improvements—involved the appeal of the common defense, and the very humble beginnings of federally supported scientific establishments. Direct congressional aid to education continued to be in land grants, specific and general, and in the distribution of surplus revenues most of which were devoted to the respective school funds. This aid involved no federal supervision or qualifying condition. The only obligation on the states to fulfill the intent of the acts was a moral one, and that was too often regarded indifferently. At this stage federal participation involved in effect outright gifts rather than grants-in-aid, subsidies rather than subventions.[22]

By whatever authority controlled, the effective functioning of popular education required a modernizing and rationalizing of organization and method. Autocratic school management was as inharmonious to a democratic society as authoritarian teaching was to a scientific. The old standard of "one primer, one catechism, one rod for all children" had had nothing but simplicity in its favor, and in the Jacksonian freedom even the children had their hour. The educational awakening of the thirties directed by leaders like Horace Mann, Henry Barnard, James G. Carter, and William Russell was a protest against the old in method as well as in administration and support.[23] The most advanced European practices, especially of Switzerland and Prussia, were presented in celebrated reports[24] and, against long and persistent opposition, adaptations were made to American schools. Acceptance was gradually won for such elemental propositions as that teaching skill was not wholly or mainly a matter of physical strength, that interest seriously motivated provided the strongest incentive to learning, and that specialized equipment and attractive surroundings were essential for achieving the best results. Less formalized textbooks were made available, and teacher-training was improved by journals, lyceums, institutes, and normal schools. The general public was becoming literacy conscious. Shrewdly and realistically, with all of the curricular adjustments and innovations that such an aim might imply, Mann emphasized the economic values of general education.[25]

Improved methods came mainly from the broadening of the curriculum both at the lower and higher levels. By the twenties the classical autocracy was being challenged by daring pioneers—most notably at Union, Amherst, and Vermont—with proposals for a very moderate range of electives and optional nondegree courses; but even these limited departures from a straight and narrow prescription met with such intolerant opposition that they failed to make any marked impress on the traditional curriculum and organization.[26]

The innovation that was ultimately to work the greatest revolution in modern education was the movement to develop the natural and physical sciences as regular and coordinate subjects. The formulation of fundamental principles of scientific learning in the late eighteenth and early nineteenth centuries had provided the materials and pointed the method, but for a long time science came into the program tentatively and on sufferance as among the lesser tables of the academic law. Teaching was in didactic formula and subject to controls of demonstration and inhibitions of conclusions that meant the negation of true scientific method. As late as his inaugural in 1869, Eliot could make the utterly damning charge that "prevailing methods of teaching science, the world over, are, on the whole, less intelligent than the methods of teaching language."[27] The spectacular rather than the significant tended to be emphasized in demonstrations, as in the case of the old chemistry professor whose student, tiring of his lectures, asked when he would do more of his "tricks."[28] In the popular view, as reflected in fictional and sensational news portrayals, there was much of mystery, not to say magic, connected with the scientist and his laboratory. When in 1849 Professor John W. Webster at Harvard essayed the perfect murder by seeking to exterminate the *corpus delicti* in a chemical furnace, many no doubt felt that there was a natural connection between the crime and its setting.[29] Before the establishment of standards and standardizing agencies there was indeed much of charlatanry and chicanery under the guise of science, both pure and applied. But in spite of all handicaps and limitations the sciences as subjects of study were making an assault upon the traditional curriculum that would not be repulsed.

For those who would draw distinctions more or less invidious between science in its pure and applied states, it should be moderating to reflect that while the development of basic principles was essential to the making of applications, it was the demand for applications in various special fields that led to the initiation of most direct scientific investigations. Thus the incentive and justification for chemical experimentation was largely in connection with medicine, soils and plants, and minerals. Geology and physics as well as mathematics were needed by the engineer, whether military or civil. Botany and entomology gained chief support in their horticultural applications.

The professions, learned and technical, had need of scientific principles and of a method to give them assured standing in a changing social order. The "learned," as the term was traditionally employed, were as a class entitled to that designation only by courtesy. Professional training, when available, was to be had only in narrow, dogmatic, and highly formalized "schools" of thought and practice, but for the overwhelming majority, lawyers were office-read, physicians, apprentice-trained, and ministers, emotionally inspired. Not until the end of the fifties was there any appreciable improvement. By that time there was evidence not only of a marked increase in the number of professional schools but, within the restricted limits of most of the subjects, of a better organized and more thorough instruction. A hopeful indication was the growth of a more critical attitude within and without professional circles.[30]

Technical training made its way slowly but inevitably. The frontier both postponed and intensified the need for it as self-sufficient cultivation and hand industry were superseded by diversified farm and factory, and primitive transportation by the agencies and utilities of modern trade. Yankee inventive and organizing genius awaited only increase of population, social stability, and the consequent growth of markets. From the time of Benjamin Franklin and Benjamin Tompkins, the utilitarian possibilities of the new science had been appreciated. De Tocqueville, after calling attention to the natural interest and unusual opportunity of the new republic in the practical utilization of science, concluded, "It is evident, that, in democratic communities the interest of individuals, as well as the security of the commonwealth, demands that the education of the greater number should be scientific, commercial, and industrial, rather than literary."[31]

This emphasis found supporters from the latter half of the eighteenth century. The Philadelphia academy and its university successor, while not going as far in practical emphasis as the founder desired, was a pioneer in instruction in science as well as in secular control.[32] Early universities recognized the basic occupation in nominal chairs of agriculture, a study to which Washington would have given prominent place in his national university. But the first technical field in which there was provided systematic instruction on the higher level was that of military science. The academy established by Congress at West Point in 1802 was America's first real technical institute; its graduates became not only army officers but explorers, engineers, and scientists in various fields.[33] Lesser military schools followed the model with varying degrees of attainment. The most influential was a direct offspring. A former commandant, Captain Alden Partridge, founded at Norwich, Vermont, in 1819 the

American Literary, Scientific and Military Academy which emphasized science, mathematics, and physical training in content, and practical projects, optional courses, and a flexible term in method and organization.[34] Numerous other military academies followed, especially in the South, and the military influence was strong in certain of the state universities.

Meanwhile, the commoner occupations were not wholly neglected. The manual labor schools and the female seminaries were incidentally vocational, while the lyceum movement in New England and private benefactions in Pennsylvania provided centers of direct practical training. The Gardiner Lyceum in Maine, a private establishment with state aid, gave instruction in agriculture and mechanics for a decade (1821–1832) during which several future leaders in the land-grant movement were students or instructors.[35] The Agricultural Seminary at Derby, Connecticut, had attractive plans but endured barely a year.[36] In the urban sphere, the Girard College for the vocational education of orphans and the Franklin Institute, a sort of instructional and investigational engineering clearinghouse, had the same general purpose.[37]

By far the most notable and influential venture in technical education in this explorative period was the Rensselaer Institute, started at Troy, New York, in 1824. The benevolent-minded founder's broad design, expanded from a manual labor school plan, included every vocational interest. His "principal object" was "to qualify teachers for instructing the sons and daughters of farmers and mechanics, by lectures or otherwise, in the application of experimental chemistry, philosophy and natural history to agriculture, domestic economy, the arts, and manufactures." Fortunately for so general and inclusive a scheme an able scientist and great teacher, Amos Eaton, was secured to head the enterprise. Eaton's relations with Van Rennselaer suggest an interesting parallel to those of Andrew D. White with Ezra Cornell as among the rare cases of continuing harmonious cooperation between resident patron and administrator. While the original plan was never fully developed—the domestic training was not established, and the agricultural course did not continue beyond the formative years—the developments in organization, methods, and especially in emphasis, constituted a turning point in technical education. The institution may make a strong case for a remarkable number of "origins"—systematized individual laboratory work, field experimentation, observation trips, scientific research on a graduate level, and varied extension activities were all to some degree anticipated. Most striking departure of all was its open and confident break with all past subject-matter traditions in American collegiate education. The relations of this pioneer in technical education to the land-grant movement in leaders, subject emphasis, and methodology are clearly established.[38] But Eaton and his fellow workers were many years in advance of their time.[39]

It appears, then, that by the forties the nation's chief educational need was an adequate provision for vocational training which awaited mainly the course of economic and social evolution. Only when the limitations of primitive exploitation were sufficiently manifested could there arise class-conscious interests and movements which would compel the creation of institutions at the higher as at the lower levels adapted to popular needs and desires, people's colleges as the crowning feature of a democratic school system.

CHAPTER II

THE INDUSTRIAL MOVEMENT IN STATE AND NATION

The forties—"roaring," "fabulous," "hot air," as variously depicted by the sensational chronicler—owed their special turbulence to numerous and persistent, though often ill-advised, efforts to deal with the cumulative economic and social maladjustments which by this decade were being experienced even in the land which throughout the western world was symbolic of opportunity. The panic of 1837 had brought to disillusioning culmination the era of youthful, carefree plunging and unreasoned confidence. Primitive abundance, of easy appropriation and simple organization, was giving place to settled production and capitalistic control, with consequent inequalities. Modern class divisions were beginning to appear. The political revolution of the preceding decades had provided the means for the protection and, as soon as there should be sufficient sentiment for such action, for the positive advancement of the common man. European radical philosophies and organizations, reflecting the more intense industrial struggle along with agrarian limitations, found in America the freest and most practicable conditions for social and economic as well as political innovation.

Educational reform and extension were inevitable phases of the general movement. With the increasing application of science to the industries, the broadened social vision of certain educational leaders, and the growing class consciousness of farmer and labor groups, the emphasis was more definitely vocational than ever before. Like the other great reform efforts this "Industrial Movement" passed through the emotional vagaries of the forties into the more stabilized thinking of the fifties only to be obstructed by the sectional conflict and in turn to be unnaturally accelerated by the war for the union.

In its broadest scope and truest aim, this movement to apply the findings of the new sciences and the technique and organization of the new education to the changing business and social order marked the most socialized phase of the educational awakening. It was an effort to keep education in touch with the world of affairs, to give it reality and hence vitality. That the traditional instruction was wholly out of harmony with the needs and desires of mid-century America there was evidence on every hand. Secondary training was meeting a persistent demand for a broader program and a wider availability, and college enrollments were declining markedly at the very time when actual and potential need for technical training was increasing. Cold statistics gave verification to Francis Wayland's sententious summary of the plight of the old-line college in his report to the Brown corporation in 1850: "Our colleges are not filled, because we do not furnish the education desired by the people. . . . We have produced an article for which the demand is diminishing. We sell it at less than cost, and the deficiency is made up by charity. We give it away; and still the demand diminishes."[1] The need for technical education was patent, but in seeking it social inertia and established interests occasioned obstructing delay, dissipating conflicts, and eventual adjusting compromises.

Opposition from the old order, while having the persistence of the traditional and vested, was not highly effective. The main hindrances and confusions arose out of the differences and indifferences among the varied adherents of the movement and their constituencies. The scientists, however benevolent their ultimate design, were mainly concerned with the extension and verification of their subjects as a necessary condition of their application. The agitators, in contrast, were desirous of securing more direct and amplified instruction and of gaining immediate practical advantage. Popular writers and lecturers who sought to reconcile the two points of view generally failed to secure the confidence of either side.

By the fifth decade applied science was being put on the modern experimental basis as a result of the teachings and writings of such masters as Liebig at Giessen and Munich, Boussingault at Paris, and Johnston at Edinburgh. American students sought these centers of special training and original research, and with the effective support of immigrant scientists provided on their return the basis for a native technical education.[2]

With its shifting areas and changing methods of cultivation and husbandry, the domesticating of the factory, and the extension of its canals, railroads, and telegraphs, the America of 1840–60 had peculiar needs for inventive and managerial talent. As Wayland reminded his board, "Lands were to be surveyed, roads to be constructed, ships to be built and navigated, soils of every kind, and under every variety of climate, were to be cultivated, manufactures were to be established which must soon come into competition with those of more advanced nations; and, in a word, all the means which science has provided to aid the progress of civilization must be employed if this youthful republic would place itself abreast of the empires of Europe."[3]

But with the lack of institutional foundations and organizations, private and public, and with the traditional lack of appreciation for the expert, careers for the select group were decidedly uncertain. Quacks and dangerously under-learned amateurs brought confusion and discredit. Liebig's work had aroused a zeal for analyzing soils and fertilizers that was exploited by "consultants" of doubtful competence; new agricultural practices became the hobby of medical leisure; theologians and sentimental journalists made a fashionable fad of horticulture and landscaping; and self-trained practicing civil engineers rendered their services without the restraints and checks of the higher mathematics.[4] Legislatures in several of the eastern states gave recognition to the value of the new ideas and methods by providing for a state chemist or "agriculturist" who was to make analyses of soils, fertilizers, feeds, and other products and, in some cases, to serve as an itinerant lecturer before the regional societies.[5] Such establishments, however, were bound to be ineffective except in helping to show the real needs. The intermittent agricultural activities in the Patent Office under agents of varying competence provided no greater professional opportunity.[6] The scientists were challenged to give popular demonstrations of the utility of their theories and techniques, and this required a working agreement, at least, with reform leaders seeking through technical education the material betterment and the consequent enhanced social standing and political influence of their particular groups.

During this decade of reform and innovation, such champions were vociferous if not always coherent. The labor groups, having learned the futility of merging their cause in that of general uplift and amelioration, were coming to see that they must look out for themselves. Education was now sought not merely for general training but for special competence in craftsmanship as well. Organizations, lecturers, and official journals emphasized that special training was both a protection against losing a job one had and a means to getting a better one.[7]

A similar appeal was made to the group-consciousness of the farmers. Local and state societies, hitherto restricted to a small circle of gentleman farmers in the older states, became general and popular. Agricultural papers numbering a score in 1840 had increased to three dozen by the end of the decade, providing organs of increasing attractiveness and service to all areas and branches of the occupation.[8] Politicians were appealing more directly and pointedly than ever before to the farmer vote; anticipating the complaints of the Granger and Populist movements, they stressed the discriminations and disparities from which agriculture suffered. Characteristic of the time, the remedy was held to lie, not in governmental regulation, but in self-help supplemented with a modicum of public aid. Professional education was expected to give competence in production and business management, social recognition, and political influence. The states, it was charged, were lavish in subsidies for the training of the overcrowded and too often predatory professions; the nation provided elaborate military and naval instruction; but the basic occupation with its peculiar scientific and managerial requirements was abandoned to primitive empiricism. Consequently, there was an increasing conviction that the more socially and intellectually gifted should seek something better, and the prevailing education, reflecting this attitude, was urban-minded, in content and emphasis, socially and economically.[9]

The "industrial classes," themselves, farmer and laborer, while all too conscious of their difficulties and disabilities, especially in the years of depression, were by no means convinced that special occupational training was the solution. Craftsmanship as a life career was unsettled both by progressive mechanization and by attractive, if often illusory, proprietary possibilities. The typical farmer, with frontier background or foreground, was governed by established tradition which gave tolerable guidance for operations within human control and reconciled him to a fatalistic acceptance of the inscrutable and unmodifiable manifestations of nature. Learning beyond the basic R's was regarded as superfluous and distracting. This indifference and inertia was reinforced more positively by popular disinclination to support new educational ventures, either by private contribution or taxation.[10] In the public land West, to be sure, the proposal from almost any cause to secure an additional portion of the state's assumed vested share of the national estate met with general approval, however much contention there might be over the disposal and administration of the proceeds. But directly or indirectly, the proposal to vote oneself or one's children an education never had the personal appeal of voting oneself a farm.

A line of lesser resistance in educational innovation, then as in later times, was the public schools. They were already established in the northern states with equipment, such as it was, and teachers, such as they were: why not vocationalize them through or by addition to the rudimentary subjects? The president of the New York Agricultural Society in his address in 1846 inquired rhetorically why they might not introduce into their primary schools "a class of studies which are designed to teach the scholars the properties of the earth on which we dwell, the variety and composition of plants and grains which are grown, the laws by which they are regulated and governed."[11] Already an enthusiastic deputy state superintendent of public instruction was devising a plan to this end, and a convention of acquiescent county superintendents endorsed agricultural teaching by dialogues and conversations as well as the development of reference libraries.[12] The agitation continued, in the East and Middle West, throughout the prewar period. Premature elementary texts were written, "science cabinets" were secured, and it was proposed to train applied science teachers in the new normal schools. There were even enthusiasts for vocational motivation of the basic subjects in vocabulary, illustration, and moral lesson, but as saner educators recognized from the start, such premature specialization provided no effective technical skill and knowledge and was detrimental to thorough elementary instruction. It was evident that technical education, at whatever level and by whatever agency provided, must, at the least, build upon the elementary school foundation.[13]

With the prevailing attitude toward the scope of governmental activity, initiative in modernizing the curriculum came from the privately controlled colleges. Their departures were in part defensive concessions to the signs and trends of the times and in part progressive adjustments. At Yale the science instruction inaugurated by Timothy Dwight and the elder Silliman (the pioneer promoter of American scientific interests) was developed by 1847 into the school of applied chemistry under the younger Silliman and his brilliant pupil, John Pitkin Norton, who had taken advanced work at Edinburgh and Utrecht. Following Norton's premature death in 1852, the agricultural research was continued by John Addison Porter and Samuel W. Johnson, the latter a Leipsic graduate who had had considerable practical experience as an analytical chemist. Chairs of civil engineering and metallurgy were added in the fifties. These precarious ventures in applied science were given permanence and security in 1860 by the Sheffield endowment.[14] Meanwhile at Harvard in 1847 the Lawrence Scientific School was founded with Agassiz, who was especially interested in the agricultural applications of geology and zoology, as the dominant influence. The Bussey Institution of agricultural research, provided for in a will probated in 1842, marked a significant early interest, but it was not to be organized until 1870.[15] At Amherst, under the sympathetic guidance of Edward Hitchcock, a distinct agricultural course was offered in the science department in 1852 by William S. Clark, a Göttingen Ph. D., and J. A. Nash.[16] The moribund Delaware College prolonged its existence for almost a decade (1851–59) by the addition of a scientific course in which agricultural instruction involving an experimental farm had a leading and appealing place.[17] During the decade general science and civil engineering courses were provided at Union, Dartmouth, Brown, and the University of Michigan.[18]

These scattered beginnings, momentous as they were for the foundation of agricultural and engineering sciences, touched but a small, select group of students and made no direct impress on the masses of farmers and mechanics. The increasing enthusiasm for technical education, prior to the general acceptance of the principle of public aid, was reflected in numerous projects as varied as the individuals and groups sponsoring them. Proprietary and local subscription agricultural schools became well-nigh epidemic during the forties and fifties both North and South, although most of them had no permanent influence.[19] The Cream Hill Agricultural School, founded at West Cornwall, Connecticut by S. W. and T. S. Gold, combined theoretical and practical agriculture, horticulture, and military training with the standard academic subjects; it continued in somewhat modified form for a quarter of a century and provided a model for the state's separate land-grant college.[20] The "school" of James J. Mapes near Newark, New Jersey received unusual contemporary notice by reason of the prominence of the proprietor and certain of his students. Along with his activities as journalist, state "agriculturist," and commercial consultant, this versatile enthusiast for the new agriculture gathered a small group of research students at his experimental farm. Influential leaders in applied science such as Colonel George E. Waring, Henry S. Olcott, and Patrick Quinn were associated with Mapes.[21]

By far the most famous and influential of the privately launched pre-land-grant ventures developed appropriately in that swarming region of social agitation and innovation, Central New York. The People's College was in its inception a labor project. One of the characteristic types of labor organization to develop during the hard times following the panic of 1837 was the order of Mechanics Mutual Protection, which placed main and peculiar emphasis upon "a more general diffusion of the principles and sciences governing mechanics and the arts, to elevate our brethren in their varied capacities and thereby give them the greatest proficiency in their several callings"—a professional training for the craftsman which would give him economic and social parity with the learned professions. The New York convention of 1846 recommended that each lodge or "protection" provide a series of lectures on trade subjects by competent "protectors."[22]

Among such lecturers the ingenious, idealistic cabinetmaker, Harrison Howard, merits a place among American educational reformers. His workers' education plan, formulated after a thorough study of the publications of Weld's Manual Labor School Society and the available reports of European industrial schools, was issued by his local protection in the spring of 1850. This quaint document epitomized the combination of sound and liberal principles with the utopian visioning which characterized so much of the labor movement before the full implications of the new industrialism were faced realistically.

Postulating the basic need of general and technical education for raising mechanics to an equality with the professions, Howard advocated a series of regional schools with one central college as the head and culmination of the system. In a plant complete from workshop and the latest scientific apparatus to assembly halls and "saloons for social reunion" he would provide instruction in "Natural Philosophy, Chemistry, Geometry, Architecture, Drawing, etc., not neglecting any other branches which are taught in our best Colleges and Universities." Manual labor, combined naturally with instruction, would "be regulated in such a manner as to be conducive to the health of the student as well as to sustain the College without pecuniary assistance from other sources." The cost of building, equipment, and support for the first year he proposed to have provided by dollar subscriptions from the mechanics of the state. His public estimate of this expenditure was $100,000, but his vision for the ultimate design was indicated by his penciled annotation, *"Will cost a million but I dare not say so now."*[23]

Reformers in varied fields were favorable to the aim and general plan. Greeley suggested the inclusion of agricultural training, location in the open country, and increased emphasis upon student support, to all of which Howard readily agreed, and the influential editor became an active and aggressive supporter.[24] Prominent politicians, no doubt seeing in the scheme an innocuous appeal for labor and farmer votes, gave more or less perfunctory endorsement. A People's College Association was formed in 1851, held annual conventions for some years, and conducted a campaign of lectures and solicitations with Howard as field representative.[25] The charter "for the purpose of promoting literature, science, arts and agriculture," secured in 1853, fixed the capital stock at $250,000 and provided that the college should be started when $50,000 was paid. The board was directed to provide for "the teaching of sciences most immediately and vitally essential to agriculture and the useful arts" and "to make ample provision for instruction in the classics." Agriculture, manufactures, and industrial arts were to be organized as a regular part of the course, and every student and teacher was to devote from ten to twenty hours each week "to bona fide useful labor in some branch of productive industry." Women's education was not specifically mentioned in the charter, but the prospectus of the previous year had promised that all studies should be "open equally to both sexes" and that special provision would be made for their instruction in household and industrial arts.[26]

Howard as official advocate demonstrated, along with crusading zeal, a clever opportunism. Educational groups were assured that what was proposed was supplemental, not competitive, that the industrial classes who were not provided for under the present system were merely seeking their equivalent in professional training.[27] Military instruction, as preparation for militia service, seemed essential to an inclusive course of study, but at this time Greeley was strongly opposed to any element of military training in industrial education. With much care Howard worked out a formula which, after being amended to exempt conscientious objectors, the *Tribune* chief was persuaded to tolerate. But the issue remained provocative among the constituency. In his lecture notes on "Tactics," Howard added the cautionary suggestion, "Handle the above carefully in Country Places, only refer to West Point and the order Military Duty produces etc."[28] The moral restraints and religious nurture that were to be provided on a nonsectarian basis were telling points for parents.[29] Women's interest and influence were appealed to gracefully, if a bit guilefully.[30] Most of all, special labor and business groups and regional interests were deliberately cultivated.[31]

There was need for all possible tact and conciliating finesse. Labor groups were even then jealous of their authority and jurisdiction. Farmers were naturally suspicious. Ill-advised zealots were tempted by the supercilious attitude of certain old-line schoolmen to immoderate and unreasoning attacks upon colleges and academies.[32] Left wing reformers sought to use the movement. The convention of 1852 was besieged by the "Women's Rights Ladies," with a delegation of such determined feminists as Lucy Stone, Elizabeth Cady Stanton, Susan B. Anthony, and Amelia Bloomer, who sought to stampede the gathering into a superfluous declaration at a time when the issue of coeducation was already threatening division. The abolitionists also made their usual plea for racial equality, but they had to be content with the use of the generic "persons" in the charter.[33]

With the opposition without and the divisions within the movement, the most available as well as realistic argument was that of preparedness for a changing and unsettled economic order. The new industrial processes, the new agricultural technique, and the fluctuating commercial system required special and extended training for technical competence and managerial foresight that could best be provided in an institution having its whole program adapted to the situations of contemporary life. The graduates of such a college, argued a shrewd politician, would learn to deal directly with affairs and not be "like sprouts grown in the shade, in ignorance of anything but books, with no practical knowledge, and like Mr. Micawber waiting for something to turn up before they can enter upon the duties of life."[34] Greeley sounded the challenge with characteristic forthrightness: "Our present financial collapse results directly from the public want of such training as this College is destined to supply. We have not only professional men in abundance, but civil and military engineers in sufficiency; yet the captains of industry, who are to double our grain crops and teach us how to exterminate the devastating insects that rob the farmer of his anticipated harvests, are yet to be furnished. We need an education which will win the attention and aspirations of our enterprising youth from filibustering in Central America and plotting paper cities on the Yellow Stone to the fertilizing and beautifying the green hills and rural valleys that surround their childhoods' homes; we want, in short, a People's College."[35]

But the hard and unsettled business conditions which indicated the need and opportunity for the proposed education put an end to all hope of popular financing. In 1855 the general promotional campaign was suspended. With all the emphasis upon the special groups to be served through their own cooperative effort, the movement had never been kept to a narrow class basis. Mechanization and capitalization had not yet gone far enough to raise impassable barriers in economic society, and before the days of social politics a philanthropic paternalism from motives both of self-interest and benevolence persisted. This particular people's movement had been directed and financed to a considerable extent by business and professional men. The president of the association was the superintendent of a railroad which aided the cause, as did other roads, by providing free passes, and along with the labor and agricultural society leaders on the board, there were bankers, merchants, and lawyers. Now at the critical stage, in 1856, the whole enterprise was saved by a western New York millionaire, Charles Cook, who provided the remainder of the guarantee fund, a farm for a site, and alluring promises of future endowment, in return for the location at his home town of Havana. The following year the Rev. Amos Brown, a Dartmouth graduate who after a distinguished career of academy teaching had been active in the creation of a state agricultural college, was selected to head and organize the unique experiment.[36]

The cornerstone laying in 1858 was one of the most notable educational convocations of the period. In addition to Cook, as the president of the day, Brown and other local educational and political celebrities, and the ceremonial grand master of Masons, Mark Hopkins and Greeley were the main speakers. Brown appealed to old and new in the claim that the college would be "both a disciplinary and professional institution." Speaking as a clergyman no less than as an educator he found the enterprise providentially ordained and guided, and named as its crowning disciplinary study "the revelations of the Bible."[37] Not so concerned with the formal disciplinary aspects, Greeley tersely summarized the aims as a thorough and appropriate education for any business or industry, the "perfect combination of Study with Labor," and "Justice to Woman."[38] Hopkins admitted that an education in which physical science and its practical application was the dominant note was superior in certain respects to one in which the classics and metaphysics prevailed and that the new emphasis might thus serve as a salutary corrective of the limitations of the old.[39]

As for the rest, the addresses and after-dinner speeches indicated the usual lack of comprehension and reasoned interest of "men of affairs" for educational innovation. A political journalist and former county superintendent of schools in responding for the press displayed the confused notion of the whole movement in verbose encomium which reads like a Dickensesque caricature of pedagogical vagaries: "In this institution the student will not only read the lofty verse of Vergil's Georgics, but will reduce his rules to practice while following the 'trailing-footed' oxen spoken of by Homer. The Differential and Integral Calculus will commingle with the ring of the anvil and the whir of the machine shop. The mechanic's toil will be diversified by the Histories of Tacitus or the eloquence of Cicero and Demosthenes. The elevation which mental training and intellectual power confers will be somewhat lessened by being blended with the more common and ordinary industrial occupations of every-day life, while the physical man will be correspondingly elevated, refined and ennobled."[40] Underlying all the discussion, whether understanding or not, was the recognition of popular purpose and direction—a sentiment that found fitting summary in ex-Governor Myron Clark's toast: "The People's College; it is of the people, and for the people, and will be sustained by the people."[41]

Like most of the independent ventures of the industrial movement this most pretentious one failed of realization in the pre-war years. The patron contributed over three-fourths of the building fund, but while the official announcements carried the promise that "The Hon. Charles Cook . . . has signified his purpose to bestow upon the Institution a large portion of his ample estate,"[42] the endowment was postponed. Unfortunately, the expectation led to a one-man control which split the board and alienated other supporters. While admirers referred to Cook as an upstate Peter Cooper, it appeared increasingly doubtful whether his interest extended beyond the personal gratification of making his remote country village (where he had secured the location only after a hard and costly fight) what he vaguely termed a "little Oxford." By the end of the decade it was evident that the institution's main hope lay in public aid.[43] Its importance for the land-grant movement was in the formulation and discussion of the fullest and most practicable plan of a technological university from the Rensselaer foundation to the Morrill Act.

The nearest counterpart of the People's College idea in the Middle West was the Farmers' College founded at College Hill, near Cincinnati, Ohio, in 1846 by Freeman Grant Cary, a member of the famous literary family. In the fifties Cary sought to broaden an old-line college, in scope and appeal, into a technical university, and through his lectures and journal, the *Cincinnatus* (1856–61) became a leading champion of industrial education. But while a farm and a small endowment for a chair of practical agriculture were secured, resources were inadequate to make it a true farmers' college except in name. It remained a center of agitation rather than of demonstration and, like other more or less promising ventures of the period, sought an extension of the federal aid which had been first applied in this state.[44]

Thus, all these varied efforts to provide popular technical schools and colleges on a basis of independent support made evident the necessity of governmental aid. The frequent rumors of millionaire patrons did not materialize; bequests were made only to the established colleges or for the founding of new institutions on the old lines. Van Rensselaer had no successor before the land-grant period. Following the pioneer proposals of the early century, movements for state agricultural colleges with or without federal aid paralleled the course of agricultural societies and the rise of a permanent, class-appealing agricultural journalism both of which gave major place to this cause. The New York society, one of the oldest and most active, was an early and persistent advocate. Following its reorganization and permanent establishment in 1841, in a period of growing agricultural unrest, there was at last a possibility of the gradual realization of the premature proposals of Elkanah Watson, DeWitt Clinton, Simeon DeWitt, and Jesse Buel. Foremost in presenting plans and reports of experiences at home and abroad were such journalists as Luther Tucker in the *Country Gentleman,* Dr. Daniel Lee in the second *Genessee Farmer,* A. B. and R. L. Allen and Orange Judd in the *American Agriculturist,* and J. J. Mapes in the *Working Farmer,* leaders of the state society like B. P. Johnson and John Delafield, and their scientific advisers, J. P. Norton and S. W. Johnson of Yale.

After long discussion in journals, society meetings, and legislative hearings, Governor Fish in 1849 recommended the chartering of the desired institution, but due to educational and regional rivalries, it was not until 1853 that the New York State Agricultural College was incorporated on a joint stock basis. The act required location on a farm of not less than three hundred acres and the teaching of theoretical and practical agriculture and engineering. Delafield, the moving spirit, was named president of the board, his farm at Oaklands was selected as the site, and preparations made for stock subscription when the sudden death of the leader necessitated a new start.[45] Amos Brown as principal of the Ovid Academy had established a subscription professorship and public lecture course in applied botany and chemistry which under the direction of William H. Brewer, an early Sheffield graduate, had been markedly successful. Now with local backing he proposed to combine with the new state enterprise. When in 1856 the legislature provided for a loan of $40,000 to be equaled by private subscription, the Ovid supporters exceeded the requirement and purchased a farm of nearly seven hundred acres. Brown, however, was not to carry on here; opponents blocked his selection for the presidency, and, as noted, he became the head of the rival enterprise at Havana.[46] After temporary management by the president of the state society, instruction was started in 1860 under the direction of Major M. R. Patrick, a West Point graduate, and a faculty of three who instructed less than thirty students in a three-year course of elementary agriculture and engineering along with mathematics, English, government, and philosophy. Patrick resigned before the end of the first year to enter the army and thus put an end—permanently it was to prove—to the Empire State's first official trial of industrial education.[47]

The Keystone neighbor, planning more modestly, was to build more enduringly. After persistent advocacy by the state society led by Judge Frederick Watts and Hugh McAllister, the legislature in 1854 created "The Farmers' High School of the State of Pennsylvania" which was located well out in the country in Center County, whose citizens donated a farm and $10,000 to match the initial state appropriation. During the next five years buildings were constructed, farm and orchards developed, preliminary testing and experimentation undertaken by the superintendent, and instruction started in 1859.[48] The presidency, by the fortunate culmination of long and deliberate planning, went to one of the ablest and most versatile applied science scholars and administrators of the time.

Evan Pugh after preliminary experience as blacksmith's apprentice, student at the famous Whitesboro manual labor school, and academy proprietor in Pennsylvania had gone to Germany for graduate work in chemistry. After three years at the leading centers of scientific research he secured a doctor's degree in chemistry at Göttingen in 1856. Before returning to America he carried on special research in plant physiology under Lawes at Rothamsted. At Leipsic in 1854 he formed an intimate and congenial friendship with his fellow student, S. W. Johnson.[49]

During the following years, after Johnson's return, the two young scientists carried on a detailed and spirited correspondence on the needs and possibilities for agricultural education in the United States. Contemptuous of existing organizations and methods they regarded themselves as champions of experimental science and missionaries to the neglected farmer. From the environment of university laboratory and experiment station, their vision lacked nothing in comprehensiveness. Pugh's "ideal plan" for his state involved a central college with branch schools in each county, investigation stations in each township, and observers on every farm. The college was to train not only farmers and farmers' wives but research specialists and teachers for the rural schools. Contrary to prevailing opinion, from his experience at Whitesboro, he was convinced that manual labor for student support was wholly impracticable. An agricultural journal was felt to be an essential adjunct to their educational scheme. Quite in the modern professional manner, Pugh proposed that since so many colleges were taking up agriculture it was their duty to provide the needed textbooks, and modestly he suggested ten in the fields of their main interests.[50]

To launch his career Johnson was desirous of having a college established either in New York or Pennsylvania; Pugh's interest was in his own state and he proposed with youthful selfconsciousness, if the legislature proved indifferent, to inform the public that his foreign study had all been with the aim of the agricultural improvement of his state and to seek the inauguration of his plan by general subscription.[51] Fortunately, legislative action made this test of public interest unnecessary. After the failure of various plans for state and institutional employment in his native New York, Johnson received an appointment at Yale, starting his career as pioneer experiment station worker and organizer, and from this strategic center he used his influence to secure the appointment of his friend by the Pennsylvania board.[52]

The primitive country school marked a sorry deflation from Pugh's grandiose plan and he apologized to Johnson, amid the venerable Yale traditions, for the statement in his catalogue that Pennsylvania was to have the best agricultural college in the world. He had adopted a somewhat popular plan and appeal rather than one more strictly scientific and dignified not from choice but from necessary expediency. In any case he pledged himself to stand against the effort to secure popularity by making the school a center for promoting pseudo-scientific analyses that had been exploited by commercial quacks.[53] For the time the school's work was highly creditable. In spite of modest name the claim of work of collegiate grade was justified. The first class in 1861 was awarded the degree of bachelor of scientific agriculture and the following year under charter authorization the court changed the name to the Agricultural College of Pennsylvania. By 1862 the state had appropriated over one hundred thousand dollars for buildings and support, and about a third as much more had come in land and subscriptions from private donations. Hard days were ahead in the years of war and readjustment, but so soundly and consistently had the college been established under leaders like Watts and Pugh that its claim to be the appropriate beneficiary of the federal land grant would not be effectively contested.[54]

In Maryland, after varied proposals by the state society for establishing agricultural professorships in existing colleges and unsatisfactory experiment with itinerant lectures by the state chemist, an act was passed in 1856 "to establish and endow an agricultural college in the State of Maryland." Support was to be provided by stock subscriptions supplemented by a $6,000 annual appropriation. A specified condition was experimentation upon the farm. The farm was secured and the college organized in 1858, and the following year instruction began with a regular classical course and a special scientific one including the "science of agriculture." The determining influence in the founding of the institution at this time was the generosity of Charles B. Calvert, whose model farm near Washington was, in effect, donated as a site. While the institution was mainly supported and controlled by the stockholding corporation, the state continued its annual subsidy through the period of independent status.[55]

Massachusetts agricultural and horitcultural interests under such exceptional guidance as that of Marshall P. Wilder, Edward Hitchcock, Henry F. French, and George B. Loring proceeded deliberately but surely to the desired educational goal. Following long discussion in journals, societies, and the legislature, the governor was authorized in 1850 to appoint a committee to investigate the whole subject. This commission's elaborate report, including Hitchcock's findings on European schools, recommended, in addition to a state board and increased aid to societies, the chartering of an agricultural college to be maintained jointly by state and private support, an academy with an agricultural department, and aid for agricultural instruction in the common schools. No definite action was taken on the educational proposals until in 1856, after specific recommendation by the board, there was created a body, headed by Wilder, called "Trustees of the Massachusetts School of Agriculture" which was charged with "holding, maintaining, and conducting an experimental farm and school thereupon, with all needful buildings, library, apparatus, and appurtenances, for the promotion of agricultural and horticultural art within this Commonwealth." Local stock promotion was held up by the war and the planning commission, authorized in 1861 upon petition by interested places, suspended action in expectation of the federal grant.[56] In the other New England states the development of applied science in privately endowed colleges and academies prevented an effective movement for state support.

In the agrarian, state-conscious South there was among leading planters a clear recognition of need—in this as in other lines of modernization—but a lack of popular interest and of sustaining resources. Early chairs of agriculture and engineering in the state universities had not been progressively developed, and legislatures proved indifferent or unfavorable to proposals for specific technical departments. A private endowment at the University of Georgia provided an agricultural lectureship which was held from 1855 to 1862 by Dr. Daniel Lee whose experience as agricultural editor, agricultural society leader, school proprietor, and statistician for the Patent Office gave assurance of competence. But the board's appeal for the expansion of this foundation into a full agricultural school was unavailing.[57]

The Kentucky state society at its second meeting in 1840 adopted resolutions which led to the introduction of a bill at the next session of the legislature for "establishing an Agricultural College and Model Farm, and appropriating six thousand dollars per annum for ten years from the State Treasury, in support of the same." The measure passed the senate but failed in the house.[58] Again in 1857 the society's board resolved that as the well-being of the profession depended upon increasing the understanding of the branches of learning that were related to it as demonstrated by the fact that "many" states had established and endowed agricultural colleges and model and experimental farms "greatly to the edification and improvement of the farming population and thereby greatly to the benefit of the whole community," the legislature was "requested to take similar wise and liberal action."[59] Popular indifference, apparently, postponed an establishment that would have been peculiarly appropriate for the state of Henry Clay.

In the Old Dominion, as a logical phase of the state's notable agricultural revival, there was persistent agitation for technical education. By the fifties the results of four decades of pioneer improvement led by John Taylor, Fleming Lewis, and Edmund Ruffin were being made known through books, journals, and agricultural societies. Further progress necessitated systematic instruction and research, but to secure the needed appropriations public interest had to be aroused.[60] In 1853 Ruffin was awarded a prize by a regional agricultural association for an essay on "Agricultural Education." His plan anticipated in essentials the land-grant agricultural college in state support, manual labor, experimentation, and military organization.[61]

The proposed system was further and more specifically elaborated three years later by the president of the Virginia state society, the distinguished planter, Philip St. George Cocke, who submitted an ingenious, comprehensive plan of state agricultural education. Two distinct classes were to be provided for: those with leisure and means for a complete university training to fit them to manage their estates and to become leaders in agricultural policies; and the large group of young farmers with limited preparation and resources who needed practical training to become skilled cultivators of their own farms or plantation overseers or managers. To meet these different needs the system should include an agricultural division or college of the university with three main professorships—the scope and divisions of whose departments were carefully and competently specified—agriculture, the basic sciences, and veterinary practice and surgery. The more popular and practical school, located with a view to health, economy of maintenance, and observational opportunities, and requiring for admission a grounding in elementary mathematics and basic science, would provide direct demonstrational training in all branches of agriculture, elementary mechanics, and accounting.

Pupil participation was to be emphasized. An essential part of the school would be a farm in charge of an experienced farmer "for the purpose of practice, illustration and healthful exercise, and by means of which the students might become familiar with the various machines, implements and animals, and with some of the practical operations of farming." Strict discipline was expected to train in habits of dependability and "laborious application to study and business." As a measure of such discipline as well as of public service, the students were to be "organized into a military company or corps, and drilled and instructed in infantry tactics, so as to make them good citizen-soldiers as well as good farmers."

The estimated required endowment of $200,000 was to be raised equally by farmers' subscriptions and a state appropriation. Of this fund, $60,000 invested in 6 per cent state securities, "together with tuition fees, would provide salaries sufficient to command the services of the ablest professors" for the university chairs. The remaining $140,000 would thus be left for equipping and maintaining the farm school. Cocke felt that with the prevailing interest in agricultural improvement as shown by the renewed support of the state society there would be no difficulty in securing both the needed subscriptions and the appropriations.[62]

In his address as president of the society the following year, Ruffin urged a grant of at least twelve thousand dollars per year, and definite efforts followed to inaugurate the instruction. The attempt to secure a chair at the state university proving unsuccessful, the military institute, where throughout the decade a department of applied chemistry had been conducted by a West Point graduate with marked effectiveness, became the main hope. After an investigation of European scientific schools in 1859, the superintendent formulated a plan for a technical and military institute to be organized into the three divisions of agriculture, engineering, and the fine arts. Private gifts of $30,000 and legislative appropriations for buildings and support made possible the starting of the school of agriculture with two professorships, but the coming of the war at this juncture brought a permanent suspension of the promising enterprise.[63]

In the West precedents of land grants for schools and universities made similar aid for technical institutions both natural and available. Lack of popular interest in regions where undeveloped resources encouraged exploitation rather than improvement together with the opposition of existing colleges, public and private, were the main obstacles. Michigan, pre-eminent in state university development, was the first to provide for the industrial addition. The new constitution of 1850 directed the legislature to establish an agricultural school "as soon as practicable" and authorized the use of unappropriated lands for such an establishment at the university. A specified aim of the normal school founded at Ypsilanti the same year, under direct influence of the prevailing industrial emphasis, was to give instruction in agriculture and the mechanic arts, and shortly thereafter the university sought to furnish the desired training by a chair of "theoretical and practical agriculture" and provision for public lectures on the subject. But the state society under the lead of its secretary, John C. Holmes, and an alert journalist, Joseph R. Williams, both of whom were influenced by experiences abroad and in the older states, contended for separate establishment. Their argument won popular support, and in 1857 the first state agricultural college was founded on an undeveloped farm near Lansing. Under Williams' presidency the appeal was frankly to the masses in subjects taught, in method, and in means of support.[64] The future of this first state agricultural college accordingly depended upon the progressive adaptation of its program to secure and maintain the appreciation and loyalty of the constituency.

No other western state brought its project to going status in the prefederal period. In Ohio, the mother of colleges as well as of presidents, the legislature was not minded to act without national aid. Dr. Norton S. Townshend, a medical enthusiast for agricultural advancement, with associates from Oberlin and Western Reserve, sought in 1854 to establish winter lecture courses for farmers, but after failure to secure the desired state subsidy, this effort to bring science to the Buckeye farmer was abandoned.[65] At the other extreme of elaborateness was a bill introduced in 1858 for a college under control of the state agricultural and educational boards with a farm of 1,000 acres which was designed to provide instruction on a par with the best European agricultural schools. For a scheme at this tentative stage there was the ironically superfluous safeguard that the professors were "not to be paid over $5,000 for the first year, and $6,000 for the second; their salaries thereafter to be determined by the Board of Supervisors."[66]

Hoosier interests were as deliberate in moving for a college as they had been in establishing a state board. The revision of the university's curriculum in 1852 promised agricultural and engineering departments, but they failed to materialize as did the recommendation of the agricultural board for state lectureships. Discussion by the board and in farm papers had, however, brought the matter to public attention by the time of the federal land-grant proposals.[67]

Due perhaps to earlier and fuller eastern influence, Iowa went considerably further. From the beginnings of statehood there were suggestions of such a college, and with the founding of a state society and the starting of two agricultural papers, these proposals became more definite. Suel Foster, a pioneer horticulturist and chronic reformer, and William Duane Wilson, an agricultural journalist no less addicted to causes, were the most persistent advocates. In 1858, through the efforts of a group of young pioneer farmers in the legislature, the "Iowa State Agricultural College and Farm" was created with an appropriation of $10,000 which was about doubled by local bonds and subscriptions. The location and development of the farm were the only accomplishments of the first decade. Positive interest in the early years was so slight that abolition was prevented in 1860 only by parliamentary finesse.[68]

Divided counsels prevented definite action in Wisconsin. President Lathrop, one time of the Gardiner Lyceum, urged a distinct agricultural college in the university with instructional and experimental functions; leaders in the state society favored an independent institution. Bills for both purposes failed.[69]

Meantime, in spite of youth, Minnesota's society under the energetic leadership of John H. Stevens had formed a college corporation, purchased a site, and undertaken the raising of a building fund by subscription and state appropriation when the burdens of war and frontier defense put an end to the whole project.[70]

California discussed state establishment of higher education for over a decade. Agricultural interests, as expressed in the state society, desired their own college; other professional and academic groups sought a full university; the adjutant general and the superintendent of public instruction believed that an industrial college organized on a military basis would best meet the state's needs. Such divisions along with sectarian rivalry prevented any definite action.[71]

By reason of strategy of location, the volubility of its spokesmen, and the sweeping claims later to be made for the state's part in the land-grant movement, Illinois holds a peculiar interest. Failure to make definite use of the "seminary" and college public land grants before the later fifties gave the industrialists the opportunity and the excuse for seeking this neglected and badly managed fund. The need for diversification and industrialization, unusually active agricultural societies and press, and an educational zeal engendered by certain eastern colonizing and missionary groups combined to stimulate the movement. Sectional differences, economic and social, the inertia of extensive cultivation, and the tradition of sectarian higher education presented complications and obstructions. The counter-balancing of these influences prevented definite decision during two decades of heated debating and resolving.[72]

The most voluble if not effective of the propagandists was Jonathan Baldwin Turner who in interest, attitude, and method of appeal was typical of the reforming-agitator type of the Middle Period. A native of Massachusetts, he was a graduate of Yale and long a professor at Illinois College, founded by the Yale Band. His brothers were leaders of the corresponding missionary movement in Iowa. With such a background and connections his crusades and enthusiasms were sufficiently diffused and varied during his nonagenarian career to include abolitionism, anti-Mormonism, psychiatry, mesmerism, spiritualism, biblical criticism, monetary reform, inland waterways, national capital removal, land speculation, anti-monopoly, mechanical invention, horticultural, entomological, and agronomic experimentation, as well as educational extension and reorganization.[73] Long active in the free school cause, it was inevitable that this ebullient reformer, retired from teaching to experimental farming, should become a zealous advocate of education for the industrial classes.

Recanting his earlier proposal to ingraft the new education upon classical colleges, Turner formulated a plan for an industrial university. After being suggested tentatively at teachers' institutes in 1850, the full presentation was made in 1851 at a convention of farmers and mechanics called for the express purpose of considering the establishment of an "agricultural university."[74] This disquisition and prospectus, combining sensible observation and quixotic proposal, started with the assumption that society was sharply divided into the professional classes, whose education was assumed to be provided for adequately, and the industrial classes whose special training was wholly neglected. For this latter group he suggested a scheme of education that joined a modified traditional college curriculum with the exhibitional activities of agricultural societies. The actual "university" setup, so far as it can be visualized amid the discursive diatribes at contemporary society, indicated a lack of an adequate and reasoned appreciation of the scope and method of a technological institution. In comparison with contemporary proposals, Turner's lacked the social realism of those of Howard and Greeley, the systematic organization of those of Norton, Hitchcock, Ruffin, and Cocke, and the scientific precision of those of Pugh and Johnson. The interest taken in the pronouncement by social and educational reformers was apparently due to its vigorous restatement of the traditional national philosophy of popular opportunity and its rhetorical onslaught on the aim and content of an obsolescent classicism.

Probably largely because of this lack of deliberate, qualified specification the plan was widely and usually favorably discussed, and it undoubtedly gave an impetus to the industrial movement, both state and national. Encouraged by the interest thus aroused, a group of state educational and agricultural leaders, of whom Turner, John A. Kennicott, Bronson Murray, and John P. Reynolds were prominent, formed an "industrial league" which for several years conducted an active campaign of lectures and newspaper discussions and held nine state-wide conventions between 1851 and 1864.[75] The members corresponded and consulted with promoters in other states, East and West. In 1854 Cary at Farmers' College sponsored a "Northwest Industrial Convention" at which Murray represented the league and read a paper by Turner. Upon solicitation of President Tappan of the University of Michigan, Turner also presented his views in 1856 at an educational meeting in Detroit.[76]

In Illinois herself, opposing interests, sectional, sectarian, and class, proved too strong, and after the failure of various bills for different types of technical institutions, the league consented in 1857 to the founding of a "Normal University" as the first legitimate utilization of the state's land grant for higher education and, in their wishful claim, the first unit of an industrial university.[77] The chief significance of the Illinois industrial movement, as well as the source of the later historical controversy growing out of it, was to be in its influence upon the development of the federal land-grant policy.

In the two decades preceding the introduction of the land-grant bill, proposals of federal participation, either through direct establishment or through land or money subsidies to state institutions, were brought almost continuously to public attention. This movement for national technical education paralleled and to a considerable extent interlocked with efforts for national departments of agriculture and education and for federal aid for a transcontinental railroad. The general arguments for such national programs combined appeals to precedent—land grants for education, asylums, and public works, proposals for a board of agriculture, and a national university—with the alleged needs of the nation for an industrial leadership. The model of centralized organization, as well as the outstanding example of direct federal activity, was the Military Academy. Prior to the days of pork-barrel appropriations and of grants-in-aid from the treasury, the public domain was the chief recourse; but a liberally conditioned windfall from abroad, the Smithson bequest, offered the most immediately available capital fund, either for a central foundation or for regional distribution. The long and bitter controversy over acceptance and utilization of this fund—by no means settled by the incorporation of the Institution in 1846—stimulated the hopes of educational as well as of other interests.

As early as 1838 Charles L. Fleischman, a graduate of the Bavarian Royal Agricultural College, offered a memorial to Congress which after reviewing the achievements of instruction in applied science in Europe urged the establishment of schools of general science, mechanics, agriculture, and veterinary art. The next year he added the suggestion that the Smithson fund be used for this purpose.[78] The Agricultural Society of the United States, founded in 1841 largely by the promotive effort of Solon Robinson, at its second and final meeting the next year had as the leading item on its agenda the securing of this much-sought fund for a national agricultural school, library, and experimental garden "that should bear and be worthy of the name of Smithson."[79] Before a New Hampshire state agricultural convention, in 1849, Professor Sanborn of Dartmouth questioned "whether the best mode of appropriating the interest of this princely bequest for disseminating 'a knowledge of the sciences of cultivating the earth' would not be a pro rata appropriation among the several States, for the support of agricultural societies and agricultural schools."[80] Turner in his industrial university plan looked to the same foundation to provide a "National institute of science" for training teachers and investigators. The Maryland society in 1854 presented the unique proposal of an agricultural school at the Institution with an experimental farm at Mount Vernon.[81] During the same year Representative "Long John" Wentworth of Illinois, acting quite independently of the plan of Turner and his league, introduced a resolution instructing the committee on agriculture to inquire into the expediency of establishing a national agricultural school in connection with the Smithsonian

Institution with the same basis of apportionment of students as the military and naval academies.[82]

The military academy provided the readiest suggestion of the form and standards for a national school of science. Dr. Lee in the Patent Office report of 1850 proposed that Congress take the lead in establishing a school "of the scientific grade of West Point Academy" and secure foreign scientists like Liebig and Boussingault as teachers until enough American applied scientists were trained to supply the state agricultural colleges.[83] Cary would have decentralized the system with a series of nationally endowed regional schools; he recommended four as a beginning properly equipped with experimental grounds and laboratories.[84] Another proposal would have integrated national and state activity, with a national institution of the "highest order," supported by land receipts or other "surplus revenue," to train teachers and workers for schools of the "lower order" to be established and maintained by all the states.[85] Of the various proposals for national establishment and direction, that which Representative Morrill offered during his first session in 1856 has an unusual interest, in view of his future relation to the land-grant movement. The resolution provided that "the Committee on Agriculture be requested to inquire into the expediency of establishing one or more national agricultural schools upon the basis of the naval and military schools, in order that one scholar from each congressional district and two from each State at large may receive a scientific and practical education at the public expense."[86] The constitutional argument when considered at all by these advocates was invariably an *ad populum* one of special need and of superior and more effective service than that rendered by less worthy and appropriate objects of support.[87]

During the fifties the chief center of agricultural effort was the United States Agricultural Society established in 1852 with headquarters at the Smithsonian and led by Wilder, Calvert, Watts, Lee, and David P. Holloway of Indiana. The society was interested equally in promoting a federal department and agricultural colleges.[88] The main proposals on these subjects during the decade were discussed by the members and the most important that were presented to Congress had their sponsorship.

Such appeals multiplied throughout the decade; with the projection of institutions, state and private, and the undetermined scope of direct national functioning, congressional aid became the great objective. Apparently every state from Massachusetts to California that had a projected institution or even a vaguely planned scheme of industrial education was represented by one or more of these petitions. But far more significant than these appeals for individual projects were the persisting proposals for grants to all the states. In 1841 Captain Partridge of the famous Norwich academy proposed an appropriation of $40,000,000 from land receipts to be distributed among the states in proportion to representation in Congress for their new or adapted institutions where, in addition to general studies, engineering, agriculture, commerce, and military tactics should be taught.[89] John S. Skinner, the veteran editor of agricultural and industrial journals, presented a memorial to the Senate in 1848 asking for subsidies to the states for colleges of agriculture and mechanic arts.[90]

More definite and official, as well as vastly extended in amount of grant, were the resolutions adopted by the Illinois legislature at the instance of the industrial league in 1853 and presented in Congress the following year. They instructed their state's delegation "to use their best exertions to procure the passage of a law of Congress donating to each State in the Union an amount of public lands not less in value than *five hundred thousand dollars,* for the liberal endowment of a system of Industrial Universities, one in each State in the Union, to cooperate with each other, and with the Smithsonian Institution at Washington, for the more liberal and practical education of our industrial classes and their teachers; a liberal and varied education adapted to the manifold wants of a practical and enterprising people, and a provision for such educational facilities, being in manifest concurrence with the intimations of the popular will, it urgently demands the united efforts of our national strength." The governor was instructed to send a copy of these daring pronouncements and proposals "to the Executive and Legislature of each of our sister States, inviting them to cooperate with us in this meritorious enterprise."[91] A bill prepared by Turner to formulate this plan was withheld during Pierce's administration by reason of his known hostility to land appropriations for state institutions.[92]

The plan came before the United States Agricultural Society for action in 1856. The committee of three to whom it was referred were sharply divided. Henry of the Smithsonian and Byington of Connecticut presented a congressional petition in the name of the Society, urging the enactment in toto. J. D. B. DeBow presented an impassioned minority protest. While agreeing fully as to the importance of industrial universities, he deprecated the endorsement by a national organization of an exercise of federal power over which the country was so definitely and bitterly divided. He was convinced that "this Society constituted for the common good of the agriculturists of the whole Union, ought not to be put in the way of arguing against itself the prejudices and hostilities of any class or section." On the motion of a Massachusetts delegate action was put over to the next annual meeting.[93]

At the 1857 convention discussion came mainly from opponents of general federal aid or of this particular plan. The supporters no doubt felt that their case was fully established; the main argument they presented was the old one of professional discrimination: the government educated soldiers, sailors, civil engineers, and artists but—in contrast to European foresight—did nothing for farmers. The calamity of imported bread stuffs, the society was warned, was to be prevented only by such scientific cultivation as would result from the proposed colleges.[94]

The opposition rested its case on grounds both of expediency and of the proper limits of governmental policy. B. P. Poore of Massachusetts found the petition highly inexpedient and hoped that the society would not discredit itself by endorsing such a visionary proposal. According to the official proceedings, of which he was editor, "He did not think that any gentleman acquainted with the practical workings of Congress would believe for a moment that there was the slightest chance of obtaining such an immense donation for such vague purposes."[95]

George E. Waring of New York, agricultural and engineering writer and practitioner, was convinced that industrial colleges should be started only in response to regional demand and initiative, and that no congressional bounty could overcome popular indifference and misunderstanding. The only proper basis for an American agricultural college was private subscription and student labor. Publicly maintained institutions which admitted students not stimulated to work by zeal for improving their professional efficiency could "never be in accordance with our republican ideas of the just apportionment of the public money." The only legitimate field for governmental aid to industrial education was in the development of instruction in science in the common schools which reached the masses, rather than the privileged few. Begging the long controverted question he assumed the effectiveness of such teaching, at any rate in the better schools. "The elementary sciences which are applicable to agriculture are not more abstruse, not indeed so abstruse as these which are now taught so largely in the schools of New England." The only immediate need for government aid was in placing in the schools elementary books on the sciences pertaining to agriculture. "Industrial universities," he concluded, "we undoubtedly require, but in my opinion, sir, they will be of no value until they arise from the demand for them among the farmers themselves, and then, sir, they will not need governmental influence to advance their usefulness."[96] After acceptance of an amendment by a Kansas delegate including the territories in the proposed act, the plan was approved by a majority of three.[97] The lines of cleavage, political and social, which the society reflected were ominous for this as for other constructive national policies.

By this time, it is evident, the industrial movement stood at the crossroads. Definite beginnings had been made, through private and state auspices, in providing various sorts and degrees of technical education. By 1862 it was conservatively estimated that there were "twenty institutions which could be grouped under the general title of scientific schools."[98] But the whole movement remained tentative in scope and impermanent in support; there was a lack of recognized standards, systematized subject matter, effective methods, and adequate resources. Under such unfavorable conditions popular writers and politicians could point to the wastefulness and ineffectiveness of colleges as compared with practical lectureships and journals.[99] The unconscious bull of an original and ardent champion of practical agricultural education stated the situation with restraint, "There has been and will continue to be some failures in the success of Agricultural Colleges."[100] As a matter of fact, there were no assured successes while the failures were all too evident.

As in other large undertakings of common concern but with local variations, federal subsidies, allowing liberal range for state determination, seemed essential to bring regional enterprise to assured establishment. As usual, too, educational exigency had to wait upon political expediency, but by the late fifties, in spite of all past constitutional and social traditions and prejudices and present sectional division involving them, sufficient sentiment had been created to make federal aid to industrial education an "available" issue, provided it was strategically presented. It thus remained for the industrialists to take their cause to the best political market. In October, 1857, Trumbull advised Turner, in reply to a suggestion of early action, that there was a steadily growing opposition in Congress to further extensive grants to the landed states and that the pending proposal would be better received if presented by an easterner.[101] Two months later Morrill offered the bill, which, embodying the main objectives of the movement, was to unite and rally the industrial forces of the nation.

CHAPTER III

THE FEDERAL SOLUTION

For the Middle Period, as for later times, the legislative galleries, committee rooms, and lobbies of the national capital, while affording strategic points for observing the denouement of great national measures—tariffs, slavery, banking, homesteads, internal improvements, industrial education—provided but partial and confusing explanation of origins and influences. These were to be found in the conditions, interests, and prejudices back home in the grassroots and on the sidewalks of the various regions. Such issues of general interest have invariably started locally and as invariably moved to Washington (often in spite of desperate efforts of party leaders to keep them localized) to find ultimate adjustment—with the exception of the one great failure and tragedy—in a way to conciliate sectional interests and preserve federal balance. Thus, in taking or following their cause to Congress the industrialists were acting according to form, and no less so was to be the legislative solution.

The bill presented by Morrill in the Thirty-fifth Congress, while not reproducing in detail any one of the numerous past proposals—such as amount and distribution of aid and specific organization and curriculum—was a generalized synthesis of all of them, the epitome of two decades of regional agitation and experimentation. The Illinois system of land endowment was here joined to the Partridge plan of distribution in the appropriation of 20,000 acres or scrip in that amount for each senator and representative with a lump of 60,000 acres for each territory.

The purpose was sufficiently broad and general to include all the varied concepts of industrialists: ". . . the endowment, support, and maintenance of at least one college where the leading object shall be, without excluding other scientific or classical studies, to teach such branches of learning as are related to agriculture and the mechanic arts, in such manner as the legislatures of the States and Territories may respectively prescribe, in order to promote the liberal and practical education of the industrial classes in the several pursuits and professions of life." For this purpose the states were obligated to maintain the grant-fund undiminished and to keep it invested in public or other "safe stocks" yielding not less than 5 per cent. Ten per cent of the capital fund might be expended for a site or for experimental land, but no income from the grant could be used for erecting or maintaining buildings.

To secure the grant a state was required to provide a college within five years. The only supervision and suggestion of possible standardization was the formal requirement that each college should send its annual report—"recording any improvements and experiments made, with their costs and results, and such other matters as may be supposed useful"—to the other similarly endowed colleges, the Smithsonian Institution, and the agricultural division of the Patent Office.[1]

Such was the proposed solution of rival educational systems and governmental jurisdictions, marking new and advanced applications of traditional practices and precedents. To inaugurate and mature this flexible plan of federal relations, a legislative spokesman was required who would have the foresight to venture the initial step and the persistence and vision to secure continued support. Such a sponsor appeared in the new but resourceful representative from Vermont.

Justin Smith Morrill, while in many ways typical of his time and section, had elements of uniqueness that caused him to stand out among his contemporaries. A member of a Vermont family of sturdy farmer-mechanic stock, he had retired from mercantile pursuits at thirty-eight with a modest competence to devote his time to the gentlemanly pursuits of farming, reading, travel, and politics. As it proved, public service was soon to occupy his full and continuous attention. Election to the House of Representatives in 1854 started a legislative career that was to continue to the end of his long life. From the first the intellectual and artistic establishments of the government had a large place in his congressional work; next to his major financial service came his efforts for capital improvement, the Smithsonian Institution, and the land-grant colleges. Early in his public service he had regarded industrial education as a substantial cause of timely appeal to his own state and section and with hopeful possibilities as a national policy.[2]

Like so many well-read men of his day Morrill had long been interested in educational reform. His much emphasized regret at being deprived of collegiate training seems to have been a rather late development as he had been easily persuaded, after two terms at academies, to forego such an opportunity for the immediate returns of business.[3] Before his later academic contacts he held the critical attitude of the typical man of affairs toward the existing collegiate system. In 1848 in reply to notification of election to the board of Norwich University he felt that "as *Americans*" we might well "lop off a portion of the studies established centuries ago as the mark of European scholarship and replace the vacancy—if it is a vacancy—by those of a less antique and more practical value." While declining the proffered honor by reason of other duties, he saw in this pioneer technical-military institution, which he rejoiced to see returning to its original purposes and standards after a period of decline, "the only hope of carrying out some radical improvements in the old system of education . . ."[4] When he entered Congress he was apparently still undecided as to just what these "radical improvements" should be and how they should be secured, for, as noted, his only suggestion was an indefinite one for national schools of agriculture. In contrast his bill of less than two years later embodied the principles and in several places the phraseology of the leading current proposals. These questions of priority, of no concern at the time, were to be argued about in succeeding years.

In the case of a bill which inaugurated so directly a great transformation in higher education it was natural that much attention should be given to origins and, like other cardinal acts to which many minds have contributed, it was inevitable that there should be disputes over authorship.[5] During the years of struggle for existence and consequently of scant academic prestige, there was no concern with genesis and slight parental pride in an offspring with such dubious prospects; but as the movement passed the experimental stage and certain of the new colleges and universities waxed strong and confident, founding services were appraised and honors awarded. College heads hoping for added benefits through the influence of the perennial statesman were eager to recognize his full paternity. His own version in personal memoranda, letters, and anniversary addresses was in no way dissuasive to their tributes.

Whether due to an overweening jealousy for a favorite act, which he always put foremost among his legislative achievements, or to the disproportioned sense of originality which a self-taught student tends to give to his ideas—a feeling encouraged no doubt by fulsome flattery in high academic places—he saw fit in his explanation of direct sources and motivating influences to ignore contemporary plans and projects and to attribute the inspiration to his personal experiences and cogitations. As thus observationally and logically determined, his main conclusions, by no means novel, were that the public lands might be more effectively utilized, that farming methods were wastefully inefficient, that, as "the son of a hard-handed blacksmith," he "could not overlook mechanics" in his educational plan, and that the existing educational facilities were inadequate to meet these needs. Long had he meditated on these matters, deeply had he delved into statistical compilations, and patiently had he formulated arguments to meet the indifference and hostility of fellow representatives.[6]

Becomingly modest regarding other notable achievements, the veteran Senator maintained his claim for the preferred one with unvarying consistency. In a memorandum in 1874, drawn up evidently as a personal record of the land-grant act, he wrote, "Where I obtained the first hint of such a measure I am wholly unable to say."[7] He reiterated this assertion to inquiring correspondents: to Atherton in 1883, the phraseology was wholly his own;[8] to Howard in 1885, "I do not remember that I ever heard a hint of it from any quarter until it was brought out by myself;"[9] and to Hewitt in 1894, "I do not remember of any assistance in framing my Bill prior to its introduction."[10] In a final public *apologia* of his educational service he referred to the act of 1862 as embodying "the best thought I was able to formulate—good enough to be adopted by Congress—and the first to be approved by President Lincoln. . ."[11]

So simple and personal an explanation seems incredible in view of the long and varied industrial movement, the similarity or identity of the leading features of the bill with well-known phases of that movement, and Morrill's own recorded or reasonably implied experiences. He was a sympathetic observer of the Norwich plan and was no doubt personally acquainted with the founder.[12] As an intelligent New Englander he must have had at least general familiarity with the work in applied science at Yale, Harvard, and Amherst and the promotive efforts of men like Wilder, French, and Holmes. His appreciative tribute to the People's College in 1863 showed full acquaintance with that notable departure.[13] He was the official Vermont delegate at the meetings of the United States Agricultural Society at which the Illinois Plan was considered and the general problems of agricultural education discussed.[14] For two decades professional and popular periodicals as well as government reports had been discussing educational expansion and reorganization in its varied aspects, and the new Representative's speeches and correspondence show direct acquaintance with such writings, which he was reading to some purpose as evidenced by the growth of his ideas within a year from vague preliminary resolutions to a well-phrased bill.

Lack of awareness of the long-continued campaign for educational expansion and reform would indeed have been a reflection on any alert member of Congress, to say nothing of a New Englander purporting to be an authority. The obviously appropriate course for a practical statesman in formulating such a measure would have been to compare and collate all the leading plans and experiments and select from them what appeared most fundamental and available. To disregard such experience and guidance would have marked him an irresponsible innovator who could not have continued to represent the Green Mountain State for upwards of half a century. In view of the long, widely extended, and popularly discussed experiences with industrial education, Dr. True's judgment appears to be as conclusive as it is moderate: the "measure was in fact the culmination of the long movement for agricultural and technical schools . . . and it is altogether likely that Morrill derived the ideas incorporated in his bill from various sources connected with that movement."[15]

For the same reasons rival claims to individual authorship are equally untenable. While various participants from Massachusetts to Michigan have been acclaimed locally as the originators of the land-grant idea the claims for the western representative of the "Morrill-Turner controversy" have overshadowed all the others. In 1907 at a meeting of the Society for the Promotion of Agricultural Science, Dean Eugene Davenport of the college of agriculture of the University of Illinois propounded the "historical query" whether Professor J. B. Turner had not provided directly the essential ideas of the act bearing the Vermont representative's name and was not consequently the true author. On the basis of such evidence as he had collected, the speaker, by profession a geneticist, felt that an affirmative answer should be given, but he agreed, pending fuller researches, to withhold final decision.[16]

The state's official unqualified dictum and challenge was issued three years later by the president of the university himself who—in spite of the ingenuous but credulous finding of his research assistant that Morrill "was the real father of the land grant act from its inception—that the idea in fact was his and his alone"[17]—posted, in a university bulletin, his "Thesis . . . that Jonathan B. Turner . . . was the real father of the so-called Morrill Act . . . and that he deserves the credit of having been the first to formulate clearly and definitely the plan of a national grant of land to each state in the Union for the promotion of education in agriculture and the mechanic arts, and of having inaugurated and continued to a successful issue the agitation that made possible the passage of the bill."[18]

To provide documentary support, of which there was an embarrassing lack, Turner's daughter shortly thereafter compiled a biography of her father including correspondence and other records of the industrial movement in Illinois which together with certain supplementary documents printed in the official history of the university supposedly covered the extant evidence. Unfortunately for the sweeping asservation of the thesis, there appeared surprisingly little bearing directly on the point in controversy, and in default of more substantial evidence, there has been a tendency to give large and at times determining place to the old-age reminiscences of Turner and his associates.

In fact the evidence is at times either inconclusive or contradictory. Thus, according to nonagenarian recollections of Turner and Bronson Murray, the Illinois group persuaded Morrill, after considerable reluctance, to become their congressional spokesman and supplied him with the plan of the bill and the arguments for its support.[19] Such a relationship is directly contrary to Turner's own precise statement in a review of the industrial campaign for the agricultural society in 1865: "During this interval the Hon. Mr. Morrill . . . first presented the bill to Congress . . . We forwarded to him all our documents and papers and gave him all the aid and encouragement that we could. He managed the cause most admirably . . ."[20] There is here no suggestion of Illinois initiative which, if the fact, would naturally have been much stressed by Turner and his associates.

All other evidence is to the same effect. Less than two months before the bill was introduced, the Illinois interests at home and in Washington had no legislative plan,[21] and that would have been an impossibly short time in which to prepare the measure and coach the spokesman. Most conclusive is the nature of the bill itself which differed so radically from Turner's general plan and the specific askings of his league. In contrast to equality of grant favored by the West there was the compensatory proportional distribution sought by eastern interests. The Illinois plan guaranteed a certain minimum endowment; the bill left the states to realize what they could from the grant. Turner was doubtful of the inclusion of classical studies in his university, and the league's memorial called only for "liberal and varied" studies, but the easterner's bill gave the old "disciplinary" subjects an express safeguard. Naturally Turner felt and asserted that the bill as introduced needed "*some* amendment."[22]

Turner's contemporary attitude, in contrast to the egoism of old age, was one of humble gratitude to the Vermont spokesman. In 1861 his assurance of continued interest brought a formal and rather reserved acknowledgment to one who had been presumably "an old pioneer in the cause of Agricultural education." This exhibit, as his only known letter from Morrill, has been much emphasized by the defenders of the "thesis."[23] Lack of an influential, not to say a determining, relationship is shown still more conclusively by the Professor's letter to the Senator in 1872 when the bill for increased support was pending. After expressing the gratitude of the Illinois friends of the cause, Turner added, "You may not know or you may have forgotten amid your many cares and labors that I always felt a deep interest in this subject and watch its progress with great solicitude; so do a great army of our very best men in the west, who are wholly outside of all political circles and interests."[24]

The same discrepancy appears between the contemporary record and Turner's old-age illusions regarding his relations with Lincoln, who has inspired so many sincere fantasies. Both Dr. Bailey and Dean Davenport were told by the venerable educator that he had taught Lincoln mathematics and that between lessons the two young enthusiasts "dreamed out together the hope for a new education in the practical things of life."[25] The real influence, while indirect, was one of which any teacher might be proud and naturally come to distort, even to the study involved, in nonagenarian retrospection. In a letter from Washington in 1862 he reported a recent visit with the President: "He also told me his only instruction in the English language had been from me, through the Green brothers of Tellula, Illinois, while they were students of Illinois College and he was a hired hand working for their mother in the harvest-fields."[26]

With the most definite and active organization engaged in the agitation, it was but natural that the Illinois group centering in the state society should have been highly conscious of their pioneering efforts in the general crusade. But in their contemporary self-gratulation, it should be noted, it was the state organization as a whole with a definitely recognized band of leaders rather than any individual to whom credit was accorded.[27] Any special prominence that Turner attained at the time was due not so much to constructive suggestion and practical organizing effort as to hectic enthusiasm and picturesque volubility. He, like all the other "fathers," whether inspirational agitator or constructive organizer, contributed in greater or less degree to an organic act which in basic principles epitomized a quarter century of observation and discussion. There had been and continued to be throughout the formative years hard work and sacrifice for all participants, and when the new system was fully established there should have been glory enough for all. As Davenport, with all his partiality for the claims to precedence of his adopted state, was led in deliberate conclusion to concede: "As a matter of fact, there were many men and many centers of influence that contributed to the general result; and just who or what was chiefly responsible for the particular form which the movement finally took in the land-grant act, we shall probably never know."[28]

The number and variety of these leaders and centers were manifested by the support extended to the bill immediately upon the announcement of its introduction. There appeared at the capital a distinguished and resourceful group of educational lobbyists, all representing wishful and more or less hopeful promotions. Gilman observed, perhaps with a shade of irony, "There were busy and devoted men in New York, Pennsylvania and Illinois who spared no effort within their power to secure a national appropriation."[29] Morrill, though jealous in his claims to authorship, in contrast always paid full and frank tribute to his legislative aides.[30] "Brave old Ben Wade," as Morrill appreciatively characterized him, led the support in the Senate. Marshall P. Wilder lent his distinguished and venerable prestige. Amos Brown, financed apparently by People's College backers, worked tirelessly and effectively upon doubtful members. In connection with his candidacy for the presidency of Cornell, ten of the New York delegation, Fessenden, Wade, and others, certified to Brown's decisive influence in the passage of the first bill and the enactment of the second.[31] Morrill's grateful acknowledgment would seem to disprove the charge of Brown's brother that the Senator was bitterly jealous of the veteran educator.[32] Evan Pugh led the Pennsylvania group with characteristic zeal and with effective if not determining influence on the final result.[33] Joseph R. Williams, of the Michigan venture, provided the material on European schools for the minority report and Morrill's speech, and probably influenced western votes.[34] Other prominent aides were Cary of the Farmers' College, apparently about equally concerned over the promoting of a land-grant act and the circulation of his paper;[35] Holloway of Indiana,[36] who as commissioner of patents was soon to urge a new industrial department; and Kennicott of Illinois, who was to be an active candidate for the headship of that projected establishment.

Turner merely gave his absent blessing; he was not on hand during the consideration of either bill. Called to Washington in the fall of 1862 by the illness of his son, he had intimate conversations with the President and other notables, but in his vivid letters to his family, printed in his daughter's biography, there are no references to educational legislation.

The United States Agricultural Society at its annual meeting in 1858 adopted a unanimous resolution endorsing the bill.[37] At the meeting the following year Calvert reported for the committee on a department of agriculture that they had not urged this measure as it seemed certain that the present Congress would refuse to act favorably, "and the agitation of the subject might endanger the success of the 'Morrill Land Bill,' in which many of the agriculturists of the country took a deep interest." After considerable discussion this meeting passed resolutions which, without specifically mentioning the bill, endorsed its general principles.[38] Letters received by Morrill from various sections indicated that efforts were being made to arouse local interest and to secure memorials from legislatures and societies.[39]

Morrill needed all the support that the cause could rally, both outside and inside Congress. Like the other nationalistic projects of the decade, the college grant policy ran athwart the new sectionalism. The opposition secured initial advantage by reference to the hostile public lands committee, rather than to the agricultural committee of which Morrill was a member. The matter-of-course adverse majority report presented by Cobb of Alabama was accompanied by an elaborate minority report prepared by Walbridge of Michigan with the advice of Morrill and educational experts like Williams.[40]

A measure appealing mainly to the interests of agriculture and labor was put at an obvious disadvantage through the sectional alienation of the most unified and influential agricultural group and the lack of a labor bloc. Support had to be sought in other directions. Old-line Whigs like Crittenden and Bell welcomed such an appropriate application of Clay's American System.[41] Easterners, especially New Englanders, ever jealous of western favors, saw in the proposed distribution a partial compensation for past regional grants for education and transportation. With becoming sarcasm a Vermont correspondent wrote Morrill that his bill was defective in not applying the grant mainly to the western Democratic states and excluding New England which hitherto had developed her railroads and other enterprises without national aid.[42]

Morrill's elaborate speech—his first major effort in the House—offering a substitute bill which omitted grants to territories and applied the double minimum principle in the selection of railroad lands, was an able summary and synthesis of current protests against agricultural disparity and discrimination.[43] Wasteful cultivation and soil depletion constituted the great national danger as it had for all peoples since the horrible example of Rome. The findings of the great modern scientists and their application in European technical schools pointed the solution. While other interests, military, professional, and commercial, had been the objects of governmental solicitude, the basic interest of all had been signally neglected. Mechanics and miners were given honorable and laudatory if relatively incidental mention. The labor cause and the current movement received no understanding consideration in the whole debate.[43a] Constitutional precedent was found in earlier land grants.[44] That made to Kentucky in 1827 for an asylum for the deaf and dumb, with the support of Buchanan, Polk, and other prominent Democrats, seemed especially pertinent but could easily be overemphasized. Morrill's assumption that all of the presidents prior to Pierce would have approved his bill in principle and form will be taken by the historian, as it was by the contemporary critic, with considerable reservation.

The opposition, centering in the South, rested its case mainly on a constitutional plea. The majority report contended that the proposed grants would be an invasion of the domestic rights of the states, and this argument was expounded in the conventional reasoning but vigorous statement of Cobb in the House,[45] and Mason of Virginia, Clay of Alabama, Davis of Mississippi, and Green of Missouri in the Senate.[46] Senator Pugh of Ohio inserted Pierce's veto message of the bill providing a grant for the indigent insane as the final word on the issue.[47] Cobb's dire prediction might seem prophetic of later proposals and policies for education and relief. If the bill passed, he held, the states would have the right to ask that common schools be provided by Congress, and the poor might ask for grants of land "to aid in the erection of buildings to shelter them from the inclemency of the weather."[48]

An effort was made with considerable success to revive the old appeal for a southern-western coalition. Middlewestern sentiment was divided, and the newer states were generally opposed.

Speculation by the absentee scrip-holder was represented as a ruinous menace to the landed states, and amendments were actually proposed to exempt Missouri and Minnesota from the operation of the act.[49]

While the division involved more of a sectional than a party alignment, Clay's contention that it was in the main a Republican and Know Nothing measure was borne out by the vote. But there was no formal party committal and the scant majorities, five in the House and three in the Senate, were due undoubtedly to the pressure of the college lobby upon the doubtful and indifferent.[50]

The safety man for the states' rights interest, on this as other measures involving federal action, was in the White House. When delay portended unfavorable action, northern administrationists who felt that a veto would be inexpedient sought last minute intervention, but found themselves forestalled by the southerners.[51] Buchanan's veto message[52] was to become a classic of individualistic reasoning. In an illogical and extended obiter he argued the inexpediency and ineffectiveness of the proposed system before the judgment of unconstitutionality was pronounced. Financially, he held, the loss to the federal treasury from land sales through the glutting of the market by the addition of the land scrip to the military bounties would be particularly embarrassing during the existing depression. At the same time, in his view, the scrip manipulation would subject the new states to the depressing effect of land speculation by absentee capitalists.

These criticisms and warnings, pertinent for a carefully planned system of disposal, lost much of their force in the face of a traditional practice of careless alienation. As President Orton of Ohio pointed out fifteen years later, grants for higher education were not to be set in contrast with an ideal use of the domain but rather with the notoriously wasteful and corrupt dissipation of the nation's heritage.[53] In the same way the plea for maintaining unaltered the original division of powers in order to "prevent conflict and mutual injury" was lacking in realism both for the pronounced trend toward industrial concentration and for the increasing tendency of the states to seek national aid. The plea would have come with better grace, too, from a president not so openly motivated by a zeal to defend the interests of one section against those of the others. But, on the other side, he argued, the grants might very likely fail of their object as the federal government had "no power to compel the execution of the trust;" the state legislatures could no more be compelled to found professionally helpful colleges of agriculture and mechanic arts than they could to return the surplus funds deposited with them in the thirties. This recognition of the obvious futility of general subsidies to fix and maintain standards would seem to have been conclusive answer to the charge of federal encroachment. In practice in all cases of federal educational grants prior to the introduction of the modern system of grants-in-aid, there was no authority to enforce compliance by the states.[54]

Least deserving of attention of these claims of inexpediency was that of the injury or ruin that would be sustained by the poor but worthy existing agricultural colleges when brought into competition with "an indefinite number of rival colleges sustained by the endowment of the Federal Government. . ." Such solicitude overlooked the likelihood that established technical institutions would secure their states' apportionment and the fact that a healthful rivalry which would lead to higher standards and enlarged service was essential to progressive development.

The constitutional barrier, which in the existing stage of national consciousness made all other considerations merely academic, was assumed rather than demonstrated. The policy proposed, the President averred, would mean raising revenue for state as well as federal purposes and thus, so far as the money power was concerned, would break down jurisdictional divisions and create governmental consolidation. Such hysterical states' rights assumptions, identical with those presented in the congressional debate, made no distinction between voluntarily accepted aid and enforced authority, as the bill's supporters clearly pointed out.[55]

With the division so close in both houses, all that Morrill could do was to reiterate—"not in the best humor," he admitted later—his arguments against the states' rights position. Government aid, he observed petulantly, could be extended to all causes but that of the education of the masses in their life pursuits. With a final partisan fling (though he maintained that the issue itself was in no sense partisan) at the inconsistencies as well as popular unresponsiveness of Democratic presidents, he was forced to leave the matter for the time being.[56]

In spite of temporary check the organized effort for this bill was to be decisive on the final achievement. Petitions from legislatures and agricultural societies and assurances of support from private individuals came from all parts of the country.[57] While Calvert's resolution censuring the President for inconsistency was ruled out of order by the United States Society at its meeting in 1860, the protest was voiced.[58] A meeting of the Illinois agricultural and horticultural societies in June of the same year petitioned Congress and called upon the legislature to take similar action for the enactment of the equivalent of "the bill called the 'Morrill bill.' "[59] The veto was calculated in every way to win support among free-soilers and to enhance the political standing of the measure in the North. According to Turner's recollection, he had the foresight to ask for Lincoln's approval before the convention and received ready assent. Douglas, he also recalled, had made a similar pledge and at the time of his death was planning with Turner's advice to introduce a grant bill at the next session.[60] While, like the companion proposal for a department of agriculture, industrial education was not mentioned in the Republican platform, it could be urged as an appropriate measure of the free-soil program. Accordingly, when in the first regular session of the Thirty-seventh Congress, December, 1861, with states' rights majority withdrawn and immediate war emergencies met, the leaders of the composite free-soil agricultural-industrial coalition hastened to press the measures sought by their respective interests, industrial education was revived.

Early in the session Morrill offered a revised bill, which increased the grant by one-half—30,000 acres per senator and representative—made no mention of the territories, excluded the states in rebellion from its benefits, and added military tactics to the required subjects. Discussion of the first bill had shown the inadequacy of the return reasonably to be expected from the original unit and that provision for the territories invited distracting controversy. The military requirement marked a tardy acceptance by the North of an educational feature long prevalent in the South. There was an opinion, both lay and professional, that such training had given the Confederates a marked advantage at the beginning of the contest in trained or partially trained officers. Hence, the new colleges should train officers for the militia of their state, and as West Point had combined civil with military engineering, the new nationally endowed schools would combine military training with their instruction for civilian pursuits.[61]

While there was an undoubted majority in both houses who from conviction or expediency would support the bill on a final vote, a small but desperately persistent group of obstructionists necessitated skillful parliamentary management to bring it to that stage. Since reference to an aggressively hostile House committee threatened fatal delay in a crowded session, Morrill persuaded Wade to introduce an identical bill in the Senate, and upon its passage and submission to the House, forced its adoption there under the previous question rule without reference or debate despite extreme obstructionist tactics.[62] Meanwhile, discussion in the Senate and in a few newspapers with interested readers had been sufficiently extended and heated, if not generally pertinent or informing.

The old sectional cleavage—ever existent and with secession reappearing in normal form—manifested itself in this debate more distinctly and openly than in that on any other of the free-soil enactments.[63] The homestead was a party pledge, however reluctantly conceded in some quarters; transcontinental railroads had eastern promoters as well as western recipients; the department of agriculture seemed too small a matter for anything but passing warning on the dangers of centralization; western tariff opposition was caustic but as usual scattered; currency and credit acts were rushed through as emergency measures with little understanding by the average member and with consequent lack of appreciation of their potentialities for sectional interests. The college bill presented a material basis of contention. To the land-conscious regions it seemed a deliberate attempt to transfer large, no doubt determining portions of their vested-interest resource to outside rapacious speculators. On this issue the West was still divided. The states whose better lands were patented were generally favorable, but for those with large unappropriated areas, especially Wisconsin, Minnesota, and Kansas, the attitude was hysterically defensive—"a violent though not powerful opposition," according to the *New York Tribune*.[64]

To the point of crass opportunism the issue was joined on past and future relative advantages of the landed and landless states in the disposal policies. The proposed proportional distribution, the opponents held, would largely nullify the beneficent intent of the homestead. The eastern land-scrip speculator might concentrate in certain strategic counties, and while waiting for the unearned increment deprive the progressively aspiring state of prosperous farms and public-spirited communities.[65] For Kansas, whose share of the domain was felt to be inadequate, the proposed act, in the deliberate judgment of Senator Jim Lane, would bring certain ruin, and Wilkinson of Minnesota and Howe of Wisconsin were almost as fearful for their states.[66] The bill was held to be but a culminating effort of the old financial centers to control the destinies of the new. "Free West" appealing—unavailingly in this case—for the sympathy of the editor of the *Tribune* felt that the bill's "sinister designs against the new States" were "about on a par with the doings of the 'Holy Allies' at Vienna." All that remained for complete domination was a New York grand duke in Kansas and a Massachusetts viceroy in Minnesota.[67] Lane suggested the addition of social insult to material injury in the far-fetched possibility that southern freedmen might be sent in to populate Kansas.[68]

The appeal of eastern supporters and their effective allies, such as Wade of Ohio, who was impressed by the growing strength of agricultural organizations,[69] and the ex-schoolman Harlan of Iowa, who was backed by instruction from his state legislature, for this very moderate "compensation" to the older states[70] did not impress the opposition. They countered with the claim that eastern settlers and promoters, in whose interests the acts were largely passed, had shared in the benefits at least equally with western communities.[71] In turn Clark of New Hampshire was shocked at Lane's implication that Kansas had rejected the English bill in order to get more land out of the Republicans.[72]

Alike in debate and editorial there was a discouraging but characteristic lack of consideration for the educational theories and policies involved; what purported to be a discussion of these issues was mainly negative or distorted. The advocates of the bill simply reiterated the complaints of class neglect and discrimination; and made no adequate presentation of the claims of technical education as such. The opposition presented the double argument that such institutions were not needed and that, if they were, the proposed grants would be entirely inadequate to establish and maintain them. There were the traditional frontier appeals to individual self-sufficiency and exploitive enterprise. All the farmers needed or desired from government was to be let alone; all the new communities needed was to get more and bigger farms.[73] Even less did the industrial states require agricultural colleges. Wilkinson, thinking in terms of prairie cropping, sought a reduction to the absurd in the case of Rhode Island where the total recorded wheat production was only forty-nine bushels.[74]

Wright of Indiana introduced a chivalrous sentiment. Disregarding the possibilities of land-grant coeducation, he argued that if there were to be federal aid for education it should be devoted to the instruction of the neglected daughters and sisters of soldiers who, in his distressful view, "must do one of three things: either go to teaching, or sewing, or they must, many of them, lead abandoned lives, while you have this immense army in the field."[75]

Whether or not the system proposed was desirable, the grant, it was pointed out, would be wasted, at the expense of the new states and with no ultimate benefit to anyone. Lands that might be the basis of prosperous homes, the *Milwaukee Sentinel* bemoaned, would be "frittered away with little advantage to any localities or persons except those who under the titles of 'Presidents,' 'Professors,' & c., pocket such proceeds."[76] But according to Senator Howe of the same state, this designing group would fare but slimly for, he warned, "You will never get a fund out of it in the State of New York or any other State that will keep a professor of agriculture from starving one week. . ."[77]

In hopeless minority on record votes the obstructionists fell back upon emasculating amendments. The only way of escape from the impending calamities, the *Sentinel* had warned, was for the states to adopt measures that would make scrip location unprofitable,[78] and opposition senators sought to anticipate or facilitate such impediments. Lane proposed restriction of location to the territories, in contrast to Grimes of Iowa who desired greater safeguard for territorial lands.[79] Lane's colleague, Pomeroy, secured by a margin of one vote a limitation of scrip to one section per person—a method that, as Senator Doolittle suggestively observed, would realize more than that of dumping large blocks upon Wall Street—but upon reconsideration the amendment was rejected.[80] Wilkinson sought postponement of the act for two years and one was conceded.[81] As a last resort in interferences, Howe offered a money grant of $30,000 from land sales instead of the acreage unit, to which there was made the bearish objection that it might require twenty or thirty years to accumulate the full endowment.[82] The only material amendment adopted was that limiting the amount of scrip to be located in any one state to one million acres.

With the exhaustion of ingenuity for amendment by the senatorial trio and of the obstructing tactics of "Bowie-Knife" Potter in the House, approval in both houses was overwhelming, 32 to 7 and 90 to 25, respectively.[83] The opposition was almost entirely western; in the Senate the only opposing easterner was Saulsbury from Delaware and in the House the nays had one from non-cereal Rhode Island and three from New York City, whose goat and swine herders, brewery refuse dairymen, and potato growers were supposedly oblivious to the possibilities of the new agriculture.

Lincoln's approval had been taken for granted throughout.[84] From his pronounced Whig convictions on the restricted function of the executive in determining positive legislative policies, he was not likely to oppose congressional will, more especially in the case of a measure involving finance. Aside from his general attitude there was every reason—apart from his reported promise to Turner—for approving this particular act and none, whether of personal conviction or party expediency, for opposing it. The proposed grant had a potential popular appeal in the older West and throughout the agricultural regions of the East. The notoriety of Buchanan's veto had definitely confirmed the measure as a part of the free-soil "new deal," even if it was not considered of sufficient importance in getting votes to merit a line in the platform. Undoubtedly approval was automatically good politics.

But the assumption that Lincoln had some direct and positive relation to the enactment and that, consequently, he deserves a large credit for it is but another biographical exaggeration. The bill was not on his "must" list. He had no competent understanding and apparently no personal interest in industrial education as such. In his address at the Wisconsin state fair in 1859 he had expressed full complacency with the existing institutions and facilities for popular education. While recognizing the need for agricultural improvement his chief interest was in the perfection of the much-discussed steam plow.[85] Repeated efforts to discover any direct connection which Lincoln might have had with the bill before it came to him for his signature have been wholly negative;[86] there is no evidence that he ever gave the matter any special thought.[87]

Moreover, it must be admitted, the President's passive attitude was quite in harmony with the state of public opinion on the question. As usual, the enthusiasts could readily secure endorsements of their plan from legislatures and organizations, but there was no indication of spontaneous public interest. The new departure in higher education secured generally no more than incidental mention amid the war news; only the sectionally defensive western papers and the socially sensitive *New York Tribune* gave any appreciable notice, and the *Tribune* omitted the act from its laudatory summary of the session's achievements.[88]

Even the agricultural papers, after the years of agitation, failed to manifest enthusiasm or, in some cases, even to give passing notice. The *Rural New-Yorker* showed the most appreciation. It gave brief but hearty endorsement to the first bill and printed the act—as it had previously the homestead and department of agriculture acts—with the succinct comment, "Our present Congress seems determined to recognize the interests of the farming community."[89] The *Country Gentleman* printed the resolutions of the Vermont society and two brief editorial paragraphs on the first bill,[90] while both the *American Agriculturist* and the *New England Farmer* ignored it. On the final act the *Gentleman* made a brief comment,[91] and the *Agriculturist* accorded a dozen line summary with the promise, "We shall have more to say about this act,"[92] but the editor forgot to say it for over a year. The *New England Farmer* maintained a discreet silence. Reminiscences published before the colleges gained their modern prominence mentioned the act only incidentally, if at all.

After all, any more general interest was not to be expected. An appreciation of the act on the basis of the greatness of the institutions to which it was to contribute would have been wholly anachronous. The original law,[93] while offering the possibility of strengthening existing projects in industrial education and of founding new ones, in itself assured nothing. The acreage or scrip, of uncertain value, was to be secured on conditions most uncertain of fulfillment. Contrary to later assumptions regarding the immediate influence, there was real doubt as to whether the provisions would be generally accepted. So dependable a supporter as Greeley sought to discount expectation of limited utilization by the assurance that the act would be justified if it led to the establishment of not more than five true industrial colleges.[94] Superlative encomiums of the measure as the "greatest act in the history of higher education" would find no contemporary substantiation, in professional assurance or popular recognition. The possibilities of this plan of national aid were only to be manifested in the course of time as the states utilized it in accord with their particular conditions and needs.

CHAPTER IV

STATE OPTION

In replying to the constitutional objection of Buchanan's veto message, Morrill had asserted that his plan left "the whole matter to the entire control of the several States to arrange, manage, and control as they may see fit";[1] and the message itself had practically conceded the same thing in the complaint that there was no effective provision for federal direction and control of state policy. While in statement of purpose marking a certain advance over past educational grants, in direct contrast to the modern policy of grants-in-aid the act made no fixed requirement as to type of institution or, beyond broad designations of fields of study, as to content of instruction. The only positive obligations were to dispose of the land or scrip, in manner and on terms left to state discretion; maintain the fund as a perpetual endowment invested at 5 per cent; devote the income to one or more institutions which, while including the traditional college subjects, must provide instruction in agriculture, mechanic arts, and military tactics; and make an annual report of the results.

Proportion of emphasis, as between the general and applied subjects or as between the two main fields of applications; subject content; instructional standards; physical equipment; administrative organization; and control were in each of the states to find ultimate determination in the prevailing popular desire. Supplemental acts, rather than increasing federal control, made the aid more available and adaptable. These special laws extended the privileges to the former Confederate and the new states and adjusted time and financial requirements to meet the particular limitations or negligence of individual commonwealths.[2]

Freedom from either restraint or direction, necessitated by political expediency and educational immaturity, was lauded as a constructive idea by both active innovators and passive recipients. Andrew D. White, after a decade and a half of the experiment, was "prepared to maintain, against all comers, that of all the good fortune which has attended the carrying out of the act of 1862, this variety of plans and methods in the various States was the best." The system, he held, provided essential unity while avoiding the narrow uniformity that was the bane of public education.[3] The same year, in his inaugural address, President William H. Scott of Ohio recognized a positive intent to anticipate geographical and occupational differences by leaving the institutions "free to adapt themselves to their environment."[4]

But, obviously, in a system of joint support, some happy medium between a uniformity of control at the expense of local needs and progressive experimentation at the one extreme, and the absence of general standards at the other was essential to a sound federal relationship. A checking of Dr. White's sweeping assurance, in 1884, that of the colleges receiving the grant "everyone is making a noble return on all it has received"[5] would have revealed embarrassing exceptions. In all cases—even the noblest—the returns had been delayed and hampered by rivalries and misunderstandings which clearer interpretation and more definite direction would in considerable part have prevented. The lack of such stabilizing influence opened the way for rivalries in which the real interest of the classes for whom the act was specially designed was little regarded.

The consequent scrambling, maneuvering, and intriguing for the federal largess reflected the financial desperation of the majority of colleges and the misconception among educational promoters of the peculiar field and special requirements of the new institutions. Conditions typical of the Gilded Age had contributed to an inordinate multiplication of educational ventures. The period marked the culmination of sectarian zeal in establishing doctrines and extending organization through colleges and seminaries. With the more aggressive sects ecclesiastical strategy dictated new promotions without regard for the long-time needs and opportunities of higher education, and community pride and supposed material advantage and "cultural" uplift encouraged the founding and keeping of all possible local institutions of learning, even though such indiscriminate provision tended inevitably to lower standards and to foster ruinous competition. New millionaires found personal gratification, and perhaps at times a certain moral satisfaction, in giving their names to monstrosities of towers, domes, and arches, thinking in the contemptuous phrase of Noah Porter that it was "as easy to found a university as . . . to build a cotton mill."[6]

Such reckless undertakings, sectarian and individual, brought an inevitable struggle for existence with appeals for public and private aid peculiarly inappropriate to the exalted aims expressed in the donors' presentations and in the classical or biblical college mottoes. Consequently, any new educational enterprise, technical, professional, or pedagogical, no matter how inconsistent with the organization and the avowed mission, would be entered upon with presumptuous eagerness if it involved the addition of even a small amount of "new money." The unfortunate precedent of legislative driblets to private colleges from time to time in the past no doubt stimulated the belief that this federal appropriation could be dissipated for such academic doles. Evan Pugh in his report in 1864 made the cutting observation, "That Literary Institutions should, with such undignified haste, grasp at resources (secured for the endowment of Industrial Colleges) to which they had not the *slightest legitimate claim,* is a melancholy illustration of the terrible extremities to which they are driven in the struggle for existence." Their plight, he felt, should be a warning to the states to provide adequate endowment for their land-grant creations.[7]

With little chance of securing the entire fund the smaller but desperate aspirants proposed division. In New York "a score of colleges were represented by men, eminent and influential, clamoring for a division of the fund among their various institutions, though the fragment which would have fallen to each would not have sufficed to endow even a single professorship."[8] Massachusetts' unusual interest in applied science occasioned active rivalries. Governor Andrew, President Hill, and Professor Agassiz led the Harvard interests in their plan to form a "grand university," combining the facilities of the College, the undeveloped Bussey Institution, and the Institute of Technology; Amherst and Williams sought distribution of the fund among the various colleges; and the board of agriculture was strongly committed to a new technical establishment.[9]

Division was persistently sought in Ohio where there were a complicating number of semipublic and private applicants. In addition to the original land-endowed universities and the Farmers' College, several other institutions clamored for a share.[10] Missouri's overmultiplied colleges, regardless of existing program and equipment, were desirous of adding chairs of agriculture.[11] Illinois industrialists, after blocking the concerted movement of denominational college presidents for distribution, found division in their own ranks. Chicago mechanics demanded a separate college in that city, and a bill actually passed the lower house providing for a university at Urbana with a mechanical department in Chicago and an agricultural school in the southern section.[12]

Among the numerous and fantastic proposals brought forward in the scandalously long contest in Indiana was one to divide the fund equally between four denominational colleges, each of which should maintain an agricultural department subject to state supervision, and the still more remarkable one for a research center at Indianapolis and professorships distributed among not less than five existing colleges and universities, no one of which should ever have more than two of the new departments.[13]

No less absurd was the plan of Waterville College for a technical education circuit for Maine: Bowdoin, chemistry applied to agriculture and the arts; Waterville, mathematics applied to mechanical and practical arts; Bates, agriculture, zoology, and veterinary science. Three-fourths of the fund was to be divided equally among the professorships and the remaining unit applied to the support of experimentation and of special lectures to be given in turn at the three colleges.[14]

Among those who recognized that the support and administration of popular technical education was a strictly public function there were conflicting ideas of concentration and division which in some form and degree have continued to the present. State university adherents urged the economy and efficiency of centralized organization and administration as well as the cultural opportunity and curricular balance to be secured by combining technical with general instruction. In direct opposition the champions of practical instruction for the occupations maintained that industrial education could succeed only in a separately organized institution where equipment, method, subject emphasis, and social attitude were congenial to the basic purposes. In attitude and objective the classical and the technical were held to be incompatible. Unsound and antiquated but persistent academic traditions denied equal fellowship to the technical, hence in defense and self-respect it should go its own way.

Aside from these vocationally minded enthusiasts certain broad-visioned educators were doubtful of the suitability of university connection. Pugh did not think that an agricultural college could "flourish under the wing of a literary college . . . [which would] sap its vitality, rob it of its enthusiasm, take away its best students and finally appropriate its means of subsistence," and years later as liberal an educator as Francis A. Walker warned repeatedly of the dangers of unequally yoking technical education with unappreciative or unworthy universities.[15]

With trade school zealots and local boosters, diffusion schemes went to meaningless extremes. One of the varied Indiana suggestions was for no less than twelve institutions—one within the university and one in each of the congressional districts,[16] and as late as 1890 a Washington legislator proposed that the state's fund be used to establish regional farms upon which boys could be trained in practical operations.[17]

Public school interests, then as later in industrial legislation, were concerned, however irrelevantly, for their cause. There were proposals to establish normal departments in connection with the new technical institutions, and the Illinois Normal

University asserted its qualification and competence as the administrator of the new fund.[18] California's state superintendent felt that the federal grant should be assigned to any private college that would take it, as the state should not be committed to new undertakings while the public school system remained so incomplete and insecure.[19] In Indiana and Missouri there were serious efforts to divert the endowment to the common school fund. But even this plan lacked the effrontery of an Indiana proposal, to establish no educational foundation but a soldiers' home.[20]

With such a confusion of interests and jumble of ideas it is rather remarkable that original adjustments were so satisfactory. Such an outcome is to be attributed mainly to the influence of far-visioned and constructive educators who had guided the movement in the initial stages in their states and who now were able to preserve it against selfish marauders from without and erratic visionaries from within. In the end each of the established state or semi-state technical colleges received the fund, with the exception of New York where rival experiments and incompleted establishment provided no adequate foundation for the type of institution sought by the state's educational reformers. In Michigan the contest over concentration of funds had already been settled by the establishment of the agricultural college to which the land-grant fund naturally went.[21] Pennsylvania's pioneer college met successfully criticisms in the legislature and press and resisted the pretensions of a small denominational college to a share in the fund. As an analysis of the scope and needs of the industrial college contemplated by the grant and as a brief for maintaining the fund intact, Pugh prepared for his board of trustees in 1864, shortly before his untimely death, an elaborate report which constitutes the most complete and understanding contemporary statement of the financial and educational requirements of land-grant education.[22] Maryland's state subsidized college in receiving the grant was brought a step nearer to ultimate public status.[23] The "Iowa Agricultural College and Farm" after surviving the unsettled conditions of the war was now able to resist the pressure for consolidation from the university interests.[24]

In other cases state universities, due in most instances more to ineffective competition than to positive appeal, were made the original depository of the fund. In the West, Wisconsin[25] and the recently established Minnesota university were reorganized with agricultural and engineering departments. Missouri's university led by President Read, James S. Rollins, and Norman J. Colman won a long and hard fight, with the condition that three-fourths of the fund should go to the agricultural and mechanical departments and one-fourth to a separately located school of mines.[26] In the South the land-grant establishment was made in the state universities in Georgia, North Carolina, and Tennessee; in Mississippi and South Carolina the fund was shared with the new Negro colleges. Curiously enough lack of promotive interest in Morrill's own state led to the organization of the new college with the state university. The legislature promptly accepted the act and chartered an agricultural college of which Morrill himself became a trustee, but after waiting three years for a satisfactory local bid, the institutions were combined as "The University of Vermont and State Agricultural College."[27] Delaware College, closed for nearly a decade, was reopened as a land-grant college (the state becoming a half owner) which ultimately became a state university.

Locations within private institutions were in some cases a recognition of established scientific foundations and in others a matter of mere convenience. The selection of the Sheffield School was mutually advantageous: Connecticut made official connection with one of the best developed science schools of the country without any expenditure for equipment and maintenance, and the Sheffield foundation secured essential aid at a formative stage.[28] Brown, with a scientific emphasis dating from the days of Wayland, seemed as appropriate a choice for Rhode Island. The transfer of New Jersey's relatively modest fund to the venerable Rutgers was but the first step in the creation of a full-fledged state university.[29]

Other unions with private institutions were not so well considered and were to occasion misunderstandings and internal dissension. The so-called Kentucky University at Harrodsburg combined with Transylvania at Lexington, and the state agricultural college was joined to the resulting church-controlled institution.[30] Oregon, as an emergency measure to save the grant, conferred its endowment upon the sectarian Corvallis College with the designation "State College of Agriculture."[31] New Hampshire's adjustment was unique. Affiliation with Dartmouth on a basis of separate organization and support was justified scholastically by the presence of distinguished science foundations but was really determined by considerations of economy.[32]

Where the industrial consciousness was especially keen or where local interest was strong and sharply divided, the most satisfactory solution proved to be a new "A. and M." college. In Massachusetts the leaders of the agricultural board, backed by popular sentiment, were able to thwart both the Harvard and small college designs, so far as agriculture was concerned, and secure their own college, but with the fund shared with the Massachusetts Institute of Technology on a two-to-one basis.[33] After the rivalries of Maine colleges had failed to develop a constructive plan or to indicate an understanding appreciation, the state's agricultural interests, led by Dr. Ezekiel Holmes, veteran educator and journalist, and S. L. Goodale, secretary of the state board of agriculture, secured a new college that realized an aim persisting from the Gardiner Lyceum days.[34] Indiana's long and embarrassing "college for sale" period, by benefit of John Purdue's gift and special congressional time extension, had a similar outcome.[35] Kansas' pronounced regionalism assured the distribution of her educational activities among different institutions. Rather tentatively in the unsettled times of reconstruction, five southern states—Alabama, Florida, Louisiana, Texas, and Virginia—launched institutions that in form and aim reflected directly the new industrialism. Among the newest states institutional decentralization was the prevailing trend. South Dakota, Utah, New Mexico, and Oklahoma founded separate colleges in the territorial period, and Colorado, Washington,[36] North Dakota, and Montana shortly after attaining statehood.

In the remaining states the land grant determined or influenced the founding of universities which, in the deliberately considered cases at any rate, constituted an effort to "carry out the act in its whole scope"[37]—a balanced and harmonious combination of the general and the technical. The Ohio board, after resisting for a decade the pressure to divide the fund, founded a new A. and M. college on such broad lines as to facilitate its reorganization five years later into a full state university. The grant thus brought a unity to the state's system of higher education which it had hitherto lacked and might not otherwise have attained.[38] Illinois finally established an institution which in name, organization, and emphasis approximated her reformers' conception of an "industrial university."[39] California's varied higher educational interests were pooled, with a reasonable approach to agreement, in one state university.[40] Arkansas, retarded educationally as well as economically by geographical position, and hitherto making no public venture in higher education, now founded an industrial university.[41] West Virginia, always combining the characteristics of South and West, perpetuated them in her new university. Nevada and Nebraska, granted statehood for reconstruction purposes and with sparse settlement, concentrated on one institution as did territorial Arizona, Idaho, and Wyoming.[42]

In view of the state's contributions to the early industrial movement, the distinguished leadership of the contending interests, and the significance of the foundation in the evolution of the university idea, the New York solution merits special attention. Among the numerous contenders before the legislature for the imperial endowment, Cook and his lobby were strong enough to secure the fund for the People's College on the very moderate condition that within three years the trustees should provide a farm, shops, scientific equipment, an adequate library, housing for at least 250 students, and a faculty of not less than ten. The college plans, as officially announced, were most pretentious. There were to be no less than twenty-three chairs in subjects ranging from natural and revealed theology to ichthyology, and from "taste as applied to the arts" to practical agriculture, and a gradation of instruction extending from speculative philosophy and comparative science to the preparatory department. A faculty of eight, headed by President Brown in the chair of philosophy, was selected for the opening in 1864, and the catalogue gave assurance that as soon as the scrip was "converted into cash" the trustees would fill the vacant chairs. But the collegiate status of the historic enterprise was never to be fully realized; the Regents' inspection committee revealed early in 1865 that the conditions of the grant had been met in no respect. Cook, following an illness that was ultimately to prove fatal, refused to provide the expected endowment, and under his heirs the nobly conceived experiment pursued a less ambitious though honorable career as a preparatory academy.[43]

The portended failure of the Havana enterprise encouraged other creative and promotive efforts. One of them was to place a landmark in higher education. An unusually fortunate conjunction of regional politics had brought to the state senate two remarkable personalities, contrasting but complementary. Ezra Cornell, a rugged, self-made capitalist with rare social vision, had long been concerned over the needs and possibilities of popular education, general as well as technical. As a leading member of the state agricultural society and a trustee of the dormant agricultural college, he was a persistent friend of education for the farmer, and he had a broader view of the scope and mission of popular higher education than the typical agitator for this cause. More clearly than most of the educators and administrators, he appreciated the possibilities of the federal grant. To harmonize and preserve the state's two enterprises, he proposed a division between the People's College and the Agricultural College, and at the state society meeting in 1864 offered, if this were done, to give $300,000 to the latter. From this step he was effectively dissuaded by his youthful, cultured colleague, Andrew D. White.[44] As a pioneer history professor at Michigan, with Yale and German university background, White had shared Tappan's vision of a broad and liberal university and two years before had sought to join his inherited fortune with that of a noted philanthropist to found a similar university in his native central New York.[45] He now found a willing coadjutor in the idealistic man of affairs. Once convinced of the possibilities of a concentrated endowment for a far bigger and nobler undertaking in popular higher education than any heretofore tried in his state or elsewhere, Cornell went the whole way, to the limit of his resources and promotive energy and genius, to secure its realization. He made the daring offer, in return for the complete scrip apportionment, to found a new university with ample site and $500,000 endowment.[46]

This audacious new departure, so upsetting to the small schemers, public and private, was heatedly but futilely opposed by all of them combined. The sectarian weaklings made curious and desperate alliance with the stillborn state offspring. The whole plan was distorted and the motives of the donor were savagely maligned. Against such tactics White exerted his rare powers of reasoning and persuasiveness in debate and, with the aid of the zealous patron, his even more effective skill in private conference. Humanitarians, like Greeley, were won over by the inclusive and liberal basis of the proposed foundation and by the provision for free scholarships in each district. Judicious log-rolling seems to have been the final resort, culminating in an agreement to use the building of the Agricultural College for a state insane asylum. Thus the new university, bearing the founder's name—somewhat against his wish—and his all-embracing motto, was chartered. In the legislative struggle there was but one casualty. A drooping college that felt that its great expectations had been thwarted by past discrimination made a "strike" demand for $25,000 which, to prevent further dangerous delay, Cornell paid. The legislature later had the grace to reimburse the donor with this sum for assignment to the university's endowment.[47]

In locating the newly created institutions there was a rivalry often as keen and bitter as that over the disposal of the fund. The practice of authorizing and encouraging rival bidding by counties and other subdivisions while generally making for increased immediate resources led in a number of cases to enmities that militated against later state support. There was the danger, too, that immediate material advantage or special local "pull" would outweigh sounder considerations. At times these colleges, designed in the interest and for the service of the people of the states, became mere pawns in log-rolling contests involving rivalry not only of sections but of political and corporate interests. Illinois' industrial university actually went to the "lowest bidder"; the estimated offering of the locality selected was far below either of three rival sites, but special local influences overcame the disparity in assets.[48]

In a number of cases the existence of some sort of educational enterprise on the chosen site, usually quiescent or moribund, with equipment ill-adapted to the new special purpose and with wholly inharmonious traditions, exercised an inordinate influence. California, where the combined church interests that had established a college with the expectation of meeting the state's need for higher education recognized the demand for a public university and turned over their institution for the purpose, was the exception.[49] The trustees of the Kansas Bluemont College, after failing to locate the state university, were glad to devote their liability to the agricultural college venture. In Alabama a defunct church college provided the lowly base for a great "polytechnic," and in Mississippi a similar purchase was devoted to the Negro university that shared jointly in the state fund. An abandoned "institute" was one of the supposed regional assets that attached to the Purdue location in Indiana, as were a partly-built "seminary of learning" in Illinois, and academies in Virginia and West Virginia.[50] The importance attributed to these academic relics is a fair indication of the prevailing inadequate conception of the peculiar requirements of the new technology. As the groups directly concerned reached a clearer understanding of these requirements increasing demand for reorganization and re-establishment followed.

Class-conscious farmers confronted with the productive and

distributive complexities of the new industrial era demanded their own colleges to help solve their problems. Separate colleges with utilitarian purpose were a distinct demand of the agrarian crusade, in opposition to the contention of leading contemporary educators that public higher education should be as strictly centralized as the elementary instruction should be widely diffused. The national and state Granges were strongly committed to the separate college plan, and the agitation was continued by the Populists.[51] The logic of class education was reduced by the Wisconsin order to the "axiom . . . that each profession should be taught by those who practice it, and are professors of such profession. Ecclesiastics should teach ecclesiastics, lawyers teach lawyers, mechanics teach mechanics, and farmers teach farmers." In disregard of such a system of instruction and in nullification of congressional intent, there appeared, so Henry C. Adams of the same state complained, "a lot of agricultural departments tucked in under the wings of state universities, and so closely hid that the only evidence of their being was in their catalogues."[52] As a result of insistent demand a number of separations took place in the eighties and others followed the "second Morrill Act" of 1890, which precipitated decisions as to permanent establishment and organization.

The connections with private institutions had always been the most tenuous and tentative. At Brown the required use of the small income for free scholarships, available in any course, had proven a burden rather than an added resource, and following the establishment of a state agricultural school in 1888, President Andrews recommended that the fund be relinquished. With the grant of 1890, however, the situation was altered, and the resourceful executive saw the possibility of a fully developed applied science school. But such a plan came too late and, after a financial adjustment, the new school at Kingston was made the land-grant college.[53] In neighboring Connecticut the Sheffield School, while developing experimentation to a high degree, did not provide the practical instruction desired by the Grange and the state society. An agricultural school established at Storrs in

1881 by private bequest and with state subsidy became the hope of the opposition, and in 1893 the legislature made it the state agricultural college, awarding it the new fund and transferring to it the old. Yale contested the action and was awarded damages to the value of the original fund with accrued interest.[54] The Dartmouth affiliation, an adjustment of short-sighted expediency, was discordant throughout. Relations were never sympathetic, and friction soon developed. Students of the old classical institution regarded contemptuously the assumptions of the new applied scientists, and the president in petulant commencement remarks gave peculiar affront in the opinion that at most the agricultural course fitted students for "highway surveyors, selectmen, and perhaps, members of the legislature." Throughout the eighties farmers were demanding removal, and the opportune Thompson bequest made possible relocation at Durham in 1893 on the site of the future state university.[55] Ecclesiastical conflict within the "Kentucky University" led to the withdrawal of the A. and M. department and the subsequent founding of a full state university at another location in Lexington.[56] After fifteen years of nominal church jurisdiction, the Oregon legislature in 1885 took over the Corvallis College as a state institution and by legal contest secured full title.[57]

State university affiliations, in some cases, proved equally unstable. In Mississippi almost from the start the Grange was dissatisfied with the agricultural instruction and conducted a wide and vigorous campaign for separation. Following the defeat of their bill in 1877, the state convention resolved in language not to be misunderstood: "We insist that the Legislature of the State shall establish an agricultural college in accordance with the intention of the act of Congress appropriating the proceeds of the sale of public land in this State for that purpose, and that no further delay nor frittering away of the fund will be quietly tolerated by the agriculturists of the State." The legislature recognized the mandate at the next session and after careful consideration of rival local inducements, permanent location was made.[58] In the reconstruction years the income from the North

Carolina fund was so inadequate and badly managed that it was given tentatively to the university. During the economic revival of the eighties the combined activities of the public-spirited Watauga Club, the state board of agriculture, and the various farmers' organizations secured a long sought A. and M. college.[59] The Tillman movement and the bequest of Thomas G. Clemson brought a similar transition in South Carolina.[60] California, Missouri, Wisconsin, and Minnesota, after long and persistent Granger and Populist attacks, were saved from division by unusually able administrative leadership, a reorganization and broadening of instruction, and effective extension contacts.[61] In Morrill's own state, after the initial indifference, a long and bitter struggle ensued to detach the grant from the university, either for a rival or a new institution. Both sides sought the Senator's influence. In 1890 an aggressive agricultural journalist and organization leader presented a most enticing appeal. A satisfactory financial settlement such as Brown made would, he urged, really be to the university's interest, and if the new college were located centrally, say in Morrill's home town, there would be no injurious rivalry. The feeling of Vermont farmers seemed to be unanimous for the change and they were looking to the Senator for aid in founding another institution "which will be in your own state the same lasting monument to Justin S. Morrill that exists in the shape of similar A. and M. colleges in most of our other states." But Morrill, who had been an active trustee and close adviser of the president since the union, was unalterably committed to the maintenance of the university connection.[62] Wyoming, by law and popular referendum, provided in the early nineties for the creation and location of a separate college, but the legislature refused to take action and the university remained intact.[63]

In contrast to these tendencies toward separation, in Louisiana, where educational status had always been curiously confused and unsettled, popular sentiment favored the union of the land-grant foundation with the old military seminary to provide a real state university.[64] A still greater reversion was involved in the proposal made by certain Massachusetts legislators and recommended in a governor's official message to give the state's agricultural college to Amherst College. Fortunately, this defeatist counsel received no general support.[65]

Such instability reflected not only an uncertainty as to aims but an equal uncertainty as to the means necessary for their realization. Relinquishment of the fund in most cases was facilitated by disappointment over its inadequacy, and zeal for new arrangement was moderated by the same limitation. The requirements of the act, the general financial conditions of the founding period, the competition of other grant and disposal acts, and the indifference and incompetence of state officials combined to depress the value of the land and scrip. There was the pressure for immediate funds to start the colleges within the required period with consequent glutting of the market with huge blocks of scrip. The concurrent railroad grants and the inauguration of homesteading contributed further to an unsettled and bearish land market, while the background of inflation and consequent depressing deflation were undermining public and private confidence.

State officials generally had little appreciation of the possibilities of the act, and there was ineffective cooperation with federal agencies. Rhode Island assignees, seeking to forestall her competitors, made personal application to the land office immediately upon the execution of the contract, and upon delay in issue of the scrip proceeded to locate lands in Kansas, for which colonizing plans had already been made, in advance of the requisite evidences of ownership. The commissioner of the land office promptly repudiated such an anticipated transaction, and the state's interests, it was claimed, were in consequence endangered.[66] The record low of 41 cents for the Rhode Island scrip (secured from a lump sale to one of the college's official agents) was perhaps partially the result of the misunderstanding. Too often, it is evident, the easy way was taken to secure ready money from the scrip and it was consequently beside the point for such careless and short-sighted bargainers to inveigh against the "harpies and land sharks" who had secured "enormous profits" from their necessities. So long as state agents had no more initiative than to deal with land-brokerage houses, they had to expect heavily discounted endowments. Scrip sales by a number of the reconstruction governments involved waste and fraud, and the policies of some of the larger scrip-holding states in the North—notably Pennsylvania, Massachusetts, and Ohio—were inexcusably inefficient.

Considering the prevailing financial and political influences, however, the returns to the original recipient states were not so abnormally low as has often been represented. The average price was $1.65 per acre. Nine states received more than the public domain minimum of a dollar and a quarter. The public land states of Kansas, California, Minnesota, Iowa, and Michigan held and managed their lands for highly satisfactory prices—above, in two cases twice, the "double minimum" of public land rates. Some of the older states with remaining public lands found only inferior lands from which to make selection and were thus destined to small returns.[67]

New York's achievement that eventually secured from 10 per cent of the national grant about 40 per cent of the total receipts, was the reward of imaginative venturing and heroic sacrifice. Cornell's celebrated agreement—to negotiate and finance the disposal of the state's scrip with a guaranteed 60-cent return to the land-grant fund and all in addition to become an unrestricted endowment—was an essential part of his uniquely inclusive university design.[68] That there were not similar achievements in other states was due to the fact that there were no other Ezra Cornells to vision an enterprise of such "utilitarian idealism" and to inspire collaborators to see it through.

In the realm of purely public initiative a conception of the full responsibility of the state for higher education and a positive recognition of the responsibilities and opportunities of federal cooperation were lacking. Could such reactions have anticipated two generations of growing social and national consciousness, they might have resulted in the founding in each commonwealth of an intellectually strong and socially progressive institution adequately adjusted to particular conditions and needs. As it was, with the limitations of the age of reconstruction and transition, and the inhibitions of an unbalanced, though supposedly rugged individualism, these potential state-serving colleges were left to muddle through until that consciousness evolved. The "national schools of science" could take their assured and essential place in the national scheme of education only when they were accepted, with full implications, as state colleges.

CHAPTER V

TRIAL AND ERROR: ORGANIZATION AND STAFF

In a critical appraisal of "Our National Schools of Science" in 1867, Daniel Coit Gilman, then of the science school of Yale and later to become president of the University of California, made the revealing observation: "Two crucial epochs have been passed, the Congressional and the Legislative. Now comes the third, the period of development."[1] This development was long obstructed and retarded by the lack of common understanding and working agreement as to proper field, range, and methods. While a reasonable degree of flexibility, making possible adjustments to varying regional conditions and needs, was as desirable in curriculum and methodology as in institutional organization and control, failure to agree upon essentials in scope and aim retarded the establishment of recognized standards and of helpful and stimulating relations with member and outside institutions.

The varied interpretations found at least a specious justification in the indefiniteness and ambiguity of the organic act. President Buckham of Vermont, Morrill's most intimate academic confidant, thought the phraseology might "well be compared for expansive comprehensiveness with those few but potent words which give validity to interstate commerce legislation."[2] With the irreconcilable elements in the industrial movement and the experimental basis of the proposed institutions, ambiguity and inclusiveness had been deliberate, as President William H. Scott of Ohio frankly admitted in his inaugural address in 1884: "It does not require a very close scrutiny of this language to discover that it is not the statement of a single mind setting forth a single untrammeled purpose. It is the welding of two opposite views. Minds that were agreed on the general question of appropriating public lands for education, were at variance as to the kind of education for which it should be appropriated. The result was a compromise—a compromise which consisted not in abandoning the extremes for intermediate ground, but in a union of the extremes."[3] Or as Professor Foerster has succinctly stated, the expedient course was "to embrace both horns of the dilemma."[4]

The old-line classicists, convinced that "they would render God service by diverting the money" for "disciplinary" and "cultural" training,[5] or merely concerned with diverting it for their necessities, regarded the required subjects as incidental side lines. The Bowdoin plan (which according to one of her professors would have given the enterprise the most respectable burial) aimed to compress the technical subjects into a single year.[6] The Texas A. and M., under guardians of the old traditions, made the only real departure in the addition of military training; their chief exhibit of the new learning was the chair of chemistry, natural science, and agriculture held by a doctor of divinity.[7] The first faculty of the Kansas Agricultural College, inherited with the defunct denominational college and headed by a minister "of conservative views with regard to education, politics, and religion—a typical New Englander of the old school," had no sympathy for or understanding of innovations in applied science.[8] The Nebraska university made a young bachelor of arts superintendent of the farm, the chief evidence of the federal connection, and a little later gave him the added dignity of "Tutor in the Agricultural Department."[9] The Corvallis College recognized its public function by the purchase of a small farm and the addition of horticultural instruction to the teaching duties of the professor of languages.[10] The Florida State College of Agriculture had a remarkable professorship of "Agriculture, Horticulture, and Greek," held by a master of arts.[11]

The classicists at most tolerated the new subjects, so long as they were kept in their menial place; the industrialists agreed only in opposing the old philosophy. From the beginning, and to some degree throughout the formative years, the movement was divided into extreme groups. The "broad gauge" scientists postulated the teaching of fundamental principles and underlying theories as the only adequate basis for application. Such teaching necessitated breadth as well as depth, a "liberal" background as a preparation for intensive specialization. They thus stood for adding to rather than subtracting from the content of higher education. The "national schools of science," as they significantly termed the land-grant foundations, were not to be trade or vocational institutes for training working farmers and mechanics but colleges or departments for educating leaders in the sciences. As well, they held, expect West Point and Annapolis to provide privates for the ranks and seamen of the line as to look to the polytechnic for skilled craftsmen and proficient mechanics. Manual dexterity and physical adaptability were irrelevant acquirements for industrial experts and managers; knowledge of principles and methods was everything. Laboratory practice, consequently, should not stress acquisition of routine skill but involve rather demonstration and research; farm and shop should not be model but experimental.[12]

Such an emphasis was in harmony with the contemporary "new education" movement which was seeking to modernize and socialize the curriculum by an emphasis upon science and the modern languages. The science schools of Harvard, Yale, and Dartmouth, along with early polytechnics in the East and the University of Michigan in the West, were the pioneer centers, while Cornell and the stronger state universities sought to fulfill the land-grant requirements on this basis.

The outstanding educational leaders of the period were the champions. Eliot defended the aims and values in his notable *Atlantic Monthly* articles in 1869 and in his inaugural address of the same year; Gilman, before launching his graduate university (Johns Hopkins), had with satisfaction "seen a school of science grafted upon one of the oldest and most conservative of classical colleges" (Yale) and had "helped to rescue a State University from the limitations of a college of agriculture and enlarge it to meet the requirements of a magnificent commonwealth" (California); Walker carried the idea from Yale to the more intensive application at M. I. T.; and White gave formulation in his inaugural and detailed exposition in addresses and magazine articles.[13] Even Noah Porter—to whom Ph. B. must always have signified a barbarian philosophy and S. B. a dubious *satis bene*—conceded, on the basis of the Sheffield plan, that the modernized course might be "better adapted to a certain class of young men the texture and habits of whose minds and limitations of whose time seemed to preclude them from the longer and the more valuable courses of the college and the professional school." The new, if lesser light in the academic firmament was definitely fixed and must be so recognized. "He cannot be awake to the necessities of the times, and the true enlightenment of the largest number, whose zeal for the Old education disqualifies him for intelligent and cordial sympathy with the New."[14]

In distinct contrast in aim, content, and method were the "narrow gauge" survivors of the labor mutuals and manual labor school movements who continued to stand for the direct, "practical" training of farmers and mechanics. For such training productive labor on farm and in shop was regarded as absolutely essential for manual dexterity, good moral habitude, and current maintenance. They would thus reduce higher education to the lowest terms and give it the widest extension. In these literal people's colleges instruction should be adjusted to the average district school standards. There might be no royal road to learning but they were confident that there was a democratic. The older colleges were for the select few rather than the masses. Their graduates were turned from the pursuit of the socializing, stabilizing basic industries into the overcrowding learned professions. Indictments overrating prevailing scholastic interest and achievement complained that "Digging out Greek roots, discussing knotty points in metaphysics or ancient history, or discoursing upon heathen mythology are more congenial occupations. The effect of the training of our classical schools seems to be adverse to fitting a young man for following the quiet, laborious life of the farmer."[15] The trial of industrial education, they were convinced, could not safely be made in such an aristocratic environment or in accord with the wholly inappropriate organization and method.

Such popular, prejudicial appeals came from varied sources. The Illinois lower house in 1869, taking note that complaints were made that the "leading objects" were being departed from, resolved that their industrial university had for "its leading and essential objects the teaching of such branches of learning as relate to agriculture, horticulture, and the mechanic arts, and the consequent promotion of the industrial classes in the various pursuits of life by imparting to them a liberal and practical education." The board's chief duty was held to be to adjust and adapt the whole system "to the educational wants of students who are looking forward to the adoption of farming or mechanics as their chosen avocation in life."[16] Governor John Brough of Ohio, in his message of 1865, assumed that Congress intended to provide practical manual training for the laboring classes, hence the instruction should be "plain and practical, not theoretically and artistically scientific in character."[17] In the same spirit Governor Merrill visioned the Iowa college sending forth "in annual procession, a line of educated intelligent husbandmen;" and leading board members were pledged to start and recruit such a procession. One of them proclaimed the institution open to "any of God's people" but especially designed for the state's working people; another, in intrusting the keys to the president, expressed the fervent hope that training in the "practical industries" would ever be the main objective.[18] Likewise, Governor Roberts of Texas thought that an agricultural college was "for the purpose of training and educating farm laborers," while "Blue Jeans" Williams of Indiana was convinced that higher education of any sort and degree was a deterrent to honest labor.[19] Professor Ezra Carr of California, a Rensselaer pioneer, concluded that the only justification of the federal grant was *"to make more farmers and mechanics."*[20]

Premising this objective, content and method followed logically. A Philadelphia agricultural paper gave especially realistic directions: "Instead of introducing the student of agriculture to a laboratory and chemical and philosophical apparatus, we would introduce him to a pair of heavy neat's leather boots and corduroy pants, and learn [*sic*] him how to load manure and drive oxen. We would put him through a course of really practical farming, and we would select as professors such men as the Cornells of Bucks county, and the Conrads of Chester county, who could not perhaps make critical analyses of soils but who could raise good crops of corn and potatoes, and wheat and barley."[21] The *American Agriculturist,* after warning against too elaborate equipment at the beginning, gave its formula for successful establishment on the bases of far-reaching assumptions: "Set a number of earnest men, capable of teaching agriculture, down upon a good farm, with a good large house and barns upon it, and the cooperation of a good farmer; put up a few temporary buildings, if need be, for lecture rooms now, and perhaps for stables by and by; give the Faculty a little money to spend upon books, apparatus and fitting up; let them know that they shall have more as fast as they can show results; let all permanent improvements be made with a view to the future and leave the Faculty as unhampered in regard to matters of instruction and discipline as possible, and success of the most gratifying character will be almost certain in any State of the Union."[22] The English Royal Agricultural College at Cirencester was recommended by some as a model of occupationally motivated instruction.[23] This craft and trade school notion long persisted: after a quarter century of discussion and experiment there were still those in the new state of Washington who would have devoted the college fund to practice farms for boys.[24] Farmers' organizations consistently, though seldom understandingly, thus clamored for real farmers' colleges that, in effect, would take awkward boys and girls from the farms and send them back master farmers, model homemakers, and community leaders.

In this contest between the rival groups of industrial educators, federal authorities made no helpful contribution to the definition and adjustment of the terms of the act and had no authority to enforce such ideas as they might have. The law creating the "Department of Education" in 1867 had provided that in his first report the commissioner should present "a statement of the several grants of land made by Congress to promote education, and the manner in which these several trusts have been managed, the amount of funds arising therefrom, and the annual proceeds of the same, as far as the same can be determined." In accord with this requirement Commissioner Barnard circularized the various colleges established or aided by the act of 1862 for the fullest obtainable statistics on origin, organization, finance, courses of study, and methods of instruction. Detailed descriptions of the Sheffield School and the Massachusetts Institute of Technology were appended as models. The authorities concerned were reminded that "These institutions as a class are so new in this country, and so much thought has been expended upon them, and at the same time so much remains to be ascertained in respect to their practical efficiency, even in the states where they exist, that a comparison of their various charters or acts of incorporation, programmes of study, regulations, funds, buildings, and collections is imperatively called for." By prompt and full response they would "contribute to the solution of a problem of momentous interest to the people of the United States. . ." The statistics from the various states, including current laws, along with descriptions of certain European technical schools, were published in the first report,[25] as a basis, supposedly, for determining the most desirable and practicable system. The early heads of the agricultural department, which had more possibilities of growth and expansion of functions, with consequent political sensitiveness and a tendency to follow rather than to guide the constituency, were emphatically committed to the popular occupational view.[26]

Both groups appealed to Morrill but to little definite effect. Atherton maintained that "scarcely anyone except the author of the bill showed any clear understanding of its real scope and meaning,"[27] but it soon developed that if he understood he was most reticent in his revelations. As an educational writer in the eighties pointed out, while Morrill's speech of 1858 gave the fullest statement of his intent, it was definite only upon two points, the relations of extensive cultivation to agricultural decline and the European evidence of the corrective value of education.[28] To judge by this speech and later utterances, his plan at the beginning, beyond that of benefiting and raising the relative status of the farmer and mechanic, was as indefinite as that of the average contemporary reformer; and his interpretation of the scope and purpose of the institutions, to which his name and fame were to become attached so intimately, changed decidedly with the years. From the original intent of securing entry for the main occupational subjects to the established collegiate system, his design expanded to a plan for national schools of science in which agriculture and mechanic arts should have preferred standing, further broadened to the balanced all-around education of the industrial classes, and finally sought the extended scope of university instruction by a greater emphasis upon pure science and modern language and the addition of the applied sciences.[29] The influence of scholars and administrators like President Buckham and Judge Benedict of Vermont, White, Gilman, and Brewer upon Morrill's developing educational theory is apparent.[30] Above all, in later years, Morrill's land-grant education philosophy seems to have been shaped and adjusted by the needs and exigencies of his own state university, with its notoriously slow development of applied science instruction, and its long struggles against rival colleges and Granger and other unfriendly agricultural groups, involving serious threat of separation.[31]

Whatever his personal views, as the reputed, and in time traditionally revered father, he tended to tolerate and in most cases to give rather indiscriminate blessing to all of the offspring regardless of their contrasting organizations and aims. In the early years farming enthusiasts, without recorded contradiction, cited statements indicating that a college farm and required manual labor were basic in his plan,[32] while the Sheffield group in the intimacy of a personal visit secured an admission that a farm though desirable was not strictly essential, that manual labor was suitable mainly for physical exercise, and that their school was fulfilling the intent of the act both in letter and in spirit.[33] During the first year of the new act Charles Cook was adjured that the success or defeat of the whole plan depended largely upon the action of the People's College board;[34] twenty years later Dr. White was assured that his university was "an institution of learning which more nearly approaches my cherished ideal of what our country most needs than any other hitherto known."[35] In the debate on the proposed new grant in 1872 he asserted that there was abundant proof that most of the thirty institutions were successful and that six or seven were "preeminent in character and usefulness." Those of Michigan, Iowa, Kentucky, Illinois, Massachusetts, and Connecticut were "doing work of priceless value" and Kansas and Missouri were not far behind.[36]

Without benefit of outside direction or guidance it remained for the institutions themselves to reconcile the extreme positions of the "purely educational and the merely mechanical" and of "science without practice and practice without science."[37] While relative direction was determined by local background, prevailing interests, and consequent leadership, the tendency was increasingly to recognize, at least in theory and assumption, both claims. To restrict industrial education to the narrowly vocational, it came to be realized, was to limit rather than to extend popular opportunity at the higher educational levels. The most practical agricultural colleges came to recognize that without an adequate scientific content and methodology they had little to practice and, consequently, no special service to render their supporting constituency.

On the other side there were social obligations to extend the new education as well as an expedient need to placate special influential groups whose desires, if somewhat unreasoned, could not be ignored. Ex-President Hayes, who was largely responsible for the working agreement between his university and the state board of agriculture, noted in his diary after a conference with the university secretary: "The university to be improved and popularized. Farmers, mechanics, and military men to be especially considered in the university! Good."[38] A conciliatory but assured interpretation and exposition of the scope of the land-grant act conceived the "industrial classes" as including the higher educable groups, whether "technical" or "liberal."[39] But such an admirable conception of a modernized university had to contend at the beginning and in most cases for several decades against unfavorable conditions and unsympathetic and indifferent attitudes, within and without.

The general public was little enough concerned with the scope and method of higher education, general or technical. The nation was not yet college-going conscious; the campus was a cloistered domain apart from ordinary existence. In most communities the college graduate was so rare as to be a marked man, whether or not marked for anything in particular. Student teachers of country schools during the long vacation of winter amazed the back country inhabitants with their tales of college prank or achievement, and not infrequently awakened in some youth of the household longing and aspiration for the adventures and supposed opportunities of the higher learning. The president and professors, while condescendingly regarded in "practical" affairs, like the clergy, commanded in matters intellectual high esteem and poor support.

There was, however, for the average individual a compensating and counteracting attitude of forced indifference. The self-made tradition remained strong. With the intellectual resources of the district school, supplemented by self-training and the true American initiative, one could secure all else worth having. A popular writer and lecturer in an obituary eulogy of Lincoln in a business magazine drew the moral that "The child of the lowly and of the exile can gain an education free as air, and good as that which Victoria can give her titled children, with the treasury of her Kingdom at her command. The sons of coal heavers and porters become millionaires. The store boy of one generation becomes the princely merchant of the next."[40]

Eliot lamented in his inaugural that as a people we did not apply the principle of division of labor in the realm of the intellect and had slight faith in special training for professional service. "The vulgar conceit that a Yankee can turn his hand to anything we insensibly carry into high places where it is preposterous and criminal. We are accustomed to seeing men leap from farm or shop to court-room or pulpit, and we half believe that common men can safely use the seven-league boots of genius." He felt that the "lack of faith in the prophecy of a natural bent, and in the value of a discipline concentrated upon a single object" amounted to a "national danger."[41] A quarter of a century later Francis A. Walker sounded the same warning: "The ghastliest mistakes of life are those of self-made men theretofore successful, whether in war, in politics, in professional practice, or in business."[42] From the classical camp Porter berated the blatant self-educated type, seen most conspicuously in journalism, who "indulged a jealous contempt of all disciplinary training whatever" and found "in their own success a satisfactory argument for the uselessness of any other than the so-called practical or useful studies, as well as the decisive refutation of all that can be urged in the defense of any other."[43]

Farmers, the especial "industrial class" for whom the new training was designed, were generally lacking in appreciation. President W. O. Thompson, misled apparently by the agitation of farmers' organizations in Ohio, was led to assert that the movement sprang, not from the social reformers and professional educators "but from the rank and file of the people themselves."[44] The evidence is all directly to the contrary. The invariable experience of administrators and educators was that the farmers themselves were the hardest to convince of the need and possibility of occupational training, and editorials, letters to agricultural papers, and discussions in state and local societies and by other farmer meetings were all to the same effect—an indifference, suspicion, or open contempt for the new-fangled methods of learning to farm.[45] Success in cultivation and husbandry was a matter of applying faithfully the good old traditional methods. Experience, not book learning, was needed.

Ambition for collegiate training which was spreading in rural communities was directed toward general or professional rather than technical instruction and was desired especially for the boy who was "too smart" to keep down on the farm. The average farmer was confident that he could teach his son all that he needed to know about farming operations—and far more effectively than any professor. The silk-hatted, kid-gloved, cane-twirling supervisor of farming operations was a caricature hard to live down. The whole idea of formal study in connection with farming as he experienced it was ludicrous in the extreme to the country wit. "What you goin' to do with that college up there?" inquired the Massachusetts farmer. "Are you goin' to larn 'em to rake arter?"[46] Many felt in their self-satisfied complacency like the New Hampshire legislator of the twenties who opposed an agricultural society appropriation with the claim that the farmers of his part of the state already knew a lot more than they could practice.[47]

While easterners, "glorying in their goads,"[48] tended to keep to the ways of their fathers, the westerners found land exploitation more immediately profitable than improved methods. Turner confessed in 1863 that the college act had come ten years before he had expected it and it might be that long before the state was ready for it.[49] Popular skepticism was encouraged by writers from whom more constructive counsel might have been expected. Donald G. Mitchell (Ik Marvel), evidently feeling that the pen was mightier than the test tube, expressed the opinion that a few thousands spent for farm papers would do more for agricultural improvement than all the expenditures for colleges.[50]

The expenditures in any case could not be lavish, even according to the budgetary standards of a period when the average endowment of the leaders was not over half a million. Pugh in his notable land-grant college plan suggested a total budget of $47,000—including sixteen professorships at $1,500—which was to be secured by the income from endowment and tuition at $50 per year.[51] He regarded his estimates, especially for salaries, as conservatively restrained, but they were not to be generally attained in the formative years.

The essential needs of technical education, based upon the

standards of the traditional one-building, crudely equipped, president-professor college, were in the early years greatly underrated. The able secretary of the Ohio board reported that the trustees believed that an initial appropriation of $50,000 "judiciously expended" would place the college "in such a position of efficiency and usefulness that there will be no need for a long time to come, if ever, to apply for more State aid, unless on some unforeseen and special occasion."[52] A Maine legislative committee as late as 1881 was confident that the college could gradually become self-sustaining and advocated progressive reduction in appropriation looking to that end.[53] A record for voluntary economy was set by the Oregon board in the hard times of the early nineties in actually declining a $5,000 legislative grant.[54] This is recorded as unequaled in Oregon history and it is doubtless so in that of all state colleges, for it was soon evident that technical education was the most expensive type, both in outlay for equipment and plant and in cost of instruction.

The productive endowments were in most cases inadequate and state appropriations for the current needs of federally created institutions were generally sparingly given, in the spirit of the Maine statesmen just cited. Unfriendly legislatures at times created critical situations by cutting off or temporarily holding up expected support.[55] Against such tactics resourceful executives and professors might play the political game with more or less effectiveness, and alumni representatives were increasingly helpful;[56] but until reasonably regular provision was assured there was a demoralizing uncertainty. The prevailing practice was to provide free tuition for the state's own students, but some were forced by their necessities to violate this tenet of popular education. Massachusetts' board felt greatly handicapped in attracting students by the necessity of making such charges, and it was even recommended that a percentage of the state dog tax be devoted to the financing of free scholarships.[57] Inadequacy of endowments, lack or uncertainty of state appropriations, and the reluctance of private benefactors to contribute to a public enterprise resulted in a precarious or hampering dependency throughout the trial years.

Universities with potentially large endowments might seem to be raised above the common lot, but they, too, had to be "carried" during the lean, expectant years. Cornell much more than fulfilled his personal obligations to his university and at great sacrifice of time, money, and immediate reputation held the investment in timber lands for a more favorable market. Meanwhile, the university was sorely pressed to maintain the portions of its elaborate program that had been undertaken. Leading board members felt that it would be better to have a million in hand for present necessities than three or four times that amount five or ten years later. Willard Fiske well expressed the faculty sentiment in a letter to President White: "Mr. Carpenter has been at work on Mr. Cornell for the past two days and says that he has succeeded in making a good sketch of him. I wish that he might be painted in the act of selling two hundred thousand acres of land for a million dollars."[58]

The founder did not live to see the vindication of his foresight; he died in the midst of the panic with his personal fortune wrecked in an inland railroad venture which he vainly expected would bring business to his home city and additional millions to his university. It remained for Henry W. Sage, as able a financier as he was a generous and discriminating philanthropist, to bring the dream to substantial reality. Cornell's greatest material contribution to his foundation was in winning to its support a group of benefactors through whom the essential features of his university idea were to be realized.[59] The more opulently endowed state colleges and universities likewise had to wait for the slow returns upon their timber, mineral, and prairie investments.

Small and inadequate as the endowments were in the early years, their management involved much confusion and dispute. The typical governing board was almost as ineffective in financial management as in educational direction. Selection by governor, legislature, or in a few cases by popular vote, brevity and uncertainty of tenure, legislative interference—at times to the point of abolition or reorganization—and local and group pressure all worked against administrative competence. Quite apart from educational understanding and vision, the popular ideal of hard-headed business men who would safeguard, invest, and direct the expenditure of public funds in the most economical way was not generally realized.[60] It was in spite of, rather than by reason of, the system and standard that there were so many conscientious, self-sacrificing members.[61]

Under the best of conditions the requirements of the act were difficult to meet strictly, and most of the states were technical violators in some particular. In a few cases the funds were lost through gross carelessness or fraud and had to be replaced later, but the trouble usually arose not from any criminal intent but from incompetent management and inadequate support. Nevertheless, in a period of recurring exposures of financial corruption and of general farmer and labor unrest, legislative investigations of college finance and management were in line with popular distrust and afforded opportunities for scandalous attacks by disgruntled or bigoted opponents with consequent discredit to the institutions involved and in some measure to the whole land-grant cause.[62] The only solution was an assured living income and a sound budgetary policy, competently administered.

With capital funds limited and with mistaken notions of fitness, physical plants tended to be varied and primitive makeshifts, as inharmonious as they were inappropriate. Contrary to the sensible advice of the *American Agriculturist* that the colleges should be established in well-settled regions as the students had experienced enough of pioneering on their home farms,[63] most of the new institutions, from necessity or choice, were located on forest clearings, abandoned homesteads, or the open prairie. Porter referred advisedly to institutions that figuratively and literally were not yet "out of the woods."[64] Physical pioneering provided all too literal setting for the educational. The first agricultural college, according to a description as realistic as picturesque, was located "on the very margin of the cultivated portions of our country, where the 'forests primeval' are just vanishing before the encroachments of civilization."[65]

The others, with regional variations, were equally raw and

rudimental. An observer of the undeveloped site of Iowa's venture in industrial education felt that "it must have been selected as a place of exile, where students would some day be banished, remote from civilization and its attendant temptations, to study nature in its native wildness." He was later convinced that "no more unpromising College enterprise was ever launched into existence—even in the 'wild west.' "[66] An unkempt ridge between ravines and a "ragged cornfield surrounded by rail fences" constituted the original Cornell campus overlooking, not the "bustling town," but a village that Goldwin Smith regarded as a "rough place . . . barbarous so far as the comforts of life are concerned. . ."[67] At a much later date the Washington experiment in higher technical education was enveloped in a luxuriant cabbage patch.[68] Undeveloped transportation facilities intensified isolation; campuses were snow-bound in winter and mud-bound in spring. The long winter vacation, in addition to other advantages claimed for it, brought relief from drifted, wind-swept spaces where natural forces were little tempered by architectural and landscaping moderations and adornments.

Collegiate architecture in this country had traditionally been simple and austere to the point of the ascetic. Porter, champion of the old discipline though he was, felt that marked innovations in harmony with modern comfort and hygiene might desirably be introduced. "The institution need be none the less severe and exacting, if the students were allowed to breathe a respirable atmosphere or to sit on comfortable benches." As it was, "The hopeful son of Tim O'Flaherty is better accommodated at the age of ten in the palatial public school-houses that are voted him by our sovereigns than is the delicate son of a millionaire in the class-rooms of colleges which have educated thousands of the intellectual primacy of the land."[69] Unfortunately, the reaction from primitive and puritanical austerity, in accord with the spirit of the time, brought superficial display rather than artistic appropriateness; local pride sought gaudy show more than educational efficiency in the new city schools, and rococo ornateness characterized the collegiate monuments to the new millionaires.

The land-grant colleges, supposedly dedicated to plain living and high thinking, were not free from this sorry exhibitionism. Early Kansan aspiration was represented in a remarkable barn —"a broad-corniced, massive-looking stone structure, with numerous wings, towers, stairways, elevators, and offices." Never completed for the original purpose, it served successively as classroom, drill hall, and museum.[70] Maine's general-purpose frame building was termed "semi-gothic" in recognition of gingerbread decorations and spike-adorned gables.[71] Washington was spared the excesses of a two million dollar "castle" only by the fact that available funds proved to be limited to sixty thousand.[72] The Iowa board, in seeking to combine economy, simplicity, and dignity, desired "no costly dome, or curious winding stairs—but a solid stone foundation, a plain brick superstructure of four stories, with pilasters, dental brick cornice, projecting roof with brackets, with portico over the doors at each end: all of good respectable appearance, about good enough for the farmers of our State, *and good enough for anybody else.*"[73] Square brick buildings of three or four stories with mansard roofs and decorated cupolas on the front corners became the typical reconciliation of utility and showiness.

Leaders with the taste and foresight to appreciate the strategic opportunity that the new expansive and diversified campuses afforded were limited by makeshift appropriations and lack of organizing experience.[74] Frederick Law Olmsted developed an elaborate plan of grounds and buildings for an institution to be organized on a military plan. Though several eastern boards employed this artist as expert consultant none of them followed his full design, since funds were lacking for developmental programs and his key proposals ran counter to traditions and prejudices.[75] Interest in military organization and regulation waned rapidly under peace conditions, and a dormitory system seemed to many inappropriate or inexpedient. To the Maine board of agriculture, which reviewed with suspicious alarm some of the proposals of the college board, the term itself suggested "a scholastic college or a convent, or something else of monastic origin."[76]

The Cornell trustees, while admitting the necessity of institutional housing under their peculiar conditions of location and student employment, were convinced of the superior disciplinary restraints "of lodging with quiet families."[77]

Then, as so often later, there were protests against a "bricks and mortar" emphasis at the expense of teaching personnel and equipment. Governor Low of California—where propitious climate gave especial point—urged that staff and instructional equipment be regarded before buildings.[78] Eliot deprecated the tendency "to reckless preliminary expenditure upon buildings and mechanical fittings" and the trustees' "deplorable propensity to put what should be quick capital into more or less unsuitable bricks and mortar."[79] Garfield gave popular statement to this view in his references to the instructional inspiration of Mark Hopkins in settings of varying degrees of primitiveness, finally reduced to the aphorism of the teacher and his log.[80]

For applied science undertakings too often it was the log without Mark Hopkinses, with organized subject matter and established method. So long as the basic sciences remained in a transitional or tentative stage, applications were necessarily unformulated and unsystematized. Textbooks and reference works well adjusted to undergraduate comprehension and interest were lacking, and special instructional techniques were wholly undeveloped.[81] Laboratories, where utilized, remained largely demonstrational; Eliot's plea for science teaching "in a rational way, objects and instruments in hand—not from books merely, not through the memory chiefly, but by the seeing eye and the informing fingers,"[82] was only gradually heeded.

Libraries, rather than functioning in the modern manner as reference laboratories, were still largely storehouses of a narrow range of compendiums of the learning of the past supplemented by the ever-available "government documents," with closely restricted regulations of student use.[83] Visual instructional aids had not had sufficient demand to lead to provision for systematized equipment. From one of the oldest and strongest colleges Porter could argue that classrooms should be attractive and convenient "and liberally provided with every accessory in the way of apparatus and illustrations. No classical room would be any the less agreeable if its walls were hung with attractive maps and photographs."[84]

The chief lack, however, was in personnel. Latent scientific principles might be ascertained, formulated and applied; manuals might be prepared; and demonstrational and experimental equipment and techniques devised, provided there were competent educators and investigators to combine their efforts in the endeavor. To find and direct such talent, to provide the facilities for their work, and to supervise the whole course of institutional development, there was needed such peculiar and dominant executive leadership as to constitute, in Eliot's view, for technological institutions in general, the "supreme difficulty." Successful establishment, he believed, must be largely the work of one man,[85] and in a period of multiplying colleges and expanding commercial enterprise, available executive talent that could be attracted to the new collegiate venture was relatively limited. When the Iowa organization committee went into the field they found a dozen other colleges seeking the same type of leader, and the astute chairman was led to conclude that it was easier to select a president of the nation than a successful chief executive of an industrial college.[86]

The "old time president," however suitable for the old college, was out of place in the new. Eliot thought the prevailing practice of selecting clergymen for college presidents as inappropriate as would be their appointment as members of the higher courts; the teaching profession, in consequence, was "robbed of its few prizes and subjected to such indignity as soldiers feel when untried civilians are put over their heads." Whatever the experience in the sectarian realm, a clerical leader of a polytechnic would be the height of absurdity.[87] Turner, making still more extreme comparison, held that "To put an elderly clergyman at the head of an agricultural school was like placing General Scott in charge of a theological seminary."[88] Nevertheless, the A. and M. colleges, especially in the Middle West, drew liberally upon the traditional source of supply for presidents as they did for members of the faculty,[89] and it must be said for the clerical executives that their organizing and directing ability proved equal to the average, while their sermons and community addresses often made a special appeal to rural audiences. The most conspicuous failures were not among men of the cloth.

From whatever sources, there was certain to be a considerable proportion of failures—whether misfitted, maladjusted, or plainly incompetent. Promising selections failed to meet the exacting tests of the new education or, as was frequently the case, to conciliate opposing groups. In Massachusetts Henry F. French's training, experience, and acquaintance with affairs was thought to insure success, but he failed to survive the preliminary organization.[90] The real founding leader, William S. Clark, combined with training in research methods a promotive zeal that tended at times to be somewhat disruptive.[91] Purdue, after failing to attract Clark, turned to a man sympathetic with and supposedly understanding of popular technical training—Richard Owen, the son of Robert Owen, who had introduced the Fellenberg system at New Harmony—but, as often in the case of the father, the son's enthusiasms were not balanced by sound judgment. The quixotisms and vagaries of his preliminary recommendations—extending to dress, diet, and prevention of homesickness—brought a storm of ridicule from which he was glad to retire. His successor, becoming the center of a fierce internal struggle, continued but a year. A disturbing influence upon early administration at this institution, in contrast to the loyal and cooperative support by the founder of Cornell, was the interference and attempted dictation by the donor.[92]

Evan Pugh, one of the most promising of the new presidents, had written characteristically and prophetically in 1855, "I am aware that the way is loaded with labor, but the inestimable results that must flow from it are worth the labor of a hundred lives like mine and I was preparing for the sacrifice."[93] The intrepid young scientist did not live to enter upon the federal aid period of the Pennsylvania college, and experiments with a former associate of Girard and an ex-state superintendent did not bring continuity or stability of policy.[94] At Iowa, after an initial administration of fifteen years, A. S. Welch, who had previously headed the new-type normal school at Ypsilanti, Michigan, became the victim of a factional contest within the faculty and board and there ensued a period of mixed counsels during which four presidents were selected within six years.[95] Reconstruction and agrarian politics in a number of the southern states brought insecurity of executive tenure as well as instability of institutional establishment.[96] The newer states, rather than profiting by the experiences of the older, were in too many cases subjected to a partisan or factional control that made for administrative incompetence and impermanence.[97]

But the executive errancy of the formative years may easily be exaggerated, for, after all, considering the difficulties, the surprise is not that there were misfits and incompetents but rather that there were so many effective and even outstanding administrators drawn to the industrial cause. In a period especially notable for great college presidents, land-grant representatives like Evan Pugh, Daniel C. Gilman, Andrew D. White, Emerson E. White, Francis A. Walker, Paul A. Chadbourne, Adonijah S. Welch, John M. McBryde, John Bascom, William W. Folwell, and Cyrus Northrup were conspicuous. One of the greatest services of the old education was in providing such leadership for the new.

Then, as later, the president's most serious problem was in getting and directing the teaching staff. In concluding a letter of advice to Folwell in 1870, Eliot observed, on the basis of his brief experience, ". . . I may say that if your experience proves to be anything like mine, your difficulties will arise, not in laying out a broad and even magnificent plan of operations, but in getting good teachers, paying them enough to live upon, and keeping up their enthusiasm for practical education."[98] Eliot had recently postulated as essential to polytechnic instruction a loyal and harmonious group of young scholars with time and facilities to keep abreast of their own and allied fields and salaries sufficient to maintain reasonably unperturbed minds,[99] and Gilman felt, characteristically, that professors were far more important than professorships.[100] R. L. Allen, the agricultural journalist, evidently assuming ways and means, insisted that in each state sufficiently attractive compensation should be offered to secure the best talent at home and abroad.[101]

There were peculiar difficulties in realizing this orthodox academic aim in technical institutions. Aside from budgetary limitations, the number of trained and adaptable teachers was strictly limited. The typical old-time college professor, like the president, had a clerical background—a natural state of affairs, Porter thought, when one recalled that "the men best qualified by special training" were "oftener found in the clerical profession" and that the teaching profession was "akin to that of the clergyman in the smallness of its pay and the unselfish patience which it involves."[102] This profession, as a matter of course if not necessity, provided the masters of arts and doctors of divinity for the language, philosophy, and social science departments. The technical subjects calling for men grounded in the basic sciences with specialized knowledge and practical experience constituted, next to the presidency, the main personnel problem.

Competent agricultural scientists who could make convincing applications were hard to get and harder to keep. In the discussion of the first Morrill bill by the United States Agricultural Society in 1859, Henry S. Olcott feared that competent agricultural faculties could not be secured in five years to man thirty colleges. In contrast, enthusiasts like Calvert, Clemson, and Brown were "confident that whenever and wherever Agricultural Colleges might be founded, competent Professors would not be wanting." But this confidence, it proved, was not justified.[103] President Clute of Michigan in 1889 attributed the comparatively slow growth of systematic education in agriculture to this cause. The position, he had found, required "a man of large practical ability, of large scientific attainments, and of aptness to teach. To find men possessed of these qualifications is difficult in any branch. It is doubly difficult in a branch in which science is in its infancy and in which very few men have had any scientific training. The college has often found it impossible to get men who had all the qualifications for the post. The practical men have not been scientific. The scientific men have not been practical."[104]

In the formative years there were three main sources of applied science teachers and investigators: German, British, and Scotch university graduates, supplemented, especially from the seventies, by students of the Rensselaer, Sheffield, and Lawrence schools; medical graduates with general or applied science interests; and experienced practitioners and scientific technicians without higher technical training.[105] Later generations could choose from the most promising graduates, but the founders were mainly dependent upon "converted" old-line educators, recruits from the "learned professions," and practically trained experts.[106]

The actual demands made upon the average land-grant professor exceeded the resources of any system of training, then or since. Acquisition of new subject matter, initiation of research, cultivation of public relations, along with the inevitable administrative routine entailed such varied and fluctuating activities that titles had little significance. Some of the colleges indeed were organized before departmental groupings and boundaries were definitely fixed, and professors were selected without portfolio, subject to later assignment.[107]

The classical tradition had been entirely opposed to specialization, and this attitude lingered with the rise of technical education and the multiplication of subjects of instruction. The first president of the University of Louisiana, Colonel Thomas D. Boyd, had the convenient theory that any competent professor could teach any subject—a belief which he exemplified by conducting classes at various times in subjects ranging from the classics and philosophy to engineering.[108] The first regular professor of the New Hampshire college in its Dartmouth connection, a victim of epilepsy, gave all the chemical instruction, general and applied, for both institutions and served as business manager, directing architect, and legislative lobbyist.[109] Henry H. Goodell, in his thirty-eight years at Massachusetts, in addition to his service as president, was at different times secretary, librarian, and teacher of military tactics and gymnastics, entomology, zoology, anatomy and physiology, rhetoric and English language, and history. Considering his creditable performance in these diverse fields, one may readily agree with his biographer that the bestowal of an LL. D. by the neighboring college was "with sufficient cause."[110] E. W. Stanton of Iowa, an engineering graduate of the first class, in addition to a half century of continuous administrative service ranging from student clerk to acting president, taught English, mathematics, business law, and political economy and sociology.[111] His colleague in the humanities later recounted his dignities as "Professor of English Literature, Latin, History, Rhetoric, Grammar, Moral Science, Agricultural Theology, and everything else of a literary character that my Atlas-like shoulders were able to bear." And, lest he grow stale at the week end, the president made him responsible for the "chapel services of the Sabbath day."[112]

In some of the newer states, subject grouping suggested the vagaries of high school combinations at their worst. An Oregon professorship embraced elocution, common law, physiology, and mechanical drawing.[113] And perhaps unique in collegiate adaptability was the South Dakota professor who for a single year's work could report instruction in German, bookkeeping, penmanship and orthography, political economy, the Constitution of the United States, and the history of civilization; institute lectures on farm accounts; and, in extracurricular service, management of the men's dormitory and stewardship of a boarding club.[114]

The presidents, in addition to administrative duties including the personal supervision of all the instruction, were expected to teach their particular specialty or specialties which, except in the case of certain scientifically trained executives, were usually philosophy and the branches of the social sciences in process of formulation, along with such odds and ends of both theoretical and practical subjects as were not otherwise assigned.[115]

Occasionally, a land-grant educator objected to having his versatility and ingenuity put to such extreme test. The distinguished professor of botany at Michigan, after reporting that he had for one term guided the freshman class in world history through Swinton's *Outlines,* added the complaint, "Although the class seemed interested in the study, I hope never to be called on to teach another class in this subject. I believe I am capable of doing something else which will be of greater benefit to the College and the State, while there are others who can teach the history better."[116] He did, under protest, repeat the course at least once and perhaps by this experience was inspired to become the college's official historian. Even the adaptable Colonel Boyd of Louisiana came to the conclusion that there were limits, for in recommending that applied mathematics and astronomy be separated from the chair of natural philosophy, he made the incontrovertible observation, "I believe that I can speak from some experience when I say that the true secret of efficient instruction is good teachers, able and conscientious, each restricted to one subject of study."[117] A professor already burdened with a mathematics department and the duties of cashier was subjected to unreasoned criticism by colleagues and students for lack of expertness in civil engineering when this branch was thrust upon him as an economy measure.[118]

A quarter century later in discussing the problems of engineering organization in state institutions a leader in technical education was led to assert that "For the governing board to direct the president to distribute the studies among the several professors is to develop such an institution on the plan of a country school, where any man may be expected to teach anything at any time."[119] In certain of the newer struggling institutions there were striking instances of just such demoralizing conditions. As late as 1888 a willing science man, after reporting for the year classes in physiology, physical geography, botany, chemistry, physics, geometry, and trigonometry, as well as service as station botanist and chemist, offered the highly restrained suggestion, "First-class college work cannot be done under such a pressure of duties. . ."[120]

For such varied and exacting labors land-grant salaries tended in general to be low as compared with the better colleges, though there was a lack of any standardization among them, except as competition for staff members led to gradual coordination. Regent Peabody of Illinois in 1882 warned that "Something must be done to bring the wages of our professors up to the standards which such men secure, east and west."[121] At best the "standards" were not high. A few years before, the Massachusetts president complained that their professors, "men of high culture and capable of doing the best of work," received salaries "far smaller than are usually paid in the High and Grammar Schools of our large cities."[122] Faculties dependent upon state appropriations were subjected at times to downward "adjustments" and to delay in payment.[123]

To these expected conditions of hard work and relatively low pay there was often added the supreme academic hazard of uncertainty of tenure. Owing to the diverse elements brought together in a technological institution and the lack of agreement as to scope and emphasis, internal conflict was far more prevalent than among the like-minded if opinionated scholars of the older colleges. Legislative investigations led to sensational exploitation of these differences and encouraged personal attacks and departmental intrigues. Politics—party and personal—were notoriously influential in effecting appointments and removals. Inadequate and often uncertain compensation, moreover, induced and gave a specious justification to the practice which President James held to be, of all academic perversions, the most demoralizing—nepotism.[124] This abuse, all too prevalent, unsettled tenures, packed faculty votes, and lowered and disrupted standards generally. Thus, in a distressing number of instances, sweeping changes were made, both in administration and faculty, with no regard to the "good of the service."[125]

The social issues that were later to provoke the most heated conflicts over freedom of teaching were not fully developed, although the signs of some of them were appearing;[126] but farmers' organizations and religious groups, as well as the persistent old-school educators, were constant and vociferous in their destructive criticism. Legislative visiting and examining committees were often unreasonably and unsympathetically censorious. The alumni, fast becoming self-conscious and opinionated, found much not to their liking.[127] Even the undergraduates, encouraged by outside suggestion and attention, became at times bumptiously critical, assertive, and in extreme cases, openly rebellious.[128]

Against such subversive influences the teacher lacked any group support and protection. Before the establishment of professional organizations, professorial victims, either of private or public institutions, did not have even the dubious satisfaction of seeing their "case" publicized by an investigating committee.[129] Their only recourse was an appeal to public opinion through the press or by legislative hearing and the much more effective resort to political or personal influence—if they had any. In most instances the record of these tragedies has been preserved, if at all, in personal letters—written in retirement. Reasonable security of tenure and policy awaited professional assuredness. Only when land-grant educators, individually and collectively, could speak as those having authority, if not as the classical pedants, could they win respect and support, academically and socially.

CHAPTER VI

TRIAL AND ERROR: CURRICULUM AND STUDENTS

To all the other trials and limitations under which the pioneer land-grant educator labored—so long as he kept his job—there was added a student preparation so inadequate as alone to postpone the attainment of systematic applied science courses on a true collegiate level. In a period when preparatory standards in the most advanced regions were most inadequate and the "gap" or "missing link" between the elementary school and the college was the despair of constructive educators, a program of popular higher education was doomed to low and flexible entrance requirements, as all that the new academic traffic could bear. The new colleges in most cases were thus obliged to take their students from whatever source and intellectual stage available. The entrance requirements of the typical A. and M. college were the common branches to which a few added and others "recommended" algebra. In accord with the democratic spirit, pupils of from twelve to fourteen years might go to their state college "directly from the district schools, ungraded, unlettered and unwashed."[1] For those lacking in these elemental essentials—even after liberal "conditioning"—most of the western and southern states provided subcollegiate departments which in sparsely settled areas served as town high schools.

Expedient, provisional, and makeshift as such a basis for collegiàte training was, it had positive defenders. Thus, as late as 1893, President McLouth of South Dakota, one of the most ardent champions and promoters of the practical, maintained that "The conditions of admission to these colleges should be such that those young men and women who have finished a good common school course, are proficient, i. e., in reading, writing, spelling, geography, arithmetic, and grammar, could enter upon the studies of the first year."[2]

Among those not so eager to anticipate popular desires, and especially where conditions allowed greater discrimination, there was consistent effort toward higher and more uniform requirements. Some of the universities, against the protest of agrarian and industrial leaders, insisted upon one standard for all courses; others made concessions to the popular demand in double or triple standards. In either case there was a growing dissatisfaction with the preparatory situation. The Massachusetts board indicated its dilemma in 1873: "While it is important that the standard of admission should not be so high as to discourage the farmers from attempting to educate their sons, there are obvious reasons for raising it as much and as soon as the popular appreciation of college education will permit."[3] Ohio was making "in good faith, the attempt to take up the work of the common schools of the State where they leave it, but the most that can be asked of us is to adjust our demands to the better grades of these schools," since the standards of many of them were "deplorably low." They were requiring, the president reiterated, "just as little as can be safely asked."[4] Folwell of Minnesota insisted that so long as a popular basis of admission to agricultural colleges persisted they would remain secondary rather than professional schools.[5] Maryland reported a stand seemingly as heroic as it was commendable: "A limit of study has been fixed below which students will not be received into the college. This has had the effect to diminish somewhat the number of students, but it has added greatly to the character and dignity of the institution."[6] So long as it discounted or assumed the burden of preparatory training, popular higher education, both general and technical, remained nominal rather than real; democracy's college awaited democracy's high school.

With public opinion, subject matter, institutional organization, personnel, and student preparation retarding and limiting the development, the achievement of complete, systematized, balanced curricula in applied science during the preliminary years was an impossibility. Universities, usually without marked interest and invariably without reasoned plan, sought to meet the conditions of the grant by establishing new departments or adapting old ones. In most cases the advertised program was not fully attained for many years. A complete course directed by a single scientist, however ingenious and versatile, was bound to run exceedingly thin. Engineering instruction in the broader applications was more readily organized than that in agriculture, but there remained the basic problems of delimiting the main branches and fixing the character and extent of the practice shopwork.

In the seventies and eighties a rather heated methodological dispute arose between the advocates of the elementary phase of the Russian engineering course, which involved familiarity with tools and the mastery of basic skills and procedures, and those who favored the production of completed articles for sale or shop use. The Russian system, demonstrated at the Centennial, found enthusiastic champions at M.I.T. and Maine in opposition to the commercial production system most fully developed at the Worcester Free Institute.[7] Before the issue was settled, shopwork became of minor importance except for the trade school; but the controversy reflected a basic difference in aim and attitude.

To provide competent instruction in the applications of the basic sciences to the industries was one thing; to supply master farmers or farm managers for the country and practical mechanics for the city industries was quite another. The Sheffield board assumed frankly the unpopular position of a school of general science, that would fulfill its true function not "by offering peculiar attractions to farmers as a class, or to mechanics as a class, as by inviting students who wish to become scholars in science, well-trained in the higher departments of investigation, able to stand unabashed by the side of scholars in letters"[8]—a position as academically appealing as it was popularly repellent. An adequate serving of both, that is, all, interests was unthinkable at this stage.

As a means of meeting the formal requirements of the grant, several universities offered survey lecture courses. At Cornell it was felt that the federal plan contemplated that all students should have some exposure, at least, to the special subjects, and among the nonresident professors that President White secured were inspiring lecturers on agriculture.[9] Brown's museum director was also "lecturer on special branches of agriculture," and his course on practical agriculture illustrated by visits to farms and factories was so popular that it was attended not only by the scholarship holders of whom it was required but by many other students.[10] Folwell of Minnesota proposed quite provocatively the instruction of all students in those principles of agriculture, mechanic arts, and hygiene "which every educated man or woman needs to know."[11] Tennessee developed the survey course idea the most elaborately. Candidates for all degrees were required to attend during the fall and winter terms a course of lectures on the applications of the various sciences to agriculture and mechanic arts.[12]

Whatever the value of such courses as an orientation survey of the field and method of the various sciences for general information and culture, it was obvious that they could in no sense provide a "practical education of the industrial classes" in the specified fields. This failure was recognized not only by the opponents of land-grant education in universities but by supporters like Andrew D. White, who, after disappointing efforts to give dignified and coordinate place to the agricultural department, was deeply chagrined that the popularly emphasized feature of the new education should be so inadequate and inconsequential.[13]

In the separate colleges, designed primarily for technical training by new and appropriate methods, the traditional, both in subject matter and instruction, lingered. Such "liberal" studies as English composition and literature, the modern languages, Latin, usually as an option, philosophy, political economy, and constitutional history with mathematics and the general sciences constituted a large part of the early curricula in "agriculture" and the various branches of "engineering." The technical and vocational subjects were often interspersed more in accordance with the convenience of the instructor than the progressive sequence of the curriculum.

Methods of teaching involved the extremes of didacticism and of empiricism. In accord with long-established precedent, textbooks where available were made the basis of the course, their contents recited by the student or expounded by the instructor. In unorganized fields the instructor drew upon his knowledge and practical experience or made demonstrations with available apparatus and materials. Agricultural college libraries, even more limited, especially in periodical sets, than those of the older institutions, provided little aid in reference material.[14]

It was a common charge in the land-grant colleges of this period that teachers of engineering, mechanics, and physics talked far beyond the comprehension of the average student in their explanations and demonstrations. This was generally attributed to the fact that the instructor had the professional rather than the instructional point of view—that "he knew his subject but couldn't teach it"—but the difficulty was probably due as much to inadequate student preparation, especially in higher mathematics, as to unsound pedagogy. Alert and venturesome teachers who sought to develop more appropriate and realistic methods and devices of their own, laboring under the misunderstandings and discouragements of the pioneer, made some effective beginnings in specialized instruction. Professor I. P. Roberts' experience at Iowa in the direct study of materials at hand and in comparative observations of representative farms set a milestone in the development of agricultural teaching methods.[15]

"Practice" for agricultural and engineering students, before the development of systematic field and barn observation and experimentation and the utilization of specialized laboratories, centered mainly in the manual labor requirement. Adopted by enthusiasts as an essential feature of the industrial college, in spite of warnings based upon past trials from experienced educators, the system was expected to give effective application to the principles learned in the classroom, to train in skill and dexterity, to inculcate sound habits of work, to provide the needed physical exercise, and—incidentally in theory, but principally in fact—to afford an opportunity for meeting a portion of the living expenses. After long and persistent trial the system failed to realize any of these aims satisfactorily. Educative work was not remunerative, and the labor for which payment could be afforded was not instructive; gymnastics and athletics provided more appropriate and effective facilities for physical exercise and training; mechanization in industry and agriculture made manual skill and endurance decreasingly significant; and the adoption of the laboratory method in applied science superseded any possible instructional benefits. The emphasis given to this feature of land-grant instruction—the time, effort, and money expended upon it—while in line with popular desire, served to discredit the colleges in educational and scientific standing and thus to retard the public service that they were seeking to render.[16]

As it was, in spite of all the concessions to supposed popular desires and biases, none of the institutions in the trial years met occupational expectations fully and most of them not at all. The farmers' organizations which had demanded the establishment of separate agricultural colleges and staffs with practical experience and aim were not always satisfied with the work of those so established and manned, and in a number of cases were influential in securing readjustments in curricula and changes in personnel, though their main assaults continued to be on the university connections. Unfortunately for the advancement of sound educational service, these efforts dealt largely with personalities and with immediate policies rather than with underlying principles of administration and instruction.[17] Grange and Alliance leaders were persistent in negative criticism but offered little that was constructive.

The same was generally true of the complaints of self-trained agricultural practitioners whose opinions had great weight among farmers. Peter Henderson, the commercial horticulturist, found the colleges wholly impractical and ineffective. The sciences with which the students were crammed were beyond their comprehension and proved "of about as much use to them as Butler's Analogy . . . to the average boarding-school girl." As for the "science of agriculture," a great deal of it was "awful humbug." For a horticulturist, certainly, as he had witnessed in his employees, practical experience was far superior to training in any existing college.[18] A leading agricultural professor with classical education and successful farm experience declared at the Washington convention in 1885 that it had been his "fortune to come into contact with fifty men who claimed to understand the science of Agriculture and to be educated as agriculturists and not one of them was competent to feed pigs."[19] As late as 1891 a speaker before a farmers' institute in New York gave assurance to the great majority of young farmers who did not have the time or means for training in their profession that the great bulk of profitable farming had been done "by natural ability rather than by scholarship." A well-trained agricultural chemist might fail as a farmer, and a man not able "to state wherein a nitrate differs from a phosphate" might be highly successful. And to clinch his argument for the irrelevancy of book-learning, the speaker related that he had known a successful dairyman who could neither read nor write.[20]

Agricultural journals, the chief center of the discussion, while presenting in articles and letters the opposing points of view, failed to give sound and consistent guidance, owing to concern over particular leaders and groups rather than over fundamental principles. In general the editors tended to support the popular demand for "practical" training—which aside from manual labor was not definitely described—and for direct service to the farmers in ways and by means not helpfully specified. As in the case of their protesting correspondents, the editors were far stronger in destructive attack than in constructive proposal.

The *Western Rural* sought to discredit early experimental ventures by parading the worst exhibits: "What we want is accurate knowledge in this direction. If our miscalled agricultural colleges, when they *do* make experiments, would try something useful, instead of testing the lifting power of a growing squash when the sides are cramped in a box; or instead of 'proving' that cattle winter better without than with shelter; or in lieu of demonstrating that wild cattle do not become reconciled to being stalled for three months, while with ordinary stock-feeders, five or six days are enough, then these asylums for classical idiots and political professors would stave off the impending day of reckoning between them and the people whose trust they have so outrageously abused. Pending the contemplated 'grab,' by these institutions, of the balance of the public lands, they would be doing wisely if they would find out something of practical benefit to the art they were appointed to foster."[21]

The *Rural New-Yorker,* near the close of the years of trial, gave an extreme statement of the *ad populum* argument of classical encroachment. The colleges having come before the need was recognized by the farming class, they had fallen a "prey to needy adventurers in the teaching profession" who, in accord with their training and appreciation, had developed these popular technical colleges on the old lines. The result was in every way incongruous to the true intent. "How ridiculous, these 'freshmen,' 'sophomores,' 'juniors' and 'seniors' in an industrial school, and how much worse than ridiculous the scholastic methods of the Middle Ages, trying to deal with the daily work of modern farmers and mechanics! What we want is to clean out the smug D.D.'s and the pimply-faced 'Professors,' and put in their places men who have a lively sense of the lacks in learning among men and women who have to grapple daily with the world's work in this busy age."[22]

The *Iowa Homestead,* the organ of a group that was about to effect a reorganization of their college in leadership and curricular emphasis, expressed graphically by allegorical cartoon the same protest. A dehorned bull, "Agriculture," stood dejectedly in the corner of a field in front of the agricultural college awaiting the charge of long-horned cattle labelled "Civics," "Astronomy,"

"Calculus," "German," "Latin," "Ethics," "Psychology." The caption pointed the moral protest, "Dehorned and cornered in its own pasture lot. This is 'Ethics (?).' "[23] Such extremely prejudiced attacks could have but temporary effect; the case was not to be decided on such narrow and episodical considerations.

On their side, the land-grant institutions, collectively and individually, those separately established and those in university connection, did not lack for defenders. Discriminating educators sought judicious appraisal. Professors, alumni, students, and organization leaders came vigorously to the defense of their particular institutions. Farm papers upheld favored institutions and regimes and at times the general system. The *Rural New-Yorker* a few years before its onslaught against agricultural teachers paid them unstinted tribute: "There is no class of useful men that are more deserving of praise for what they have done under much difficulty than the professors of agricultural colleges, and we take pleasure in thus expressing this our sincere belief based on a knowledge of what they have done and are doing."[24]

The main responsibility for the relatively slow growth of this phase of industrial education was placed upon the farmer constituency itself which lacked an appreciation of the possibilities of applied science in their occupation. At the same time, a consumer consciousness, at home and abroad, insistent upon regulated and standardized production as well as upon an increased variety, was not yet aroused. Consequently, opportunities for agricultural specialists both in public and commercial service were limited as compared with those in newer and more rapidly expanding enterprises. Francis A. Walker, with characteristic tendency to reduce an opinion to exact formula, maintained that the establishment of technical education in general "was to constitute a striking instance of the principle that, in some things, supply must create demand,"[25] and this "principle" found most striking verification in the case of the agricultural branch.

Meanwhile, it was maintained, the departments were more than justifying themselves by laying the foundations of a true agricultural science and by training experts in this and allied fields. Regarding the occupational distribution of graduates, it was argued that while a satisfactory proportion went into farming or directly allied occupations, far more significant in this early stage was the training of leaders in instruction and research.[26]

But with all due allowances and abatements the fact remained that the popular occupation was most on the spot in launching the democratic educational system and it was the phase in which shortcomings and errors were most apparent. It was futile to argue that agriculture was only one coordinate part of the new colleges, for in general estimation they were "agricultural," and there seemed real danger, in White's phrase, that in the popular view, the Hamlet would be left out of the land-grant drama.

Military training, the other specified subject, as developed in the "school of the soldier" in the trial period, whatever other benefits may have resulted, did little, in most states, to realize the alleged aim of providing competent officers for a citizen army. The very general requirement could be interpreted according to the sentiment of the various localities. A few sought in the first years to make their institutions semimilitary in organization, garb, and control.[27] Most, however, regarded the provision lightly, in some cases not providing the training for some years; the lack of competent officers and adequate equipment gave an alleged justification for the negligence. Former military men on the faculties or local retired officers provided the first organizers and commandants. Among the notable faculty officers were Alvord and Goodell of Massachusetts, Atherton of Rutgers, Wiley of Purdue, Geddes and Lincoln of Iowa, and Hamilton of Pennsylvania.

Aside from the obligation to fulfill the formal requirement, the great argument for progressive development was in the need for preparedness, not only against outside foes but from internal disorder and uprising. Following the labor riots of the seventies the latter danger was much stressed. The nation was changing, a president found, from simple stabilized agricultural communities to industrial centers "with their increasing armies of improvident laborers," whose passions and necessities in times of distress threatened "the very existence of society." Against such a menace a standing army was unreliable, only a citizen army of those whose interests were at stake could be depended upon.[28] Again in 1891 a zealous commandant warned solemnly of the need for creating through military discipline "a law-respecting and law-abiding body of citizens" to combat "the socialistic tendencies of the present time. Riots and strikes are of frequent occurrence, while the evils of socialism and communism are rapidly spreading over the country as they have already done in Europe."[29]

In a period when discipline still held the key place in both moral and mental training, the claims for this subject were second to none. Without such saving restraint and direction, President Orton of Ohio feared that the youth of the West were in "great danger of never learning the needful lesson of prompt obedience to constituted authority."[30] A committee of the M.I.T. board, arguing against unsympathetic professors, maintained that educationally the drill compared favorably with mathematics in developing habits of concentration and application.[31] Still more realistically for job-conscious students, an officer suggested that in the increasingly competitive business struggle, qualities of punctuality, promptness, obedience, courtesy, and straightforwardness of manner were among the most available personal assets—as evidenced by the testimony of the "head of a large mercantile concern" that he would give preference to a man with military training.[32]

The alleged physical benefits were equally emphasized. The drill, supplemented with corrective gymnastics where needed, would promote the most symmetrical development as well as provide an ideal relaxation from study.[33] At the same time it would develop an ease of manner and grace of carriage desirable for all members of polite society, and help to break "the awkward shackles of the plowboy's walk"[34] which on a university campus, especially, was distressing.

Walker, viewing the matter both as soldier and administrator, summed up the values with characteristic preciseness: "Through means of the drill thus afforded, our young men coming to the school from every variety of conditions, acquire the instinct of subordination, the power of cohesion, promptitude and precision of movement, and habits of mind as well as of physical bearing which cannot fail to be useful in a high degree."[35]

Intermittent opposition from within and without gave occasion for reiteration of these arguments and justifications. The popular prejudice of parents and students against military domination—increasing with the fading memory of war—reacted unfavorably, it was alleged, upon enrollments.[36] Farmers' organizations felt that the military was somehow supported at the expense of the vocational and they were greatly aggrieved at the appearance of "uniformed dudes" in a people's school.[37] Faculty members, while often sharing popular civilian convictions and prejudices, were also in some cases resentful of the time accorded to the drill and gave but grudging support. Administrators ranged from eager enthusiasts to doubtful and grudging conformists.[38] In the absence of federal standards the attainment of a reasonably effective compliance depended in each institution upon the adjustment of these extreme positions.

At the various conferences of land-grant leaders the scope and possibilities of this slightly understood and in some cases lightly regarded department were given extended consideration. Some ambitious executives saw in land-grant military schools the possibility of an added major field with commensurate federal support; others, reflecting popular prejudice, were fearful of subordinating or retarding the main interests with such a distraction; while most, probably, confronted with more immediate perplexities of organization, were anxious to adopt the policy that would involve the least disturbance and friction. At the initial gathering in 1871 there was much complaint of the failure of the War Department to provide instructors and equipment, with some openly expressed sentiments for the repeal of the requirement. A few with conscious pride reported a strict compliance rewarded by the expected benefits.[39]

Gregory of Illinois was one of the most enthusiastic supporters of a full military program. In the national agricultural convention the following year, he headed and apparently largely directed a committee for which he presented the most elaborate military program ever designed for the land-grant colleges. In view of the obsolescence and inadequacy of the old militia service and the rapid advances being made in military science abroad, the report postulated an urgent demand for a complete, modernized national military system. To provide such a system the single military academy needed supplemental support which might be admirably provided in the new colleges, combining, as defensive measures should, national and state initiative. "The law of Congress requiring the agricultural colleges and industrial universities to teach military tactics was," they believed, "both a confession of public need and an incipient effort to establish a system of military schools." To realize this aim, a special fund was required, and the committee proposed with a boldness and forthrightness worthy of the cause that Congress grant to each state $15,000 annually for instructional expenses in a school of military science. The War Department, after providing needed arms and equipment, would appoint commissioners to prescribe the course of study for these state schools as well as a higher course for West Point whose students would be drawn in part from the graduates of the state institutions. Such schools, it was concluded, would not only make for efficiency and economy in military training but would raise the standard and tone of the entire college program. Unless some adequate provision was made either by state or federal initiative, they recommended that the military requirement be repealed forthwith. While positive opposition was voiced by agricultural leaders the main objection was the danger of raising a side issue that might prejudice the pending movement for general congressional aid. It was suggested that the committee selected for that purpose could incorporate all special requests, and the report was accordingly tabled by a vote of 38 to 24. Later, upon the motion of Ezra Cornell, the military report was specifically referred to the committee. A motion by a Massachusetts delegate asking that the military clause be repealed was given the same disposal.[40]

The conference of presidents of state universities and colleges in 1877 included this subject on its agenda, and Orton of Ohio presented a "Report on the military system in State colleges: its enforcement or repeal." With such a champion the latter alternative could be merely rhetorical, and after his forceful and inclusive justification, the training was voted "just and wise," and the institutions concerned were urged to establish and maintain "an efficient system of military instruction, in the assurance that it cannot fail to render very valuable service, both to college and State." The dissenting opinions were against the compulsory feature and any tendency to "militarize" the colleges.[41]

The convention of 1885 showed more emphatically this jealousy of possible military encroachment. A seemingly innocuous resolution to request the president and the secretary of war to confer future commissions as far as possible upon students who had completed a full military course under an army officer was met with both deprecation and ridicule. A Texas professor of agriculture, after recounting the struggle in his college to keep the military influence properly subordinated, declared that he expressed the prevailing sentiment of his profession in maintaining that "the military must not crush out the agricultural." No less emotionally a Missouri delegate warned that the resolution held out "a glittering prize that might turn to poison." An Iowa delegate, voicing the narrow-gauge attitude, referred with cutting sarcasm to the efforts to provide training in all sorts of subjects under the guise of agriculture, and suggested that naval as well as army training be included, for which his college was equipped with a pond and an old scow. Amid such denunciations and jeers the proposal to provide definite military careers for certain of their students was rejected.[42]

But the responsibility could not thus lightly be cast off. Whatever the emphasis, the law specifically required that the training be provided and any evasion of the obligation was, as Regent Peabody of Illinois observed, "an unfortunate lesson to their students as to the doctrine and duty of obedience."[43] In the end, in spite of all grumbling and sarcasm on and off the campus, most authorities made an earnest effort to meet the spirit of the requirement as local understanding and conditions permitted, and if the benefits claimed by the enthusiasts were not fully experienced neither were the evils portended by the opponents. The War Department, from its side, found the drill as carried on in the eighties generally satisfactory but felt that in some cases the requisite faculty support was lacking and that the officers' academic status and dignity were not always properly recognized.[44]

Federal participation had been gradually extended. In 1865 retired officers were authorized to serve as military professors and the next year provision was made for the detail of twenty regular army officers and the supplying of military equipment to approved colleges and universities. In 1884 the number of officers was doubled, but only about a third of the details were made to land-grant institutions. Their officials complained of assignments to denominational colleges to the neglect of the federal government's "own children." In the case of both sorts of institutions political influence was often more effective in determining the distribution of officers than the needs and possibilities of the training.[45]

The selection of officers was generally carefully made and there was remarkably little friction with the college authorities. In addition to military instruction they taught subjects like mathematics, drawing, engineering, history, and modern languages. Special efforts were made to adjust the training to local conditions and to create institutional and student good will. In varied ways the military professors sought to make their departments of special service to the colleges. Fire brigades were organized; signaling systems were devised that could give weather reports to neighboring farmers; fairs and other gatherings were policed, and the cadets lent color and spirit to ceremonial visits and to G.A.R. parades.[46] The Illinois battalion rendered guard duty during the Chicago fire that met the approbation of General Sherman himself.[47] One officer conducted his cadets to the Centennial Exposition,[48] and another took his specially trained companies by chartered train to conduct exhibitional drills at the

Columbian.[49] The drill itself was motivated in effective ways. Especial effort was made to secure attractive uniforms and improved equipment. Voluntary summer encampments provided vacation expeditions free from Plattsburg rigors.[50] One commandant offered an annual senior prize for an essay on some phase of preparedness.[51] The limitations in this branch of land-grant education assuredly were not due to any lack of energy and enthusiasm on the part of military professors.

So successful were some of them in arousing a martial spirit that the women students sought equality of participation in this as in other activities. Garbed in "appropriate" uniforms, which as in gymnastic training harmonized with prevailing proprieties, the "young ladies" were formed into companies and battalions for drills and maneuvers, thus demonstrating the attractiveness of military training at least in its exhibitional aspects and providing another evidence of the capacity and adaptability of the sex for the new education.[52]

Equality of the sexes was not only an appropriate but to many enthusiasts an essential feature of industrial education. In his inaugural address at Iowa in 1858 President Welch, a life-long champion of equal rights, asserted that this college was dedicated "to the promotion of two great and salutary reforms," the liberalizing of the curriculum and the equalizing of educational opportunities for women, and to the latter cause he devoted over two-thirds of his address. Other speeches as well as the poem of the day depicting "The Ideal Farmer and His Wife" gave the same emphasis.[53] This was the first land-grant college actually to enroll women from the beginning.

While social inertia and prejudice, housing limitations, and the lack of applied science courses specially adapted to female occupations delayed the general establishment of land-grant coeducation, the pressure for equality of opportunity—such as it was—could not long be withstood. A number of western institutions were open to women from the beginning, and during the seventies the majority, East and West, followed the popular trend.

Socially and educationally, in general collegiate training, the experiment—on a much wider scale than before ventured—vindicated the confidence of its supporters. Reports were uniformly favorable, if not enthusiastic. "From an experience of twenty-five years in conducting such schools," President Welch of Iowa could say confidently, that the two sexes were, "of an average equality in their capacity for scholarship."[54] At Maine, in commending the first woman graduate, President Allen answered the two main objections urged against the system: "She sustained a rank equal to any in her class, and during her whole college course she never missed a recitation or college exercise on account of her health."[55] At Delaware after two years trial the "young ladies" had "shown a capacity to understand and appreciate their various studies fully equal to that of the other sex." Furthermore, the resulting "generous rivalry" had proved of "mutual advantage" and been attended with "admirable order and perfect decorum."[56] At Ann Arbor and Ithaca an English observer, Emily Faithfull, found women welcomed because, according to her interpretation, they "gave classroom conversation that delicate, chaste, and humane tone which the recognition of women among the readers of books has been giving to English literature during the last hundred years."[57]

Coeducation as a system was fully justified; the difficulty was to provide a technical education adapted to women's needs and opportunities. In the period before the industries were opened to them and applications of the sciences peculiarly in line with their interests made, the new education had little to offer to the "gentler sex." The offering of special "ladies courses," involving a combination of literature and history with the general sciences, was an emergency device, supplemented in a few cases with rudimentary instruction in domestic economy. The labor requirement was met by work in the kitchen, dining room, and laundry, and at times, in horticultural and other lighter farm operations. But the main service of the industrial institutions to women at this stage was in providing in their localities a training for the optional or successive careers of teaching and matrimony. For both objectives land-grant coeducation proved to be an available and desirable preparation.

For country boys and girls alike the unaffected simplicity of these popular institutions facilitated to the fullest extent the adjustment from home surroundings to collegiate career. The low charges—reduced railroad rates to and from the college, free tuition, and in some cases, room rent, board at cost, and incidentals reduced to the minimum—were largely met by the returns from compulsory labor and school teaching or other employment in the long winter vacation. This economic equality made for a true social democracy and retarded the formation of the inevitable academic cliques. Dwelling together on an isolated farm, with life centered in the one main building, the group in many ways resembled a large family. The resemblance was maintained in the governing system which, in accord with prevailing views, was highly paternalistic. A so-called "student government" organized in a number of colleges and hailed as a progressive innovation was often merely a convenient and economical device for policing, trial of petty offenses, and the indictment of more serious cases to the high court of the faculty. In practice there were the alternating abuses of laxity and vindictiveness which discredited the experiment and brought a restoration of the old paternal regulation and discipline.[58]

Extracurricular activities were so seriously purposed and controlled as to be scarcely distinguishable from the regular program. The main tent, in Woodrow Wilson's figure, might be said to have included the entire performance. The ideal "recreation," in social discipline and intellectual stimulation, and one fully sanctioned by established tradition was the activity of the old-time literary society. With hearty faculty support these adjuncts of the old-line college were adopted, even to their Greek names. As agencies of mutual improvement they found place for all sorts and degrees of talent and of personality. When numbers or dissensions created the need for new societies, they were readily formed; there was no lack of high-sounding classical designations. Exclusive grouping was bitterly opposed in this equalitarian society. Premature efforts to launch Greek letter fraternities sometimes met with more decisive opposition from the student body than from the administration.[59] On such an inclusive basis and in default of other activities the societies filled a unique place, and their meetings along with the "junior exhibitions" and the climactic commencement performance, for the select few who endured to the end, were the high spots of a college career. The pick of these literary productions—according to prevailing taste—found place in the homiletic college magazine along with faculty essays hardly less labored.[60]

Industrial educators from the beginning had discouraged sports as unbecoming this stage and type of education, and the strict institutional regime, manual labor, and drill left little time or inclination for such indulgence. Simple country games and informal sports provided occasional physical recreation. Baseball teams —chosen by classes or by the wider selective method of choosing up sides—played against each other and in some cases against teams of surrounding villages. On or off campus the national game was most rudimentary. Organization and rules were highly informal and elastic. Captains like frontier militia commanders were selected by the group and were subject at any time to demotion to the ranks. Expert coaching was as remote from these schoolboy contests as the menace of professionalism.

With simplicity of surroundings and moderated tempo, general matters of social control—the relation of the sexes, amusements, and indulgences seldom got far from the watchful eye and guiding hand of authority. Parents could be assured that their children would be held to as stern standards and close inhibitions as in the strictest "church school." The safeguards of regimented and supervised day in isolated rural surroundings were sometimes reinforced by special prohibitory state laws as well as by institutional ordinances governing extramural relations. With all these natural and legal defenses against moral contamination, the typical land-grant college might have exulted with the New England preparatory school that it was situated at least "seven miles from any form of sin." Secured from without, discipline was maintained within, sternly if not always impartially; the disturber of peace and harmony was suspended, the rebel and the "immoral" were expelled. No less stringent conformity to the moral conventions was demanded of the faculty.[61] They were required apparently to show not only the circumspection of Caesar's wife but the propriety of his maiden aunt.

In such a moral atmosphere what an annual report referred to as the "Claims of Religion" did not suffer neglect. Daily chapel and at least one Sunday service, usually provided by the college, were compulsory, and voluntary participation in Bible classes, student prayer meetings, and "Y" activities were valued, in lieu of more worldly distractions, for social contacts, as well as for continued or newly awakened spiritual satisfaction. Evangelical awakenings if less consciously stimulated were at times as strongly manifested as in church colleges. The Pennsylvania official report of 1875 took notice of a revival that had swept the campus as one of the leading events of the year.[62] Instructional emphasis in the departments of philosophy, usually in charge of a clerical professor, frequently supplemented and supported the chapel teachings and the efforts of student organizations.[63] In spite of uncharitable and bigoted references to the "godless state schools" where faith was undermined or completely destroyed by the materialistic teachings of atheistic scientists, the proportion of religious conformists, reflecting generally the prevailing belief of their section, was high. "Free thinkers" among the scientists—usually much freer in reputation than in settled conviction—were more than balanced by clerical presidents and professors,[64] and in current controversy on science and religion for every Huxley modernist there were several Agassiz fundamentalists. At a time when the theological pool was just beginning to experience its modern disturbance, these rural campuses were not likely to be upset by the controversies over the higher criticism any more than by the controverted doctrines and dogmas in the heresy trials. In any case whatever the student's individual belief as determined by inheritance, group conformity, or reasoned conviction, resulting mainly from his study of man and the universe, sectarianism, in all of its forms and works, was to be rigidly excluded from classroom and chapel.[65]

To strike a fair balance in judging the first two decades of the land-grant experiment is most difficult. Enthusiasts and detractors both resorted to exaggeration; many achievements and limitations, treated as peculiar to the industrial, were common to higher education in general. For all it was an unstable period of transition. Land-grant institutions themselves varied so markedly in size, organization, and emphasis as to prevent the setting up of uniform rating standards. Of the system as a whole, consequently, only very general conclusions may be drawn.

The social influence was real. Quite aside from the sort of training it provided, the separate A. and M. colleges reached a stratum of students for whom higher or even intermediate training would not otherwise have been available. Entrance requirements, charges, courses of study, and social informality and equality all represented adjustments to mass requirements such as no collegiate system in this country or any other had witnessed. Whatever the results in comparison with other public and private expenditure of funds and effort, it was to be assumed that the great proportion of students was, apart from considerations of vocational expertness, broadened and socialized to a degree not otherwise possible. Making all due allowance for halcyon recollections, the evidence indicates in these intellectually, as well as physically pioneering student bodies a seriousness of purpose and a social outlook new to the academic realm.

While in moral teachings and practices the new colleges were but following the traditions of the old with, perhaps, in some cases a fuller outward conformity owing to simple surroundings and regimented schedule, there was one respect in which technical education was beginning, in certain institutions, to make a distinct and unique moral contribution—the demonstration that the "scientific spirit" was not incompatible with religious devotion and that the exercise and application of religion could be made on a strictly nonsectarian basis and with the fullest individual freedom. Such a stand, forecasted in state universities like Michigan and maintained most consistently by Cornell, while leading to bigoted and vituperative attack, was to result in the breaking of a narrow sectarian control of higher education.[66] The tolerant secularization, following slowly but surely, was not the least valuable of the contributions of the land-grant idea and movement to American education.

Educationally, results were uneven and in many respects undetermined. The federal grant had been an important and, in some cases, an essential factor in the modernizing of state universities and the establishment of new ones, with their vast and varied possibilities of public service that involved the most inclusive interpretation of "the liberal and practical education of the industrial classes in the several pursuits and professions in life." Colleges had been founded that were to develop the functions and facilities for more technical investigation and instruction and for its widest dissemination, and so, in their way, provide another answer to the nature and scope of the education called for in the endowing act.

When one applies the ultimate test of any educational system, the quality of the students trained, the land-grant showing in the formative years is highly commendable. In addition to the many who carried on their work in varied fields and performed their civic duties creditably, there was a fair proportion of outstanding leaders in business, the professions, and the public service. Best of all, here and there in the early classes were creative scientists who would provide the inspiration and direction for the research and instruction of the future.

The training of teachers for the public schools was a significant educational influence not contemplated in the original design. The system of alternate teaching and study was held to be more effective than the regular normal regimen. Some of the colleges found it desirable to introduce courses in pedagogy for the large proportion of their students who taught winter terms in district and village schools.[67] A surprisingly large number of early graduates entered this profession as a life career, and Morrill was led to conclude that one of the greatest services rendered to the nation by his foundation was in supplying teachers for educationally backward regions.[68]

By no means of least importance was the effect of the new

education upon the old. In return for their borrowings and copyings the innovators gave "fresh life and activity to the older colleges, which had sunk into routine, tradition, and imitation." In his last public address Francis A. Walker expressed the belief that "no student of American education will question that the new colleges had an immense influence in quickening the life of the old and in promoting the searching reforms from within which render them today so much more active and efficient, than in any previous stage of their existence."[69]

None the less, with all these demonstrable achievements the fact remained that thus far the special training contemplated in the act and popularly identified with the new colleges had not been adequately attained. Engineering was in the transitional stage corresponding to that in industry itself, and there was inevitable uncertainty concerning the main divisions and their content and still more in regard to the proper and most effective combination of theory and practice. Even less had the main title role subject been established to the satisfaction of the educators, the general public, or the constituency to be placated and served. At the same time the possible and immediately needful range of technical subjects was incomplete and unperfected; women, especially, found no peculiar vocational opportunity. In all fields distinctive and specialized methods of instruction adapted to the peculiar materials and objectives were undeveloped. Happily, influences were already under way which were to give land-grant education its peculiar content and emphasis, and thus enable it to realize the aims both of the scientists and of the reformers and in so doing to win public confidence and support.

CHAPTER VII

RECONCILING SCIENCE AND PRACTICE

Industrial educators had been agreed that experimentation was an essential function of the A. and M. college, but their understandings of what constituted experimenting varied as much as the conditions and outlook of their different institutions. To some almost any sort of farm observation, however elemental and inexact, was regarded as "research." There was a persistent confusion between the showily successful "model" farm and experimental plots, equipment, and livestock. The spic-and-span farm setup had a direct demonstrational appeal to the farmer and prospective farmer that the average field and laboratory experiments could not make. Contrary to frequent claims, the two aims could not be realized effectively in the same plant, and funds were insufficient to develop both types.[1] Engineering met something of the same confusion between the well-equipped and efficiently managed machine shop and the testing laboratory. In the emerging domestic science, too, there was a natural tendency, before the adequate application of the basic sciences, to mistake the proficiency of the practice kitchen, sewing room, and laundry for an addition to the sum of knowledge.[2]

Research activities in the early years must of necessity be combined with instruction, and certain administrators were fearful lest the zealous scientist should become so absorbed in his investigations as to neglect his real job of teaching his classes. Some even maintained that the Morrill Act permitted research only insofar as it contributed directly to improved teaching. At the Washington conference in 1882 Regent Peabody of Illinois asserted emphatically that legally as well as pedagogically the land-grant teacher's place was in the classroom. In his view there was a real danger of an absorption in the quest for new information that would lead to a neglect in imparting that which was established. He was confident that the "conscientious teacher" would find the academic day all too short "to conduct his pupil over the well-known ground of clearly established truth, and that the illumination which he can and must shed upon that truth will absorb all the means and time and strength at his disposal. His first and paramount duty is instruction. If his investigation will help his instruction, let him investigate; if it interferes with his instruction, let him obey the law and TEACH."[3] This plausible dictum assumed a body of "clearly established truth" in the applied sciences that did not yet exist.

Too much was expected of the conscientious instructor. The more he sought to teach his students and advise their fathers the more was he made aware of the inadequacies of "established" applied science facts, principles, and methods. His scientific integrity and his professional self-respect drove him to experimentation. The precedents, home and foreign, all indicated the systematic experimental basis of agricultural improvement. The stations of Germany, France, and England since the fifties had been the focal points of applied science and, as has been noted, the leaders in American agricultural improvement had essayed, however crudely, to test their innovations by trial and error.

Governmental activity, so far as it had gone, had recognized the investigational function. The Patent Office program under varied competence had aimed at the compilation of experimental and statistical information. The work of the state chemists and the organization of state geological and agricultural surveys had similar intent. It was the view and aim of the pioneers in applied science that the teaching and research functions were to be combined. The superintendent of the Pennsylvania Farmers' High School started his experimental plots before buildings were completed or equipment secured. The Michigan college farm was held to be for testing and comparing as well as for labor and demonstration. The law chartering the Maryland college specified certain classes of experiments to be conducted, and in the initial years analyses of commercial fertilizers were made. A similar chemical application constituted the main interest of S. W. Johnson in the Sheffield School.[4]

The organic act had given express recognition to the knowledge-acquiring function in the provisions for the purchase of experimental farms and for reports on experiments conducted. In some cases the establishing acts provided specifically for conducting experiments, and in all the states the appropriateness of such work, however understood, was recognized. The convention of land-grant representatives at Chicago in 1871 gave major emphasis to the need for stations in each state as did the gathering called by the commissioner of agriculture the following year. The Connnecticut state board of agriculture under the leadership of the Sheffield faculty urged the legislature to provide a station on the European model; but public interest was insufficient to secure the needed action, and Orange Judd, the famous agricultural editor and an alumnus and benefactor of Wesleyan, offered a thousand dollars, and the Wesleyan trustees gave the free use of their chemical laboratory on condition that the legislature provide an annual appropriation of $2,800. On this basis the first regular experiment station in the country was started in 1875 with W. O. Atwater as director.[5]

At the University of California the experimental function was recognized from the start, and with the lack of demand for agricultural instruction this direct service to the farmers of the state became the main objective of the agricultural department. E. W. Hilgard, who was selected to head the work in 1874, was convinced that at the existing stage of development the main need was for experimental investigation of immediate farm problems and extension contacts with the farmers themselves, and he secured the full committal of the president to this plan. Hilgard's experience with an agricultural survey of Mississippi proved serviceable in organizing his projects.[6]

At the passage of the federal experiment station act of 1887, fourteen states had organized such institutions, in most cases in connection with the colleges, and in thirteen others equivalent work was being conducted without definite organization.[7] The initial work of these stations was concerned largely with the analysis of commercial feeds and fertilizers—lines of the regulatory activity that would soon necessitate more effective administrative establishments, both state and national. But the range was soon extended to the introduction of new crops, new rotations, the combating of pests, and elementary developments in animal nutrition and dairy bacteriology. Distinction was usually made between experiments that would have a direct popular appeal through their immediate results and practical application and those involving more intricate and prolonged investigation.[8]

Private foundations supplemented the state enterprises in two notable cases. The Bussey Institution at Harvard began its experimental work in 1871 under the direction of F. H. Storer. Financed jointly by the institution's endowment and the Massachusetts Society for Promoting Agriculture, this pioneer investigator and writer did notable work in field tests and fertilizer analyses.[9] In 1876 Lawson Valentine, a New York financier, projected a unique experimental institution—Houghton Farm at Cornwall, New York—modeled upon the English Rothamsted station. The enterprise was organized under the direction of Dr. Manly Miles, 1879–81, and continued under Major Henry E. Alvord, 1881–88. The complete plan called for investigations in soil physics, plant physiology and pathology, and animal breeding and nutrition, with publication of the results. The main experiments actually conducted were in corn propagation with a relatively generous expenditure of $20,000 per year. Valentine's death ended the promising enterprise before the full program was inaugurated.[10]

Experimental, like collegiate enterprises initiated by the states, required national aid to become fully and securely established. The Department of Agriculture and most of the college leaders had a common interest in furthering such institutions. The conventions sponsored by the commissioners gave special attention to the movement, and in the early eighties a committee of college presidents headed by S. A. Knapp of Iowa drafted a bill "to establish National Experiment Stations in connection with the

Agricultural Colleges of the various States." The avowed aim was to enable the Department to function more fully and appropriately through these "national experiment stations." The superintendents appointed by the trustees were to report to the commissioner at his pleasure, and the program of experiments was to be determined by the commissioner, the president of the college, and the superintendent of the station. For the support of the work an annual appropriation of $15,000 from any money in the treasury not otherwise appropriated was to be provided. The committee readily justified the localization of stations by reason of regional diversities as well as the economy and instructional availability of location at the colleges. It was not so evident that the control given to the commissioner was necessary to systematize the stations' work and avoid duplication of experiments. The colleges and other state interests resented the seeming subserviency to the Department, and it was only when this objectionable feature was removed that the united support of agricultural colleges and societies could be secured.[11]

A bill making the stations distinctly state institutions under the control of their own boards, drafted by Commissioner Colman with the aid of college leaders and introduced in the House by Hatch of Missouri and in the Senate by George of Mississippi, was enacted in 1887. The commissioner's function was made purely advisory, and it was expressly provided that nothing in the act should "be construed to impair or modify the legal relation existing between any of the said colleges and the government of the States or Territories in which they are respectively located." An amendment was added, largely through Grange influence, to permit stations organized independently of agricultural colleges to receive the benefits of the act. The final act returned to the previous policy of acquiring the fund from public land receipts. With the general availability of the grant and the growing political strength of the agricultural interest, there was no positive opposition to the measure. The main risk was indefinite postponement through precedence of other interests, but the application of strategic influence upon congressional leaders brought hasty action near the close of the session.[12]

The so-called Hatch Act had possibilities which were to make it a turning point in the acquisition and teaching of agricultural science, but immediately there were retarding influences both in lack of appreciation and in misapplied zeal. In the absence of strict federal supervision undeveloped colleges used the added money to establish the regular undergraduate teaching program. In some cases the second college subsidy in 1890 released for the first time the station funds for the true purpose.[13] Competent staff members and especially directors were hard to secure, and among pioneer specialists harmonious and equitable administration was peculiarly difficult to attain. There were attempts on the one hand to overburden the teaching staff with the research activities and on the other to control the funds for the disproportionate development of certain subject interests.[14] But in the face of the great opportunity now presented, the nucleus of research leaders who had launched the state stations was able to overcome such temporary obstacles. Research workers were trained, internal dissensions gave way before liberal-minded leadership, and federal relations were made more definite and intelligible by the creation of the Office of Experiment Stations.

The following decade marked the establishment of the stations' work on essentially the modern lines of effort—original research, verification, and inspection. The findings contributed directly to the fundamental achievements in scientific production. The dairy industry was revolutionized by the perfection of ensiling and soiling systems, the invention of a practical, simple device for milk testing, and the application of chemistry and bacteriology to the manufacture of its products. Animal breeding, nutrition, and pathology entered upon their modern phases. Soils were analyzed with more precision. Crop selection, adaptation, and improvement were greatly extended, and diseases and pests combated.[15] Farm management and economics applied to agricultural business as subjects of systematic research still awaited the rise of contemporary problems of tenure, credit, and surplus disposal.

The stations brought system and gave direction to the land-grant colleges, and more than any other factor assured their continuation. The various stations and the federal department collected and verified information which could be organized into systematic and definitely graded courses; "agriculture" was resolved into its basic constituents, and these were separated into divisions and subdivisions. Specialization was on the way to minutiae, and the B. Agr. and B.S.A. were coming to have a distinctive and increasingly distinguished meaning. Scientific standing brought academic recognition and acceptance. At the same time the practical benefits of the testing of fertilizers and stock foods and the findings of experimental plot, feed lot, and orchard were being realized by the farmers themselves. By convincing demonstration of the direct relation of scientific practices to the annual return, they were led to respect the methods of "book farming" and to encourage their sons to penetrate the profitable mysteries.[16]

The content, method, and spirit of the station were also transforming the methods of teaching. From dependence upon translations of foreign manuals and a few stray treatises by American pioneers, textbooks in applied science multiplied from the eighties and assumed their dominant place in undergraduate instruction. In addition to the traditional general treatises for students and reading farmers, leading agricultural specialists were seeking by the nineties to capitalize or promote the interest in their fields by texts and reference books.[17] Engineering teachers were no less productive. The president of the Society for the Promotion of Engineering Education reported in 1894 that technical manuals had multiplied to such an extent that students were being tempted to cram their information, but a fellow worker the same year felt that there was a strong demand for "concise pithy manuals on nearly every engineering subject which can be sold at a reasonable price," and he was confident that there were "plenty of men eminently qualified to write them."[18] In succeeding years professional ambition, pecuniary necessity, and publishing enterprise verified this claim for all divisions and subdivisions of applied science.

The same period marked the systematizing of laboratory and

field work. While nominally such instruction had been provided from the beginning of the land-grant enterprise, down to the eighties organization and equipment were in most colleges hopelessly inadequate. The stations set new standards of organization and technique, both for agriculture and the mechanic arts. The old manual labor requirements, with incidental observation and practice, were now giving way to systematic instruction in laboratory and field. In agricultural practice the determination and verification of underlying principles rather than the attainment of manipulative skill was coming to be emphasized.[19] There was a similar trend in engineering.

For collegiate instruction the engineering laboratory paralleled and in some cases preceded the corresponding development in agriculture. As early as 1861 at the Massachusetts Institute of Technology, William B. Rogers had recommended engineering as well as basic science laboratories. But it remained for Robert H. Thurston, a Brown graduate, to organize the first testing laboratory at Stevens Institute in 1871. In 1885 Thurston became director of the newly established Sibley College at Cornell, and provision was made for complete laboratory equipment according to existing standards. By that time similar developments were taking place in the leading engineering schools. For some years there was disagreement between the supporters of specialist research and of student instruction as to the proper utilization of the expensive equipment. In the end the claims of both interests were recognized and adjusted much as they had been in agriculture, except that definitely organized experiment stations were developed at a considerably later period through exclusive state support.[20] Civil engineering, the pioneer branch, extended its surveying practice realistically in a number of cases by holding summer camps in strategically situated localities.[21]

Veterinary medicine gave increasing attention to clinical instruction, and even the nascent domestic science departments sought a laboratory equivalent in practice and experimental kitchens.

Applied science research led to the clearer differentiation of graduate study. While in most land-grant colleges there had from the early years been nominal "post graduate" students, the study in general involved a time extension and a quantitative accumulation of credits rather than a different level of instruction and original achievement. With the systematizing of research in applied science, as in other fields, graduate requirements and degrees could have real significance.[22]

The military, like other lines of study, reflected the standardizing trend. Drill halls were built, the courses were given more definite place in the program, and the professors of military tactics placed upon more equal status, all in accord with the recommendations of the War Department. In 1889 the new Association of Agricultural Colleges gave special recognition to this required subject in the appointment of a committee to confer with the War Department on methods and content of instruction. As a result of the conference the Secretary of War formulated more explicit regulations for details of officers and range and content of courses.[23] Following this reorganization the military departments assumed essentially the form and position that they were to hold to the World War.

While the physical benefits of military drill continued to be emphasized, there was a growing recognition of need for cooperation with physical education in securing symmetrical development and correcting special defects. Systematized gymnastics and specialized gymnasiums were being introduced to provide the exercise hitherto secured on the farm and in the shop. German systems of gymnastics had been introduced in special schools in the sixties, and Amherst had established a gymnasium at the beginning of that decade. By the eighties classes in physical education and correction were becoming general.[24]

A much more spontaneous as well as spectacular substitute for the labor requirement on the physical side was provided by organized athletics. The seventies and eighties marked the rise in the eastern colleges of intercollegiate sport in which land-grant institutions, while starting somewhat tardily, were to have a conspicuous part. The only recognition Noah Porter gave to athletics in the discussion of a rather inclusive list of college problems in 1870 was in an incidental reference to boat races as one of the topics of idle conversation in dormitories;[25] by the end of that decade athletics had become a matter of major interest and concern in the older colleges.

Rowing was the first contest to be organized into intercollegiate associations after an earlier stage of college racing clubs. Baseball, that had previously had only intramural or in some cases amateur neighborhood status, became the leading contest of the eighties when modern American football was introduced.[26] With the arrival of modern sport came its all too familiar problems and controversies. Athletics and the athlete became major alarms in presidential reports. The new football in particular was condemned as "barbarous and brutal."

Against the system as a whole most of the conventional modern criticisms were recorded. Such benefits as intercollegiate sports provided went to the select few, funds intended for physical education were diverted to the teams, and the mass of students received their exercise vicariously. The excitement aroused by the contests was unsettling and demoralizing to the regular college program; trips were too extended, games were too frequent, and standards were so variable and flexible as to make amateur status uncertain. Conferences involved plottings and intrigues worthy of seasoned diplomats. In negotiations and contest it was all too evident that the spirit of good sportsmanship had not become a tradition in intercollegiate relations.[27]

In spite of these alleged abuses there was a popular feeling that institutions of higher learning were being ranked, especially by prospective students, on the basis of their athletic records, and an enterprising journalist sought a possible correlation between scores and enrollments. While the presidents consulted were confident "that in a matter of so grave importance as a choice of a college, a consideration so insignificant as a loss of a boat race or a ball match would have no material weight with a young man desirous to secure a good education, and still less so with his father," Barnard of Columbia was led to the reluctant admission, "It is still, however, undoubtedly true that a young man will reflect with pride on the fact that the college to which he belongs can boast an honorable athletic record, and though this consideration may not have often a prevailing influence, it is hardly to be doubted that it counts for something."[28] A logical if drastic solution would have been the abolition of all intercollegiate contests, but the lure of winning teams was increasingly hard to resist.

Land-grant colleges, naturally opposed to such vain glories, when they once entered into them came to take promotive pride in these achievements. When the Massachusetts college won the eastern regatta in 1871 the mercurial president exhibited a joy unrestrained, and the board's annual report cited the victory as conclusive evidence of the physical and intellectual superiority of country-reared youth and of this type of collegiate training.[29] Andrew D. White felt that "reasonable devotion" to athletics was commendable, and he was especially pleased with the prowess of his university's crew.[30] The general public, it appeared, needed but slight exposure to be changed from censorious critics to ardent rooters.[31] There was a growing conviction that the main solution was in better-trained teams, standardization of rules, and a general regulation of contests that would secure the socializing values without the antisocial abuses. During the nineties when modern athletic contests and organizations had arrived, East and West, these more wholesome and appropriate relationships were coming to prevail. Organized sport, both intra and inter, was but one evidence of the trend from the individual to the social, not to say mass, emphasis.

Among these modernizing trends in higher education in which the new type college joined or took the lead was the persistent, if often vague, demand for citizenship training. The whole industrial movement had been based upon this aim, however understood at different periods, and it was given specific emphasis in all statements of the objectives of land-grant education. In seeking additional support in 1876 Morrill argued that these federal-state colleges might become the most influential agency in promoting national unity and enlightened self-government.[32] Andrew D. White deplored the lack of proportionate political leadership of farmers and mechanics, and to overcome this disparity proposed that courses in history, political science, and public speaking be made a definite part of technical education. In his own university he inaugurated theoretical and practical training for public service, in addition to a major emphasis upon the social sciences.[33] Likewise, Gilman in his California inaugural in 1872 pleaded for the social training of technical students: "It is important for their own culture and for the public good, that they should have a clear notion of what constitutes the State in its best form. Whether merchants, manufacturers, farmers, or miners, they are quite as likely as lawyers, and much more likely than physicians and clergymen, to be called to the councils of legislation, and to pronounce opinions there on difficult questions pertaining to human society, law, finance, property, education, crime, pauperism, and the policy of the national, state, and local governments." Both these internal issues and the growing realities of international relations called for "the study of history not as dry annals, but as the record of living forces and human experience, the study of political economy, of social science, of civil liberty, and of public law . . . made attractive by the voices of original and profound teachers, who can gather up the wisdom of the old and apply it to the requirements of the new generations."[34] Again in 1884 an Iowa senator, in urging the broadening of the scope of the agricultural college, derided the pretensions to liberality "with her doors locked against history."[35]

With the growing emphasis upon these studies they were readily admitted among the added "cultural" offerings. The recommendation of an ultravocational visiting committee that this group of studies be deferred to an additional term for those who cared to make that sacrifice for them and better still that history and literature be read on the side in books that "could be named," along with the opinion that all of value in modern languages could be obtained in translation, was fortunately not the prevailing attitude.[36] But too generally narrow content and formal presentation tended to depreciate and devitalize the offerings. The subjects usually had gone to the president along with philosophy, and the instruction had involved the memorizing of traditionally selected and organized facts and principles in desiccated manuals.

With the awakening interest in citizenship training in its various phases, trained specialists, in accord with current standards, were secured, and their reports were introducing a modern professional phraseology—collateral reading, student reports, topics, problems, and even seminars, along with the inevitable pleas for increased and extended library and visual equipment. In modern emphasis if not altogether in organization and method, civilization surveys oscillated between sociology and history.[37]

Throughout the social science program a "current issues" consciousness was manifested. Apparently there was as yet no appreciation of the possibility of adapting special phases of social organization and development to the interests and needs of the different technical fields.[38] Such application, however, awaited only the shift of emphasis already under way from unrestrained production and exploitation to problems of consumption, distribution, and social control. This change would necessitate the gradual training of applied social scientists in place of the emotional or doctrinaire enthusiasts who pioneered in the problems of agricultural business and of rural social uplift.

The development of the new industrialism was bringing economics into its modern dominance in the social science domain. In the the opinion of J. Lawrence Laughlin,[39] the Civil War had made the nation economics conscious, and both positive developments and negative criticisms were popularizing at the same time that they were complicating its problems. The New Hampshire visiting committee in 1890 had an especially favorable impression of the political economy class, the students of which "appeared as though they had found delight in this branch." On a range of topics from basic theory to current applications, the members discoursed "as though they had devoted time and careful study to these important subjects." The committee, composed of a clergyman, a physician, and a farmer, were particularly gratified to find the conclusions "based upon a sense of right and duty" and more stress upon "principle than mere theory."[40]

Social theory tended to be based upon a moral standard identified in most cases with the established order. The chief approach to liberalism was in the neo-classical free trade doctrines of leading economists and social philosophers. Alumni and administrators were becoming fearful that these teachings were being carried to dangerous extremes—even as mere academic theories. Frankly and naively the Vermont president, as he confided to the patron senator, proposed to bring credit and material reward to his university by combating these heretical ideas. In his opinion a college which would secure a professor of economics committed to protection would "draw to itself patronage and money." Business men were charging the colleges with responsibility for the industrial collapse, and they "would rally to the support of an Institution which should ably defend and maintain the protection doctrine." Without mincing matters he made his proposal: "I wish we could find a bright, active, growing young man whom we could put into the chair, and who by publishing and lecturing would give us prominence in the financial world. Endowments would follow, I am confident."[41] Morrill, who had urged that Greeley prepare an elaborate textbook on economic theory to vindicate protectionism against the Manchester school,[42] endorsed the letter laconically, "Wants Professor of Polit. Economy to teach protection."

Aside from this more-or-less temporary favor for the "British heresy" which they generally imbibed from their instructors, land-grant student opinion in the early years—with its background of landed proprietorship and with the resulting indoctrination in traditional individualistic philosophy—was predominately hostile to disturbing innovation. When the literary society or public exhibition orator turned from the preferred classical and inspirational themes to present realities, social agitators and protestants of all sorts and shades were apt to be disposed of summarily if not altogether conclusively. The ills of the social order which the most obtuse complacency could not ignore would all respond readily to the educative process. The order itself was sound and secure: business enterprise, the good old parties, the faith of the fathers with their appropriate institutions and recognized spokesmen—the unreasoned assurance of a gilded age already beginning to tarnish.[43]

By the eighties the new forces were beginning to penetrate even academic complacency and conformity. The farmer and labor movements were creating a new cleavage and consciousness; a literature of protest was raising doubts of the powers that were in all realms, and a social gospel was awakening eager if often vague and ill-directed desire for uplift and betterment. These doubts, protests, and aspirations began to find reflection in orations and debates in local and intercollegiate contests and in vigorous if crude essays and editorials. Modern student newspapers, which were replacing the old faculty-guided magazines, had the modern zeal for news—to the point of making it if the campus appeared too depressingly calm. Intercollegiate relations on field and forum became a dependable feature, and such contacts gave a basis of comparison and helped to establish a collegiate standardization in essentials as well as in trivialities.

With widened outside contacts made possible by the development of transportation and communication facilities and with the changes incident to increased enrollment, the old paternalism, whether applied directly or disguised under a pseudo-student participation, gave way more and more to the practice, not usually definitely formulated, of treating the student—within limits of course—as a responsible adult citizen, with the rights and obligations involved.[44] Such a change prepared the way for the gradual attainment to a measure of real student participation —somewhat retarded in state institutions by the governing requirements of the code. In any case governmental interests did not stop with college politics—class, society, or student governing body. The new student generation had an active if not generally understanding interest in local and national party politics. They were no longer content merely to form party clubs and participate colorfully and vocally in mass meetings and parades. They took part in caucuses and started an agitation for nonresident student voting that was to influence eventually the adoption of the absentee ballot.[45] Student interest in public affairs was to remain largely spasmodic and emotional, with alternations of lethargic indifference and hysterical enthusiasm.[46] But in contrast with the earlier aloofness the student and his "profs" alike were getting about, extending their contacts and increasing, more or less effectively, their public activities.

Land-grant colleges shared these civic ventures with the other colleges of the period. Their special contribution was in the intermingling on a common social level of all branches and grades of study including the main industrial interests of succeeding periods, and in the direct contacts that the colleges made with their states at large[47] in the systematic dissemination of the findings of its experimenting and resident teaching in all lines of active interest. It was only with the full inauguration of such inclusive and extended programs that the true and peculiar mission of the land-grant colleges could be realized.

CHAPTER VIII

ANY PERSON IN ANY STUDY

The verifying of subject matter and the systematizing of method made possible not only richer and more effective collegiate training but opened the way for the widest extension of the field of instruction. Ezra Cornell's aspiration for an institution where the instructional needs of any person might be supplied[1] was generally regarded as a utopian dream of social enlightenment, but expansion, division, and adaptation of the field of knowledge, on and off the campuses, tended to an approximation to that ideal, involving a transformation of values as fundamental as that in content. The traditional dogma that collegiate training—aside from the professions for which it was the true introduction—must all be at one certain level, continue through the quadrennial cycle, and eventuate in certified parchments that represented a standard, in subject matter and gradation, that kept within a minimum range of tolerance, was now being challenged by baser standards represented by new degrees which, like Tom Sawyer's vari-colored Sunday school prize cards, had, with the academic elite, a descending scale of currency.

In a scientific, socially utilitarian age such distinction could not persist, and the third president of Cornell's foundation could uphold his philosophy if not his literal scheme in the assertion that a people's university must hold all subjects equally reputable and provide instruction in all alike, with social utilization the main test—"greater than the humanities is humanity."[2] Such a conception of a university was to make possible in his own institution the development of schools of philosophy, classical studies, and cultural history along with chairs of farriery, aquaculture, and hotel management, and a gradation of instruction from the exhibitional appeals of farm and home week and the demonstrational train to the creative achievements at the post-doctoral level. This was to be the trend in the fully developed land-grant universities, and the colleges were to expand and extend proportionately within their particular field. But first the scope and bounds of that field must be determined.

By the eighties the conception of land-grant education as an addition to, rather than a subtraction from, the scope of higher education was being expounded vigorously if sometimes crudely. Governor Ben Butler, in transmitting the Massachusetts report for 1882, sought to dispel the mistaken notion that the college was only for agricultural training with the assurance that "For practical instruction, to every branch of professional life except perhaps theology, the *curriculum,* and the methods of imparting knowledge to the pupil, are as beneficial as those of any other institution of learning."[3] Regent Peabody, speaking for the ambitious Illinois university, that was soon to discard the limiting adjective "industrial," held that the founding act permitted "every form of human learning which it has fallen to the fortune of mankind to devise or acquire."[4] At the same time a New Hampshire professor in a thoughtful survey reasoned that for adequate instruction in agriculture itself there was required as a basis for technical training a background of the humanities and of the exact and natural sciences.[5]

A versatile teacher and administrator of Massachusetts, with the vision of the enthusiast if not the exactness of the expert, pictured his curriculum as a rising structure: "With this broad definition of agriculture—itself a science, complete in itself, yet touching all sciences and all branches of knowledge,—and taking as our guide the law that the teacher of agriculture can but indicate these points of contact and leave to others their explanation, we have endeavored to rear our superstructure of agricultural education: agriculture, our foundation; botany, chemistry, veterinary, and mathematics, our four corner-stones; while the walls are built high with horticulture, market-gardening, and forestry on the one side, physiology, etymology, [*sic*] and the comparative anatomy of the domestic animals on the second, mechanics, physics, and meteorology on the third, and a study of the English language, political economy, and constitutional history on the fourth. These separate lines of study, each distinct in itself, yet each aiding in the interpretation or solution of the difficult problems met with, require a four-year course. They proceed hand in hand, and the completion of a study in one department is coincident with that in another. Mutual help is the watchword; each for all and all for each, in the laying broad and deep the foundation, and building up the solid structure."[6]

By the nineties agriculture had become a coordinate division or, in some of the larger universities, a school or college, and subject specialization came with diversified farming. Starting with the original chairs of agricultural chemistry, horticulture, applied botany, and "agriculture," which purported to cover the whole range of farm practice, division and subdivision were soon under way. Dairying was early detached from the omnibus department, followed by animal husbandry, and veterinary science.[7] The latter was in some cases to develop into a separate division or school.

With the improvements in breeding and the application of more reasoned methods in handling herds and flocks, and especially with the growth of regulatory measures for controlling contagious diseases and meat and milk inspection, there was an increasing demand for professional veterinarians. Proprietary initiative provided the pioneer colleges in the fifties, but of this group only the New York Veterinary College headed by Dr. Liautard had permanent significance.[8] Both Cornell and Illinois established distinct departments at the beginning. President White in his prefounding recruiting journeys was fortunate in securing the Scotch scientist, Dr. James Law, who in addition to laying the foundations of a great professional college rendered invaluable service to the state and federal agricultural departments.[9] The first distinct state school of veterinary science was founded at the Iowa Agricultural College in 1879 under the direction of Dr. Millikan Stalker. Ohio followed in 1884, Cornell in 1894, and Washington in 1896.[10] If general practice was limited, government service provided employment for the limited number of early graduates.

While the demand for agricultural training in its various branches was developing slowly and hesitantly, the other title role member of land-grant education met enthusiastic response from the first. The term "mechanic arts" was sufficiently inclusive and flexible to serve the progressing demands of a dynamic era in which industry was being transformed from the simple factory stage to the complexities of mass production. In contrast to the older occupation, opportunities outran available training. In the technical transition from the agricultural to the industrial era, engineering direction and service was needed at every point—and needed immediately. "Railroads, bridges, water works, sewerage works, and mining and metallurgical plants were demanded over the face of the continent. Hundreds were crowding or were being pressed into service with little or no proper education. Chairmen and axmen speedily became transit-men and 'engineers.' "[11] Professional anxiety as well as gratification was reflected in the declaration of Robert H. Thurston at the Columbian Exposition that "*Upon the thorough education of our engineers depends very largely the future progress of the nation.*"[12] Certainly eager recruits were not lacking. Without exception the new institutions reported engineering enrollments far in excess of the agricultural. This was true even in the dominantly agricultural states as soon as industrial departments were organized. So striking was this disparity that agricultural organizations and at times the departments themselves complained, invariably without justification, of administrative favoritism. Assured employment at relatively high salaries in contrast with the lack of openings for agricultural experts, along with the novelty and glamour of many phases of the new work accounted adequately for the attraction of these courses.[13]

The "great formative epoch in the American engineering education" from 1870 to 1885 witnessed a remarkable growth in enrollment and a differentiation of the profession into its main branches.[14] In this establishment the land-grant institutions had a determining influence. In fact, a leading representative of this phase of the movement was led to maintain, enthusiastically but probably advisedly, that the land-grant achievements in engineering science constituted a "very large part of the present possession of engineering education in America if not of the entire world."[15] The increase of engineering graduates from less than 900 in the pioneer period before 1870 to over 3,800 in the decade of the eighties was due in large part to the publicly supported departments.[16]

As late as 1870 engineering "was still a single stem . . . but with budding indications of a branching growth." That year at the Sheffield School the first department of mechanical or "dynamic" engineering was established with a West Point graduate in charge.[17] Cornell, starting with chairs of civil engineering and mechanics, began this same year to develop the systematic mechanical engineering course with the benefactions of Hiram Sibley which by 1885 led to the establishment of the notable college bearing that donor's name. Meanwhile student interest and increasing applications in industry and transportation led to the founding of the first chair of electrical engineering—the initial cost underwritten by the far-and-broad-visioned president by reason of the skepticism of members of his board for such newfangled ventures.[18] From a mere division of physics, the industrial age gave the youngest member of the basic engineering trilogy a phenomenal impetus. The regional extent of the demand for engineering instruction followed closely the extending range of industrial localization. In the Middle West Illinois and Purdue gave early and increasing emphasis to engineering in its developing fields, while the mining states stressed metallurgical study.

The remaining major division of studies, resulting from the raising of domestic science and art to assured collegiate status, inaugurated a distinct and peculiar female profession. From the fifties agricultural reformers had been demanding the education of the farmer's wife not only in the household and in the dairy, poultry, and horticultural arts, which were included in that sphere, but in the underlying principles of the organization and operation of the farm to an extent that would enable her to be an effective counselor and planner.[19] Feminist agitators had long emphasized the need for education in household management and motherhood. Catherine Beecher in her project for a complete women's university in 1870 would have included "domestic chemistry and domestic philosophy," and she berated existing female colleges for lack of provision for training in the duties and responsibilities of wives and mothers.[20] But before the scientific recognition and analysis of the problems of nutrition, textile durability and adaptability, sanitation, household organization and equipment, that were developed mainly in these new public service institutions, there was no thought of such training as the basis of a professional career. In the plan for his model agricultural college the imaginative young Evan Pugh could offer no more constructive suggestion for the training of women than the facetious proposal that they be taught to make "Liebig bread and sauer kraut."[21]

The labor requirement for women met most appropriately by the daily routine of kitchen, dining-hall, and laundry provided background practice which naturally suggested, the more skilled the training became, the development of this empirical art into a reasoned and demonstrated science. In 1875 Mary B. Welch, the wife of the first president of the Iowa Agricultural College, who had been giving lectures on cooking for two or three years in connection with the required labor service, persuaded the board to establish a department of "cookery and household arts;" and in connection with this modest venture there was developed "the first experimental kitchen ever opened in any college."[22] About the same time Kansas provided instruction in sewing and lectures on the application of chemistry to foods.[23] Illinois from 1874 to 1880 probably had the most systematized and thorough pioneer venture in this department. The technical studies, backed by a broad foundation of general science, modern language, history, and philosophy, included foods and dietetics, domestic hygiene, household esthetics, household science, "domestic economy, as of time, money, with social usages and laws of etiquette," and home architecture. According to available reports the instruction was for the period commensurate with curriculum and equipment. This most promising exhibit in organization and methodology of the new applied science was terminated by a rather unusual administrative complication. The competent and resourceful professor married the regent, and upon his forced retirement in 1880 withdrew with him, and the department was allowed to lapse for the following two decades.[24] By 1890 separate departments existed in Iowa, Kansas, Oregon, and South Dakota, and five years later the number had increased to ten.[25] General establishment awaited more definite professional opportunity and the laying of research foundations in the new applied field.

Eminent scientists were already making formative contributions. As early as 1857 Edward L. Youmans' *Household Science* furnished a preliminary prospectus and helped to bring the new application within the scientific circle. The pioneer nutrition researches of W. O. Atwater were basic as was the work of Ellen H. Richards, the "Liebig of domestic science," in the chemistry of foods. A. C. True at the head of the Office of Experiment Stations gave effective encouragement.[26] By the nineties as a result of these promotive and investigational efforts the peculiar profession of women was being prepared for the opportunities that commercial promotion, consumer protection, and child welfare measures would provide.

All the varied lines of professional application put increasing demands upon the basic sciences themselves and led to expansion, systematization, and specialization within the departments. By the end of the formative period there was a tendency in the colleges toward the organized industrial motivation of the general courses.[27] Within universities the main effect of the land-grant establishment upon the liberal arts course was in an increased emphasis on the natural and biological sciences, the extended use of the laboratory method, and rather dubious experiments with the specialized adaptation of courses in the social sciences and literature to the supposed interests and needs of different groups of technical students.

The establishment of these coordinate technical courses brought the problem of recognizing the respective rights, privileges, and dignities by appropriate degrees. The earliest technical institutions had tended to keep to traditional degrees with as little innovation as possible.[28] In contrast the practical industrialists had either completely disregarded such decorations as one of the evidences of an effete classicism or had invented the most startling innovations in academic usages.

The Illinois Industrial University, to accentuate its break from the classical tradition, in the early years refrained from conferring anything but a certificate of work completed. Such a detached industrialism could not persist. Long standing tradition and prevailing practice were not to be ignored, and the alumni, "finding themselves embarrassed by their lack of the usual symbol of graduation," petitioned the legislature for the customary investitures. Responding obligingly to so harmless and self-sustaining a request, the legislature authorized "the conferring such Literary and Scientific Degrees as are usually conferred by universities for similar or equivalent courses of studies, or such as the Trustees may deem appropriate." As the board felt some uncertainties as to the bounds of usage and appropriateness, Regent Gregory was requested to correspond with the other institutions and the result was the calling of a convention at Columbus, Ohio, in December, 1877, to consider this along with certain other matters of common interest.[29]

The main questions reported on by the degree committee headed by Gregory were: Ought American colleges to continue them; if so, which ones should be bestowed; and on what conditions? It was agreed that, with all the attending abuses, the degree system was so bound up with higher education that no college could afford to dispense with it. A counsel of perfection might suggest giving the power to a state board of examiners, but the numerous small colleges, it was certain, would never relinquish this prerogative. For the various technical degrees the prevailing and probably desirable tendency was to confer the B.S. as a first degree and the more distinct professional designation only after additional study and practice. On the all-important matter of basis for conferring degrees the committee felt that the state institutions had a great opportunity. "If they can agree upon some uniform standard, it will go far toward the establishment of a general standard for all of the respectable colleges of the country." To begin with, a general standard should assume at least two years of preparatory work above the common schools. The college course itself should extend to four academic years and involve a "due amount" of languages, mathematics, history, science, and philosophy. In course range and emphasis each institution must be allowed to consult its limiting conditions within and without, and—the usual safeguard against too rigid standardization as well as the possible opening for its evasion—"What is essential is equivalency, not identity of studies." Within such institutional discretion the conference would have eliminated limping standards by resolving that all degrees be maintained at a parity with the A.B.[30]

This convention, made up of college presidents or their representatives, had no authority or adequate prestige to serve as a standardizing body, and without such a check degree granting varied as did other practices and standards. Some, more venturesome than discrete, were restrained apparently only by the limits of available alphabetical combinations in what Gilman regarded as the academic equivalent of "tampering with the coins of the realm."[31] Thus, at a southern university the graduates of a commercial course were awarded the "degree Proficient in the Commercial School" (P.C.S.?), and for graduates of two-year courses in agriculture and mechanics there were the respective awards of G.A. and G.M.[32] (an anticipation of the modern junior college A.A.).

In all the land-grant institutions the older, general degrees were brought into competition with specialization zeal and technology consciousness. In agriculture, B. Agr. was thought to get closer to the soil than B.S.A. or B.S. in Agr., while the plain B.S. hardly got out of the laboratory. Horticultural enthusiasts finding any of them too general boasted B.H. or B.S.H. Engineering schools were divided between those who awarded the professional title (C.E., M.E., E.E., etc.) as a first degree and those who bestowed it only after a period of professional service. The latter group, after experimenting with combination of the bachelor designation with the profession (B.C.E., etc.), came around generally to B.S. with the department added by preposition or parentheses. The newer lines were forced to an exercise of ingenuity in combining letters or abbreviations. Mining made a reversal of order in E.M., or a new combination in B.S. in Mn.E., agricultural engineering adopted the professional B.A.E., while architecture and architectural engineering varied as widely in its expression as music in the fine arts group. Branches rapidly and hopefully extending but not yet wholly detached from the parental limb recognized the connection in such awkward makeshifts as M.E. in E.E., and B.E.M. in Cer. (ceramics).[33] Veterinary science, after brief trial of B.V.M. as a first degree, settled on D.V.M. or V.S., though a staff member bore the remarkable designation, from a proprietary college, of M.D.C. ("doctor of comparative medicine").[34] The different tentative awards in the domestic science or art field—D.A.B., B.D.E., B.S. in D.E., B.D.S.—reflecting the conflicting views in scope and emphasis, indicated that the latest candidate for membership in the applied science family had still not found herself.[35]

The change in policy from professional or technical to general degrees, often through several stages—some in fact starting with the general and eventually swinging back to it—led to dispensations by which the old tenors could be traded in for the most recent or, in many cases, to the arbitrary assumption, where public use was called for, of the new form without benefit of any official decree. In certain cases the awarding of a degree was a condition of an evolving curriculum; the regular course was at first only three years and the degree was awarded upon the completion of an additional year.[36] Some of the newer frontier colleges started out with a full panoply of courses and degrees before the first preparatory class was trained, while others failed to include this function in their charter, and the oversight had later to be provided for by special act.[37]

Whatever the diversities of degrees and standards of their

award, it can be said to the credit of the land-grant colleges that in the early years—aside from certain emergency awards to staff members—they generally refrained consistently from the more extreme indelicacies and indiscretions in awarding honorary degrees.[38] Some even found total abstinence the only safe policy, and considering the irresistible pressure which was later brought to bear, it is regrettable that all of the new type colleges did not adopt this as a distinctive feature.

These regular courses, however liberally adjusted, ingeniously adapted, and appropriately dignified, reached but a comparatively few of the constituencies for whom the colleges were designed. There was a persistent conviction within and without the institutions that the talent and facilities of these people's colleges should be more widely applied, that skilled farmers and mechanics as well as expert leaders should be trained. State universities, finding their agricultural ventures blocked by the small number of applicants for the regular course both from the lack of properly prepared applied science students and from the limited opportunities for those with collegiate training, introduced short, simplified courses based largely upon direct, practical applications. Tennessee, at the beginning of the eighties, provided a two-year course in "agricultural apprenticeship" in which the student recited and worked on alternate days. Free tuition and labor compensation thus enabled the industrious young farmer to pay the expense of instruction in his life occupation. The course aimed "to bring the advantage of the University within the reach of the largest number of our farming community, and at the same time indirectly to improve the quality and elevate the dignity of agricultural labor in our State."[39] Wisconsin, under the lead of the professor of agriculture, and Minnesota, under that of the superintendent of public instruction, established vocationalized nondegree courses both as salvaging and socializing enterprises. With strong support of farmer organizations and of the agricultural press, the short course in some form was tried by the leading agricultural colleges.[40]

With the appeal and service of such training there was for it as for the degree schedule the problem of standardization and limitation. So long as this work was merely a shortened and simplified adaptation of the regular course, the latter lost in popular and scholastic standing without commensurate gains in the number of special students and the quality of their training. With the raising of the regular curriculum to a parity with other degree courses, a distinct differentiation could be made, scholastically and professionally. While meeting certain needs in general instruction, the short course system came to have the greatest effectiveness in special fields like dairy industry.[41]

The full establishment of short and special courses, involving a measurable reconciliation of the attitudes and aims of the rival groups of agricultural educators, opened the way for the widest use of resident instructional staff and equipment. In 1875 the *American Agriculturist* had rebuked a youthful correspondent who inquired about an agricultural college where one might be "Learned to plow Good" for aspiring to any instruction but that of the common branches.[42] The new system reached down to the versatile skilled, if only semiliterate, who might profit by the institutional contact. And if the regular degree-destined agricultural students were inclined at first to resent the campus invasion of the "shorthorns" and the "wintergreens" their attitude but repeated that of the general science students to the coming of the "awkward ags" and the "greasy engineers," of the modern language group to the science specialists, and of the classicists to the modern language devotees; each in turn had marked a broadening conception of the appeal and function of higher education as the short course involved its wider sharing.

Even such a willing adaptation and expansion of institutional instruction was regarded as inadequate. In accord with the land-grant social ideal the results of experimental research and instructional organization must be carried directly to the farms and the industries. Industrial education to justify itself must not only go out into the highways and byways to seek recruits but must carry the instruction there with appropriate method and adequate paraphernalia. The colleges, administrators and scientists came to be generally agreed, could both train scientific experts and minister to the needs of the masses of the occupations.[43]

From the earliest stages of the industrial movement there had been conscious effort and definite organization to reach the people directly. The fairs had been rudimentary extension agencies in exhibits, competitions, lectures, and reports and discussions of actual experiences. In their day lyceums had sought to develop the general intelligence and improve the skill of farmer and mechanic. State societies and boards, through the employment of special lecturers or the addresses of itinerant state chemists, brought new ideas and suggestions to varying numbers of farmers. The farm journals provided occupational news, instruction according to prevailing information, and the opportunity for the report of experiences and the exchange of opinions. Even the consultants, for a fee and according to their degrees of competence, had helped to disseminate new ideas and especially to arouse heated discussions. The great need by the seventies was to combine systematically and effectively the findings of the new science with practical experiences.

Farmers' institutes proved the most effective agencies for bringing together the research and teaching talent of the colleges and the highest achievements in farm practice before the development of modern extension methods. The efforts of some of the state boards in the fifties in promoting regional meetings had prepared the way for the college activities. As early as 1859 Professor John A. Porter of Yale had urged in the *New Englander* that the existing body of agricultural information be made available by *"the enlistment of practical men who are not professional teachers, in the work of instruction, and their combination in such numbers, that a small contribution of time and labor from each shall make a sufficient aggregate to meet the object in view."*[44] In furtherance of this aim Porter organized the celebrated "Yale Agricultural Lectures" of 1860. The four weeks' course dealt with all phases of agriculture and combined the services of agricultural scientists, journalists, organization leaders, scholarly amateurs, and practical farmers. The registered attendance of 350 represented not only the New England and Middle Atlantic states but also Ohio, Indiana, Illinois, Wisconsin, Kentucky, Florida, and Canada. The course was so enthusiastically received that it was planned to repeat it annually with additions and improvements attained by experience and the utilization of the college's growing equipment, but war conditions prevented the further development of this notable project in agricultural extension. A few years later, however, the Sheffield School gave a different direction to extension service in providing public lectures on scientific applications for skilled mechanics.[45]

It remained for the agricultural colleges to systematize and popularize the institute movement. With small enrollments the presidents and the agricultural professors sought contact with the farmers through these meetings. Where the more scientifically minded found outlet for their talents in experimental work, those with aptitudes for popular presentation became the pioneer extension leaders. A few rare spirits combined both along with effective classroom teaching. In the early years the plan was tried of holding the institutes at the colleges, especially in the winter vacation period, but the attendance was relatively small and was drawn mainly from the locality. Regional meetings with itinerant lecturers proved necessary for effective contacts.[46] By 1890 regular institutes were established in twenty-six states. While in the majority of cases the organization was directed by the state boards of agriculture, the colleges provided the main "outside talent." From its establishment in 1888 the federal Office of Experiment Stations gave hearty encouragement to the institution which Secretary Rusk termed the "farmers' colleges."[47]

The early extension efforts were often carried on in conjunction with the Grange, the Alliances, and organizations of special producers, connections that proved both helpful and embarrassing. In any case unusual patience, tact, and skill in adaptation were required to effect a working agreement of country and campus, that would bring acceptance for the professors' newfangled ideas. Both inherited superstition and acquired sophistication had to be met and measurably counteracted. Often the successful farmer with homely narrative of his experiences and simple exposition of his empirical conclusions saved the program, and experience demonstrated that the more local initiative and responsibility were taken for the institutes the greater their likelihood of success.[48] A decade of trial led to the conclusion that these popularized presentations of the findings of the stations were steadily overcoming farmer prejudice and indifference to the colleges.[49]

Along with the institutes other rudimentary extension activities were developing. Popular station bulletins made new findings readily available for farm and home; personal correspondence answered questions dealing with particular problems; farm and local papers discussed matters of more general interest; the chautauqua idea was capitalized in farmers' reading courses; and gatherings were held that were the forerunners of the present-day institution of farm and home week.[50] In these various ways in the formative years, the land-grant college was entering upon its third main line of activity which needed only more modernized transportation and communication to be brought to full development.

CHAPTER IX

UNION AND STRENGTH

To establish securely and develop progressively those lines of research and organization which converged in the land-grant college, a public acceptance that would bring increased and regular support was essential. Organized effort, involving a common purpose and group consciousness, was required to attain such a status. There was a steady growth of this attitude. From the first the new colleges had been more cooperative than competitive. In the founding period there was an interchange of experiences, and the pioneers provided models in buildings, equipment, organization, and curricula that were consciously followed. The organizing committees of Massachusetts, Iowa, Ohio, Indiana, and Missouri visited the existing land-grant institutions for suggestions as to equipment, courses, and personnel.[1] The Tennessee course of study was based upon those of Cornell and Illinois, the Mississippi upon that of Michigan, and in his bequest for a South Carolina college, Clemson specified that it should "be modeled after the Agricultural College of Mississippi as far as practicable."[2] In his California inaugural Gilman had emphasized the kinship of all types of the new education: "We shall find worth while to note the experiences of the Lawrence and Sheffield scientific schools, of the Rensselaer Institute and the Massachusetts Institute of Technology, of West Point and Annapolis, and of the various colleges of agriculture and the mechanic arts which the congressional grant has created."[3]

After establishment it became the invariable practice for any college contemplating a marked departure in curriculum or organization or in seeking special aid from the legislature to circularize or visit the other institutions to determine trend of experiences and prevailing practices. The earlier institutions trained instructors for the later, and the original group of technical leaders migrated widely among the different colleges. While this involved more or less competitive rivalry, it made in the main for a better understanding and furthered standardizing trends. There were in the early years a number of cases of visiting lectureships and professorships, and friends of college and university days corresponded and exchanged visits. Personal academic relations not only developed a group spirit but helped to break down barriers between the land-grant and private institutions to the advantage of both.[4] Professional societies brought special groups together, and in 1880 the more inclusive "Society for the Advancement of Agricultural Science" and that of the "Teachers of Agriculture" were formed.[5]

The most direct and effective cooperation was in conferences and organizations for considering and promoting matters of basic common interest. On August 24–25, 1871, at Chicago, following the meeting of the Society for the Advancement of Science, a convention of about thirty land-grant educators met upon invitation of a dozen of their own number to consider cooperation in experimentation. In addition to the consideration of the designated subject, there were informal reports and exchanges of experiences from the different colleges represented. A long discussion of permanent organization, both on a separate basis and in conjunction with the N.E.A., led to no definite action, as there was a feeling that such a step would be premature.[6]

The following December the new commissioner of agriculture, Judge Frederick Watts, a promoter and long-time board member of the Pennsylvania college, called a convention for February, 1872, of "delegates of Agricultural Colleges, State societies and boards, to take such action regarding the interests of agriculture as they shall deem expedient." Representatives appeared from all of the states but California, Florida, Louisiana, Nevada, and Oregon, as well as from the District of Columbia and the territories of Montana, Dakota, and Utah. The gathering presided over by Dr. George B. Loring of Massachusetts included the most prominent agricultural leaders in the country. President Grant, upon special invitation, attended one of the sessions, but retired in the midst of the discussion of experiment stations without making recorded comment. The committee on convention business recommended as topics for consideration the expediency of seeking further congressional land grants, the establishment of experiment stations, the modification of military instruction, and the best methods of cooperation between the colleges and the department. Committees on equalization of grants, military education, and experiment stations made their respective reports, and these were considered at length though without conclusive decision. The convention adjourned to meet the following year, and the commissioner issued the call; but for reasons unrecorded, the meeting was not held.[7]

The next general gathering was that of presidents of state universities and colleges or their representatives at Columbus in 1877 to consider the matter of degrees and other topics submitted by executives from different regions. At the beginning the meeting formally resolved that it was merely a "conference" and not a convention. The following topics were discussed and referred to respective committees for reports: degrees, courses of study, military training, increased congressional appropriation, and scope and aim of university education. The topic on governing bodies was discreetly referred without discussion. The gathering was of chief significance in indicating trends of administrative opinion on the leading problems of the state institutions.[8]

The colleges were the dominant interest in the series of conventions called by federal commissioners of agriculture in the eighties with the aim of increasing the prestige and extending the influence of the department. George B. Loring, conspicuous as a promoter of agricultural organization and education, upon assuming the office in the summer of 1881 hastened to call, for the following January, a series of conventions of different groups meeting in successive two-day sessions: colleges and agricultural societies; animal industries; cereal crops; viticulture and wine producers. The college gathering, representing twenty-one states and two territories, gave main attention to the discussion on the development and needs of experiment stations and the scope and bounds of land-grant education. The discussions afforded Dr. Loring an opportunity for indulging in rambling disquisitions based upon his personal experiences and observations.[9] The meeting was so pleasing to him and satisfactory to the interests represented as to lead to a repetition the next year. In his call the Commissioner suggested as appropriate topics for the educators, entrance standards, the educational function of manual labor, the demand for and training of industrial technologists and specialists, the "necessity" for agricultural education, and "literary culture as an accompaniment of scientific training." All of these subjects, along with more technical ones, were touched upon if not fully covered in the papers and discussions.[10]

In opening his second gathering, Loring expressed the hope that such meetings had become a fixed custom of the department, and his successor, Norman J. Colman, seems so to have assumed, as he called for midsummer of his first year a meeting of representatives of colleges and allied institutions to bring about closer relations and fuller understanding between the department and these agencies.[11] At the close of this convention, which had stressed particularly the need for federal aid to experiment stations, a committee consisting of Atherton of Pennsylvania, Cook of New Jersey, Knapp of Iowa, Peabody of Illinois, Curtis of Texas, and Newman of Alabama was authorized to draw up a plan of permanent organization. At a called meeting of delegates of colleges and stations, October 18–20, 1887, the Association of American Agricultural Colleges and Experiment Stations was founded. The various colleges and stations with the Department were the constituting members, and the Office of Experiment Stations created the next year served further to bring into effective cooperative relationships state and federal educational and research activities.[12] The association was to prove one of the most effective influences in standardizing entrance requirements, balancing curricula, and rationalizing methods of instruction.

Hitherto, as has been noted, the relations of the colleges with the federal authorities had lacked continuity and effectiveness. The educational bureau was restrained from positive action in this as in other state educational relations by the lack of any definite jurisdiction. Commissioner Barnard's elaborate compilations of home and foreign organizations and practices did not lead to any general agreement as to type and emphasis, and as the states went their several ways in developing their own types, his successors tended to accept the various colleges as they found them and to hope for the best. To the conference of presidents in 1877 General Eaton brought congratulatory greetings from his bureau with forecasts of future congressional appropriations, and a few years later he assured Morrill that his colleges "in spite of all the difficulties that have beset them are making good progress in solving the problems of scientific and industrial education."[13]

The evolving agricultural establishment, with no greater powers of direction and regulation, had had a real opportunity of relating its promotive and investigational work with that of the agricultural colleges and state experiment stations. But thus far that opportunity had been signally neglected. "The failure to seek and secure the active cooperation of the agricultural colleges," in E. W. Hilgard's opinion in 1882, was "one of the most conspicuous omissions of the Department. Through them its most useful influence could have been exerted, and its most authentic information as to facts and wants obtained. . . . To speak plainly, the National Department of Agriculture seemed to act, in a measure, as though the colleges and experiment stations were not in existence. Instead of assisting them and summing up their work, it ignored them sometimes even in the matter of the distribution of seeds and department reports. Its traveling employees seemed at times to keep out of the way of the existing institutions, often laboriously gathering anew information already abundantly in the possession of the latter." If the department sensed an indisposition of the colleges and states to work with the federal establishment, that fact, thought this observer, should have provided an added incentive to an alert administrator.[14]

The conventions of the seventies and eighties, while attended by some interchanges of friendly gestures—such as the expression of confidence in the colleges' work and the desire for their increased aid by the commissioners and resolutions endorsing enlarged status and increased salaries for the department by the delegates[15] —were also occasions for jealousies and misunderstandings. The commissioners' prerogatives and jurisdiction were uncertain and ambiguous and they could not act with assurance. Most of them from their training and background lacked an appreciation of the research worker's point of view and even more an understanding of professorial sensibilities.[16] On their side the college representatives tended to be overfearful of federal direction or dictation at the same time that they importuned for increased aid. It must be admitted that the leadership of the anomalous "department" had not generally been such as to inspire confidence among scientists and college administrators. As late as 1888 Johnson wrote Storer in connection with Atwater's projected federal service that the college leaders had about concluded that nothing good could come out of the "Washington Nazareth."[17] The new association, coming the same year as the experiment stations and shortly before the elevation of the department to cabinet status, marked the beginning of systematic cooperation between the colleges and federal administrative agencies.

Closer relations and better understanding were particularly welcome in the culminating years of the long struggle for increased federal endowment when the colleges needed all the support that they could command at the national capital. Broadening of courses, standardizing of equipment, and competition for technical leaders involved correspondingly increased expenditure. At the same time a proportionate increase of fees was inexpedient, if not impossible. The democratic appeal of the "poor man's college" was in the main to an income group that, financially and politically, imposed an insuperable bar to any effective increase in charges. States were most reluctant to make regular appropriations for maintenance with the traditions of restricted functions, the continued opposition of private colleges, the popular notion of the lavishness of the federal grant, and the unceraínty of program. The main reliance thus was upon an increase in the federal land endowment, which, as has been noted, had proven, in most cases, so disappointingly inadequate. There was the feeling, too, that the plan of distribution had been unfair to the new and growing states.[18] Hence the colleges were no more than launched when efforts for supplemental aid were made, but the opposition proved unexpectedly strong and persistent.

In the seventies there was a pronounced reaction against further land grants. Revelations of corruption and abuses in corporate holdings created a prejudice against all similar disposals, and reports, true and exaggerated, of speculation in land scrip were especially unfavorable.[19] The indifference or hostility of the farmer constituency, individual and organized, before the stations found practical solution of their problems was discouragingly evident.

The most heated opposition to increased federal endowment came from the spokesmen of sectarian and other privately supported institutions. In the debate on his first supplemental bill in 1872 Morrill had given assurance that no jealous rivalry could be aroused between the two groups as extending fields of study and rising standards were beneficial to all educational interests. On the contrary a little later in the session he was to denounce the lobbying efforts of McCosh of Princeton, who appeared in opposition to a committee of land-grant presidents, and to compare the dour Doctor's presence in the Senate chamber to that of an approaching iceberg.[20]

The annual meeting of the N.E.A. in 1873 was given up largely to a land-grant tournament. McCosh led the assault with characteristic "Caledonian acerbity." The land-grant distribution, he held, had involved an unfair discrimination between competing higher institutions. The recipients of the original subsidy were not fulfillng the express condition, as most of them had few if any real agricultural students. European experience had demonstrated that "agricultural schools" were of no real benefit to the occupation and further use of federal resources for this purpose would thus be both a waste and an abuse. The receipts from the public lands could desirably be used for high school aid in the more progressive states and for both elementary and secondary in the backward.[21] Eliot went the whole way in opposing all federal grants, both for higher and secondary education. The fund would be but a drop in the bucket but an infecting one. "The one drop is a drop of poison. It demoralizes us and weakens the foundation of our liberty. It interferes with the carrying out of our destiny—the breeding of a race of independent and self-reliant freedmen. . . . I know of no more mischievous, insidious enemy to a free republic than this habit of asking help in good works which we ought to attend to ourselves."[22]

Vigorous rejoinders, claiming everything and conceding nothing, were made at this meeting, at the one in 1874, and in official reports and discussion in popular magazines by such outstanding champions of the cause as Read of Missouri, Atherton of New Jersey, Clark of Massachusetts, Patterson of Kentucky, White of Cornell, and Orton of Ohio. As in the past, narrow scope and artisan purpose were indignantly denied; on the contrary, it was asserted, as technological universities they were training industrial leaders, and hence the number of graduates who were practicing farmers was wholly irrelevant. From the basic consideration of national security and well-being they found public support of education at all levels essential to progressive achievement and a safeguard against sectarian and caste control.[23]

The argument was not kept to the high plane of educational principles and practices; personalities were exchanged with prejudice and passion more befitting the impetuous undergraduate. McCosh referred to his neighboring rival as the "excellent college at New Brunswick, managed by a few Dutchmen . . ."[24] Eliot saw a "humiliating spectacle" in the appearance at Washington of a half-dozen men, "representing a few institutions of education, many of them but half-born, vieing for a share in the public gifts."[25] McCosh's opinions were discounted by the other side as those of a foreigner wholly unfamiliar with American democratic institutions and practices,[26] and Eliot, the champion of the "new education," was represented as a supporter of aristocratic provincialism.[27] All opponents of educational grants were held to be, however unwittingly, abettors of the corporate interests who were seeking the domain for their own predatory designs.[28]

The academic controversy had its reflection in the House of Representatives in 1874 in the authorization by the committee on education and labor, headed by James Monroe, an Oberlin professor, of an investigation to determine whether the colleges were fulfilling the law in organization, program, and finance.[29] Certain of the college men felt that this move was a deliberate attempt to cast discredit upon the land-grant cause and were fearful of its effect upon Congress and the public.[30] Their suspicions and fears proved unfounded. Monroe's report gave full and frank vindication and commendation. The committee noted a sincere purpose and well-considered plan for meeting the letter and spirit of the law and an appropriate and highly effective development of applied science instruction and of public service contacts.[31] The report was an effective reply to irresponsible and unreasoned criticism.

More hampering in the long run than the outright opponents of federal grants to education were the competing interests that sought the aid, wholly or in part, for their own purposes. Chief of these were the public school groups, the defenders of the freedmen's interests, the representatives of economically backward states, and the supporters of the general and special vocational training of labor.[32] Politically, common school education had a much more immediate and extended availability than any sort of special training, but this was offset by the traditional jealousy of federal interference with a peculiarly state function.[33] Another diverting influence was the old national university project revived in the seventies by John W. Hoyt so enthusiastically and effectively as to gain the active support of the N.E.A. and the favorable recommendations of Presidents Grant and Hayes.[34]

The school interests started the rival struggle[35] with a bill introduced in the House by Hoar in February, 1872, to apply the proceeds of the public lands to a state public and normal school fund to be apportioned on the basis of population and illiteracy. The bill was passed in the House but failed in the Senate. Meanwhile, the national convention of 1872 debated heatedly the proposals of equalization of aid and land receipts versus land grants, without agreeing to anything more specific than Morrill's resolution favoring "an additional donation of land, sufficient to found a professorship of some of the branches of practical science."[36] The legislative committee of the convention drafted a bill which Morrill introduced in the Senate granting each state one million acres for further endowment. A few months later, impressed by the strength of Hoar's school bill, he offered as a substitute the receipts from the sale of 500,000 acres to each state and territory which passed the Senate but met an unyielding demand in the House for division of funds. For a decade and a half, 1875–90, Morrill had proposals almost continuously before Congress to divide the land fund between schools and colleges. Burnside of Rhode Island in 1879 added a new source of income in the proposal to increase the educational fund by the receipts from the Patent Office—for which Morrill, in 1884, substituted returns from railroad loans—and educational gifts to the treasury. Amendments were proposed from time to time requiring the admission of women, seeking parity of opportunity for negroes, including teacher training, and extending aid to non-land-grant technical institutions. Hoar[37] and Senator Blair[38] of New Hampshire remained the main champions for the schools.

The college spokesmen made much of the equalizing aims of the proposed aid that would insure a standard of equipment and instructional efficiency to all of the states and correct the inequalities of the original grant. At the same time the substitution of money for land would do away with speculative abuses.[39] The opposition followed closely the line of argument used against the original act. Further grants jeopardized the interests of the landed states; the scrip location marked the height of public land abuse; and the colleges had been and remained indefinite in organization and aim and ineffective in results. Against all proposals for national aid to education, there were given the traditional warnings against centralization.[40] On the contrary the supporters saw in the new colleges a great nationalizing and socializing agency in the common industrial emphasis and in the training of teachers for the more backward sections.[41] Furthermore, the prevalence of this type of education would be the most effective means of combating an increasingly disturbing radicalism, for the system which at the higher range of intellectual training would produce constructive leaders, would at the more practical level give the worker an earning capacity which, according to Morrill, would free him from the "imported barbarous despotism reigning over our trade unions."[42]

The school cause proved to be more of a hindrance than an aid. With the reaction from war centralization, public sentiment proved overwhelmingly hostile to any proposal threatening to nationalize educational control. The convention of 1882 became so embittered over the matter that the debate was expunged and the resolutions laid on the table.[43] Morrill's persistent effort to combine the two interests is one of the few instances of his lack of practical political foresight.[44] Alone the industrial cause could eventually get recognition. The determining influence was in the growing demand of the organized agricultural interests, and by 1890 this pressure had become sufficiently strong to secure decisive action. The conventions of 1883 and 1885 had given main attention to the station movement; the provision for that institution and the creation of the secretaryship of agriculture gave direct impetus to the stabilization of the colleges as a complementary development. The growing political influence of the farmers' movement contributed further to the opportuneness of a measure that would appear as a direct concession to that group and have the endorsement of their spokesmen, educational and political.

In the first session of the Fifty-first Congress, Morrill made a final effort to ally the two interests but with the colleges now in preferred position. His bill of March 25, 1890, provided that the land fund from sales and railroad loans should be devoted to the endowment of the colleges up to an annual maximum of $25,000, the remainder to be given to the common schools. Even this concession seemed undesirable; a substitute bill providing a straight college grant was offered a month later and favorably reported by Senator Blair's committee.

The framing of the new bill and the directing of the legislative strategy were largely the work of the executive committee of the new college association. They provided the arguments for the committees and managers in both houses, emphasizing the general and specific services to the industrial interests and to the nation and, at the same time, the essential needs for maintaining and extending their achievements.[45] The college group was responsible, too, for certain concessions which made the bill acceptable to the determining interests involved. The Grange and the Alliance urged that the new endowment should be preserved from any possible expenditure "in the ordinary college training in belles-lettres and the dead languages"; and at the request of these organizations the committee specified subjects that, while not in practice hampering the use of the fund, allayed the fears of the ardent industrialists.[46] A satisfactory formula was worked out for the complicated and embarrassing matter of the racial division of the fund in the southern states.[47] Efforts to extend the new fund outside the land-grant circle were resisted without arousing undue enmity.[48] On the jurisdictional side closer federal supervision was provided without abandoning any essential state function.

With all material points of difference thus provided for, only nominal opposition remained. A states' rights protest with Buchanan's veto as text was but an echo,[49] as the labor charge of class discrimination was but a forecast.[50] Charges of a college lobby were counteracted by the assurance of general agricultural organization support.[51] The Senate passed the bill without record, and the House, after adding the amendment naming the subjects, by the overwhelming vote of 135 to 39. The Senate promptly agreed to the House amendments, and President Harrison signed the act August 30.[52]

The so-called "second Morrill Act"[53] provided an additional endowment for the land-grant college or colleges of each state or territory from the receipts of the public lands, starting at $15,000 and increasing $1,000 per year until the permanent annual payment became $25,000. This fund was "to be applied only to instruction in agriculture, the mechanic arts, the English Language and the various branches of mathematical, physical, natural, and economic science, with special reference to their applications in the industries of life and to the facilities for such instruction." A proposal to insert "political" before economic, in order to require instruction in the Constitution, was met with the logical if not altogether reassuring argument that economic science could not be studied without a knowledge of governmental principles.[54] No state which made a racial distinction in the admission of students was to share in the grant, but the maintenance of separate institutions with which the funds were "equally divided" was held to be a compliance with the act. Annual reports on the finances, enrollment, equipment, and educational and research work of each college were to be made to the secretaries of agriculture and of the interior and a copy sent to the other colleges. To the secretary of the interior was given the duty of certifying to the treasury department each year whether the conditions of the act had been met, but if the payment was denied, the state involved might appeal to Congress for final determination.

The second land-grant act, like the first, came in a period of special appeal to the agricultural interest and also, like the first, was definitely related to the extension of national administrative establishment. But the later act marked a much more pronounced occupational consciousness as shown by the specification of subjects of instruction and a much more definite conception of the field of industrial education as indicated by the nature of the subjects specified. It also marked an advance in centralized control that prepared the way for modern grants-in-aid. Important as the precedent was to be, the actual restraints imposed upon the states were slight; the requirements were general and flexible, and the right of appeal to Congress left the devitalizing possibility of political interference with administrative supervision.[55]

Contemporary opinion and retrospective conclusion agree that the act of 1890 marked a definite turning point in land-grant education—the transition from the period of pioneer uncertainty and instability to one of permanent establishment and progressive achievement. While development of different institutions was very unequal, progress in different lines uneven, and many readjustments of curricula, methods of instruction, and of administrative regulation were still necessary, the formative trials were past, and the modern trend was begun. The added endowment came most opportunely for anticipated constructive uses; it brought the two main branches of technical instruction more nearly to a parity, gave reality to nominal departments and created new ones, equipped more adequately both laboratory and shop, and above all, strengthened the staffs and made more adequate provision for their support.[56] However, the federal aid itself, helpful as it was, did not in the end constitute the most important influence. The measure which, along with those for experiment stations and the secretaryship, opened the way for an expanding range of federal relationships was directly responsible for securing permanent state recognition and support.

To the nineties most of the states had confined their participation to the required physical equipment, and they had expected the colleges to live and thrive on their federal endowment. Educational aid when given came grudgingly and of necessity without system or continuity. The decade following the second federal grant marked the full adoption as state institutions with the obligations entailed. Retarded by the depression years, the more ample provision, in accord with modernized standards of institutional living, was to come with the years of recovery and expansion that inaugurated the new agriculture and the new industrialism. But acceptance of lengthened and expanded budgets came only with the growing recognition of the colleges as public service institutions that in curriculum and method, on and off the campuses, provided a new education for the new nation. Experts and managers were trained for the new industries and stations, and demonstrational services grappled with their technical and business problems.

The resulting issues of social relationships not lending themselves so readily to laboratory test and field observation[57] were none the less, according to their peculiar techniques, investigated, analyzed, and more or less tentatively appraised. At the beginning of the Spanish War year, Andrew D. White found the leading state universities training large numbers "of the best sort of young men to energy and thought regarding political, social and economic problems as never before,"[58] and in the applications of "social politics" at the turn of the century state universities and colleges were actively—and often perilously—identified with the most noted "ideas" and movements. These far-reaching activities, especially in regulatory and promotive realms, involved risks and penalties in costly error and in no less costly truth when impartially and relentlessly applied. Ultimate security, however, was to be found in the creation through indispensable service of a constituency that, directly and indirectly, embraced the masses of the people. As a sage educator has concluded retrospectively and prospectively, "the colleges and universities in America which will endure will minister to all the people, without reference to their means, and will promote every phase of honorable endeavor without regard to class or station."[59]

Expanded functions and broadened outlook were reflected in agitation to change the name from "agricultural" to state college or university or some adequate equivalent. The opening of new technical fields and the growth of modernized curricula and programs made the original designations—from the first misleading—inadequate and antiquated. As early as the seventies a few were rechristened, and by the next decade practically all were considering the change, though in some cases tradition and prejudice perpetuated the reminder of a past era until recent years.[60] Whatever the name, the real test of all the land-grant institutions was their ability and disposition to fulfill their peculiar mission in the new era, and it was in ministerng to the technical, social, and political needs of the nation come of age that they attained measurably to the vision of the true prophets of the industrial movement in becoming real people's colleges—with all their limitations a distinct native product and the fullest expression of democracy in higher education.

NOTES AND REFERENCES

CHAPTER I. THE RISE OF AN AMERICAN SYSTEM OF EDUCATION

1. "Historic Foundations of American Education," *Essays in Comparative Education,* II, 283–305.

2. M. W. Jernegan, *Laboring and Dependent Classes in Colonial America,* 66; J. A. H. Keith and W. C. Bagley, *The Nation and the Schools,* 17–20.

3. J. F. Jameson, *The American Revolution Considered as a Social Movement,* 40–72.

4. G. W. Knight, "History and Management of Land Grants for Education in the Northwest Territory," *Papers of the American Historical Association,* I, No. 3, pp. 8–18.

5. *Ibid.,* 34.

6. Cf. P. J. Treat, *National Land System, 1785–1820,* pp. 284–85.

7. Knight, *loc. cit.,* 43–149; M. C. Boyd, *Alabama in the Fifties,* 149–50; J. B. Angell in *State Aid to Higher Education* (Johns Hopkins addresses 1898), 33, 34.

8. J. R. Commons and H. L. Sumner, eds., "Labor Movement, 1820-1840," *Documentary History of American Industrial Society,* V, VI, see index volume under "education" for numerous references to labor pronouncements and arguments; P. R. V. Curoe, *Educational Attitudes and Policies of Organized Labor in the United States,* 28–29, 36–37; F. T. Carlton, *Economic Influences upon Educational Progress in the United States, 1820–1850,* pp. 73–87.

9. For an understanding survey of the academy at its best, see C. M. Fuess, "The Development of the New England Academy" in *The Creed of a Schoolmaster,* 81–115. For the manual labor movement, L. F. Anderson, "The Manual Labor School Movement," *Educational Review,* XLVI, 369–86; Commissioner of Education, *Report,* 1891–92, pp. 506–10; V. M. Butler, *Education as Revealed by New England Newspapers,* 196–98. At a manual labor school at Florence, Oneida County, New York, in the thirties, some of the boys cut down trees and chopped them into logs which were hauled to the mill by an ox team. The land thus cleared was subsequently cultivated by the students. Charles E. Brown, *Personal Recollections,* 6–7.

10. E. E. Brown, *The Making of our Middle Schools* is the standard treatise. See also C. H. Judd in Duke University, *A Century of Social Thought,* 3–33. On the dominant place of the high school by the nineties, see C. K. Adams in *State Aid to Higher Education,* 8–9.

11. Willystine Goodsell, ed., *Pioneers of Women's Education in the United States;* Marion Lansing, *Mary Lyon Through Her Letters.*

12. Goodsell, *op. cit.,* 245–46; L. S. Boas, *Woman's Education Begins,* 6, 185.

13. S. W. Brown, *Secularization of American Education;* G. P. Schmidt, *Old Time College President,* 213–25.

14. R. J. Honeywell, *The Educational Work of Thomas Jefferson;* Boyd, *op. cit.,* 147; H. B. Adams, *Thomas Jefferson and the University of Virginia.*

15. C. W. Dabney, *Universal Education in the South,* I, 245–46; Schmidt, *op. cit.,* 25; T. C. Johnson, *Scientific Interests in the Old South,* 11; E. M. Coulter, *College Life in the Old South.*

16. W. B. Shaw, ed., *A University Between Two Centuries;* Norman Foerster, *The American State University,* 20–24.

17. A. O. Hansen, *Liberalism and American Education in the Eighteenth Century;* Du Pont de Nemours, *National Education in the United States;* W. H. Kilpatrick, *Teacher and Society,* 4–6.

18. H. R. Warfel, *Noah Webster Schoolmaster to America,* 93–94.

19. Schmidt, *op. cit.,* 23, 168–70.

20. L. C. Helderman, *George Washington, Patron of Learning;* E. B. Wesley, *Proposed: The University of the United States.* For Joel Barlow's remarkable plan for a national scientific institution centering in a university at Washington, see G. B. Goode, "The Origin of the National Scientific and Educational Institutions of the United States" in *Papers of the American Historical Association,* IV, Part 2, pp. 26–29, 85–97.

21. Curoe, *op. cit.,* 41.

22. H. C. Taylor, *Educational Significance of the Early Federal Land Ordinances,* 83; A. F. Macdonald, *Federal Aid,* 16.

23. The best single source for the educational awakening in general is Barnard's *American Journal of Education.* A convenient summary of the movement is in E. W. Knight, *Education in the United States,* Chap. VIII. The most recent appraisal of Mann's contribution is in the addresses and discussions in the Antioch College symposium, *Educating for Democracy.*

24. E. W. Knight, ed., *Reports on European Education.*

25. Merle Curti, *The Social Ideas of American Educators,* 113.

26. Schmidt, *op. cit.,* 154–67; L. F. Snow, *College Curriculum in the United States,* 155–61. An interesting early proposal for a state polytechnic school was made by Governor E. A. Brown of Ohio in 1819 but apparently received no attention. R. H. Eckelberry, "An Early Proposal for a State Polytechnic School," *Ohio Archaeological and Historical Quarterly,* XXXIX, 400–10. After attending a trustees' meeting of Columbia College in 1838 Philip Hone wrote, "This old, honest institution, pursuing its steady course uninfluenced by popular notions of education, appears to be gaining ground in public estimation . . ." Allan Nevins, ed., *Diary of Philip Hone,* 344.

27. *Educational Reform,* 6. In the annual address before the New York Agricultural Society in 1844 the speaker charged that the prevailing method of teaching science in schools was as formalized and consequently repulsive to youth as the catechetical mode of religious instruction.

N. Y. State Agricultural Society, *Transactions*, 1843, p. 110. The typical old-time classical-theological view of the place of science in the college curriculum is well expressed in Laur. Larsen's diary, printed in *Norwegian-American, Studies and Records*, X, 117–18. As late as 1870 Noah Porter maintained that the elemental sciences as taught were not sufficiently disciplinary. *The American College and the American Public*, 42. For a thoughtful estimate of science teaching before 1860, see Edward Orton, "The Contribution of Mechanic Arts to Educational Progress," Rutgers College, *One Hundred and Fiftieth Anniversary*, 273–75.

28. Johnson, *op. cit.*, 28; Boyd, *op. cit.*, 153. George P. Marsh, in the House debate, April 22, 1846, on the disposal of the Smithson fund gave this repellent picture of the laboratory and its demonstrator: "But what are we offered instead of the advantages which we might hope to reap from such a library as I have described? We are promised experiments and lectures, a laboratory, and an audience hall. Sir, a laboratory is a charnel house, chemical decomposition begins with death, and experiments are but the dry bones of science. It is the thoughtful meditation alone of minds trained and disciplined in far other halls that can clothe these with flesh, and blood, and sinews, and breathe into them the breath of life. Without a library, which alone can give such training and such discipline, both to teachers and to pupils, all these are but a masked pageant and the demonstrator is a harlequin." W. J. Rhees, ed., *Smithsonian Institution*, I, 385.

29. There is a very extensive literature on this famous crime; the bibliography in the sketch in the *Dictionary of American Biography* (XIX, 592–93) is far from complete. Philip Hone's comments have contemporary interest. As a partial explanation of motive he observed that Webster was extravagant "as scientific persons frequently are." Nevins, *op. cit.*, 889–90, 906, 917.

30. The most convenient summary of the development of professional education is in N. M. Butler, ed., *Monographs on Education in the United States*. On the growth of university professional schools, Schmidt, *op. cit.*, 227. The best study of medical education is H. B. Shafer, *The American Medical Profession, 1783 to 1850*. A speaker before the New Hampshire state fair in 1852 gave a satirical description of the existing schools of medical practitioners. N. H. State Agricultural Society, *Transactions*, 1852, pp. 217–18. For the relative backwardness of medical and legal education as late as the seventies, see P. H. Hanus, *Adventuring in Education*, 41.

31. Alexis de Tocqueville, *Democracy in America*, II, 47–52, 75–76.

32. Helderman, *op. cit.*, 7–8; F. N. Thorpe, ed., *Benjamin Franklin and the University of Pennsylvania*, 215–29.

33. Helderman, *op. cit.*, 166–69; C. W. Scott, "Agricultural Education Historically Considered," N. H. Board of Agr., *Trans.*, 1883–84, p. 68; "The Engineering Schools in the United States," *Engineering News and American Railway Journal*, XXVII, 318–19, 342–45, 371–73.

34. Scott, *loc. cit.*, 68; G. M. Dodge, *Papers and Addresses*, 153; A. C. True, *History of Agricultural Education in the United States*, 82.

35. True, *op. cit.*, 35–36; Society for Promotion of Engineering Education, *Study of Technical Institutes*, 31. The announced aims are significant:

to give training in the principles and practices of scientific agriculture; to provide beneficial physical recreation; to reduce the cost of education: and to try experiments adapted to the soil and climate of Maine.

36. True, *op cit.*, 37.

37. H. N. Arey, *Girard College and Its Founder;* Henry Leffman, *Centenary of the Franklin Institute of Pennsylvania, 1824–1924;* S.P.E.E., *Proceedings,* 1896, p. 36.

38. P. C. Ricketts, ed., *Centennial Celebration of Rensselaer Polytechnic Institute,* 39, 63–64, 104–08; same, *History of Rensselaer Polytechnic Institute,* 49–51; R. P. Baker, *A Chapter in American Education,* 17–74; T. C. Mendenhall in Butler's *Monographs,* 7; *Engineering News,* XXVII, 412–14. Ethel M. McAllister, *Amos Eaton, Scientist and Educator* is a full-length biography, written from the sources, but it appeared too late for use in this study.

39. It is perhaps significant that Hone in a most appreciative and laudatory estimate of Van Rensselaer at the time of the philanthropist's death (1838) made no mention of his educational foundation. Nevins, *op. cit.*, 381.

Chapter II. The Industrial Movement in State and Nation

1. Quoted and analyzed in F. A. Walker, *Discussions in Education,* 82. Cf. a similar conclusiòn, from a different point of view, by Henry P. Tappan in *University Education* (1850), quoted by D. G. Tewksbury, *Founding of Amer. Colls. and Univs.,* 8.

2. C. J. Hylander, *American Scientists;* E. S. Dana, *A Century of Science in America;* J. B. Angell, *Reminiscences,* 102; E. A. Osborne, *From the Letter-Files of S. W. Johnson,* 88; D. C. Gilman, *Life of James Dwight Dana.*

3. Quoted by Walker, *op. cit.,* 83–84.

4. Evan Pugh to S. W. Johnson, Sept. 30, 1855, Jan. 6, 1860, copies in True Papers, Department of Agriculture Library; *Country Gentleman,* III (1854), 296; C. R. Woodward, *Development of Agriculture in New Jersey,* 133. State agricultural reports for this period have numerous addresses and essays by physicians and clergymen of the sort indicated. Some representatives of these professions rendered real service in agricultural and horticultural improvement. James W. Grimes in his *Iowa Farmer and Horticulturist* (I, (Oct., 1853), 96) paid this editorial tribute to the physicians: "Why agriculture is more indebted to the Doctors for its development and success than to any other class of individuals, not even excepting the farmers themselves. Every physician is, or ought to be, both a botanist and a chemist. He understands the structure of trees, plants, and grains and the principles of vegetable growth. He knows the constituents of the plants and the soils in which they grow and can point out their chemical deficiencies. Well educated physicians are familiar with comparative anatomy, and can comprehend and prescribe for the diseases of domestic animals. In truth all our

knowledge upon this subject is derived from them. Many of them are naturalists, and detect for us the nature and habits of the many insect pests, against which farmers are compelled continually to war, and they supply us with the means of defence. They are professionally trained to habits of close observation, patient research and reflection. The science of agriculture would present a dark and forbidding prospect if all the light and aid furnished to it by the medical profession were blotted from the record and from remembrance." For the ideas of the provocative "agricultural consultant," J. J. Mapes, see files of *The Working Farmer* (New York, 1849–1860). When J. B. Angell was employed by the Boston city engineer in 1851, he found that he was the only one in the office who had studied calculus. Angell, *op. cit.,* 78.

5. *Working Farmer,* III (1851), 217; Osborne, *op. cit.,* 70, 75, 83; A. C. True, *History of Agricultural Education,* 65–66.

6. *American Agriculturist,* XXI (1862), 104; C. H. Greathouse, *Historical Sketch of the United States Department of Agriculture,* 9; A. G. Holmes and G. R. Sherrill, *Thomas Green Clemson,* 131–40.

7. J. R. Commons and J. B. Andrews, *Documentary History,* VIII, 243–62.

8. G. M. Tucker, *American Agricultural Periodicals;* W. E. Ogilvie, *Pioneer Agricultural Journalists;* A. L. Demaree, *American Agricultural Press,* 13–19.

9. For typical and representative expressions see Jesse Buel's address in 1839, reprinted in *Farmer's Companion,* 277–80. N. Y. St. Agr. Soc., *Trans.,* 1843, pp. 113–15, 1844, pp. 47–48, 1845, pp. 34–35, 40, 1851, pp. 197–200; N. H. St. Agr. Soc., *Trans.,* 1850, pp. 44–45, 1853, p. 32, 1857, p. 174; Me. Bd. of Agr., *Rep.,* 1856, p. 51; Pa. St. Agr. Soc., *Trans.,* 1855, pp. 81–85; Ky. St. Agr. Soc., *Rep.,* 1858–59, p. 131; Tenn. Bur. of Agr., *Rep.,* 1855–56, p. 86; Cal. St. Agr. Soc., *Trans.,* 1859, pp. 444–45; *Working Farmer,* I (1849), 110, III (1851), 209–10, 222, IV (1852), 137; *American Agriculturist,* V (1846), 106–07.

10. For typical views, N. Y. St. Agr. Soc., *Trans.,* 1846, pp. 38–42, 1849, pp. 63, 70; N. H. St. Agr. Soc., *Trans.,* 1852, p. 221, 1853, pp. 72–73, 1854, p. 66, 1857, p. 26; Me. Bd. of Agr., *Rep.,* 1856, pp. 57–58; *American Agriculturist,* V (1846), 106, VIII (1849), 100, 191.

11. N. Y. St. Agr. Soc., *Trans.,* 1845, p. 36.

12. *Ibid.,* 1844, pp. 373, 376–88.

13. *Ibid.,* 376–391; U. S. Agr. Soc., *Journal,* 1854, pp. 31–48; N. H. St. Agr. Soc., *Trans.,* 1853, p. 42, 1857, pp. 187–89, 252, 309–32; Me. Bd. of Agr., *Rep.,* 1856, pp. 117, 121; *American Agriculturist,* XXII (1863), 14.

14. R. H. Chittenden, *Sheffield Scientific School,* I, 45–54, 291, II, 329; H. S. Olcott, *Yale Agricultural Lectures,* 10, 20, 177–79; D. C. Gilman, *University Problems,* 109–49; D. C. Gilman, *Life of Dana,* Ch. IX.

15. S. E. Morison, *Three Centuries of Harvard,* 279–80, 356; *Engineering News,* XXVII (1892), 460–61.

16. Mass. St. Bd. Agr., *Rep.,* 1906, pp. 344–45; *Country Gentleman,* III (1854), 24–25.

17. *Delaware Notes,* VIII, 60–62.

18. *American Agriculturist,* VIII (1849), 270; *Engineering News,* XXVII (1892), 433–34, 514–16, 541–42; A. J. Klein, ed., *Survey of Land-Grant Colleges,* I, 790. For a rather exaggerated emphasis upon the professional and vocational adaptation of the colleges in the thirties and forties, see H. G. Good in *Journal of Educational Research,* XXIX, 37–46. In 1855 Dr. George F. Magoun, president of Iowa College (later Grinnell) urged the introduction of parallel science courses in the sectarian colleges that would prepare for advanced technical study in a state polytechnic university. *The West: Its Culture and Its Colleges,* 18–20.

19. *American Agriculturist,* V (1846), 69, 109; VI (1847), 123, VII (1848), 217; *Country Gentleman,* II (1853), 88; Osborne, *op. cit.,* 30–33, 66, 69, 75, 95–103; T. I. Mankin to American Institute, Nov. 3, 1851, same to Harrison Howard, Jan. 14, 1852, Hewett Papers; N. Y. Agr. Soc., *Trans.,* 1848, pp. 382–85. True, *op. cit.,* 39. An undated newspaper clipping in the Howard Papers commenting on the rumor that Gerrit Smith was to found a manual labor university in Central New York urged that some one of the numerous projected institutions be completed before any more were started.

20. Walter Stemmons, *Connecticut Agricultural College,* 20–21, 42.

21. Woodward, *op. cit.,* Ch. VII.

22. Commons and Andrews, *op. cit.,* VIII, 243–62.

23. "Address to Mechanics Mutual Protections," Mar., 1850; "Sketch of the Mechanics Mutual Protection and the Establishment of the People's College," Manuscripts in Howard Papers; Commons and Andrews, *op. cit.,* VIII, 320–25.

24. Howard Papers; Greeley to Howard, Oct. 1, 1851, Aug. 3, 1852, in newspaper clippings in *ibid.; N. Y. Tribune,* May 9, 1850.

25. Howard's "Reference Book"; circular letter to members of County Grand Committee, Aug. 15, 1852; report of the general agent of the People's College, Aug. 1—Nov. 24, 1853, Howard Papers.

26. Certified act of incorporation, Apr. 12, 1853; *Circular of the People's College of the State of New York and Act of Incorporation,* issued 1858, 1860, 1863, *ibid.*

27. Letter to County Grand Committee; Address meeting of State Teachers Association and M.M. P., Aug. 4, 1852, *ibid.*

28. "Tactics"; notes for addresses, *ibid.*

29. People's College, *Circular,* 6; address, Aug. 4, 1852.

30. Address Aug. 4, 1852.

31. Lecture notes for meetings in different parts of the state, Howard Papers.

32. Reports of meetings, editorials, and letters in unidentified newspaper clippings, *ibid.*

33. "Sketch," *ibid.*

34. Daniel S. Dickinson's address in *Public Exercises at the Laying of the Corner Stone of the People's College,* 34–35.

35. To the secretary of the association, Nov. 4, 1857, newspaper clipping, Howard Papers.

36. Statement of Secretary Howard, Nov. 1, 1855, newspaper clipping; printed letter of secretary reporting location, Jan. 15, 1857; "Sketch," *ibid.*

37. People's College, *Public Exercises Corner Stone Laying,* 8–12.

38. *Ibid.,* 30–34. At the dinner Greeley spoke on the promotion of the Atlantic cable.

39. *Ibid.,* 22–26.

40. *Ibid.,* 49.

41. *Ibid.,* 39.

42. People's College, *Circular* (1860), 7–8.

43. "Sketch," Howard Papers; John H. Griscom to editor of *N. Y. Tribune,* Nov. 21, 1859, lauding Cook and the College.

44. Files of *Cincinnatus;* C. W. Burkett, *History of Ohio Agriculture,* 199–200. John B. Bowman's avowed aim in launching his Kentucky University at Harrodsburg in 1857 was to develop a "university for the people." M. H. Pollitt, *James Kennedy Patterson,* 84, 99–100. At the founding of the University of Rochester in 1850 there was a proposal to establish an agricultural department to meet the needs of the rural constituency. One plan contemplated selling perpetual scholarships to farmers at $150 each. While the needed funds were not secured, the new institution was put on record as belonging to the popular education movement: "The University of Rochester has designed from the beginning to shape its course of education to meet the wants of the people, and to make the subject of the great principles of agriculture a prominent one in it." In 1860 the president recommended the establishment of a winter short course in horticulture. J. L. Rosenberger, *Rochester,* 62–64, 143.

45. N. Y. St. Agr. Soc., *Trans.,* 1843, p. 102, 1844, pp. 44–45, 57–60, 1845, pp. 37, 43, 62, 1846, xxiii–xxx; 1847, pp. 479–89, 1849, pp. 63–83, 1853, pp. 529–35; *American Agriculturist,* III (1844), 53–54, VIII (1849), 62, 86–87, IX (1850), 86–87; A. J. Downing, *Rural Essays,* 412–15.

46. U. P. Hedrick, *History of Agriculture in the State of New York,* 419–20; N. Y. Agr. Coll., *Charter,* etc., 7–8.

47. *Reports,* 1859–65; *Charter Ordinances, Regulations and Course of Studies,* 11–12; U. S. Agr. Soc., *Monthly Bulletin,* I (1858), 23; Pugh to Johnson, Aug. 2, 1857, True Papers; N. Y. St. Agr. Soc., *Trans.,* 1856, pp. 58–65.

48. T. I. Mairs, *Some Pennsylvania Pioneers in Agricultural Science,* 170, 174–75, 180–81; National Agricultural Convention, 1872, *Proc.,* 42; F. Watts, *et al., The Agricultural College of Pennsylvania,* 13–39.

49. Osborne, *op. cit.,* 88.

50. Pugh to Johnson, Feb. 22, Mar. 16, Sept. 30, 1855, Oct. 18, 1859, True Papers.

51. Feb. 22, 1855.

52. Osborne, *op cit.,* 66, 69–70, 83, 92, 94–103, 139–41. The New York project in which Johnson was most interested was the graduate University of

Albany, chartered in 1851 but never fully organized. A. C. Flick, *History of the State of N. Y.*, IX, 113–15.

53. To Johnson, Jan. 6, 1860, True Papers.

54. Pugh to Johnson, Jan. 14, Mar. 13, Oct. 17, 1861, *ibid.;* Osborne, *op. cit.*, 142; *American Agriculturist*, XXI (1862), 167, XXII (1863), 36; *Country Gentleman*, XIX (1862), 16, 321.

55. *Country Gentleman*, XI (1858), 353; U. S. Agr. Soc., *Journal*, 1859, p. 51; B. C. Steiner, *History of Education in Maryland*, (Bureau of Education Circular, 1894), 325; Holmes and Sherrill, *op. cit.*, 123–26; *Dict. of Am. Biog.*, III, 428.

56. Mass. St. Bd. of Agr., *Rep.*, 1906, pp. 345–66; L. B. Caswell, *Mass. Agr. Coll.*, 2–3.

57. E. M. Coulter, *College Life in Old South*, 51–52.

58. Ky. St. Agr. Soc., *Rep.*, 1856–57, p. 7.

59. *Ibid.*, 216.

60. Kathleen Bruce, "Virginian Agricultural Decline to 1860: A Fallacy," *Agricultural History*, VI, 3–13.

61. There is a digest and extended quotations in *Southern Planter*, XIII (1853), 217–19. See also R. M. Brown, "Agricultural Science and Education in Virginia before 1860," *William and Mary College Quarterly*, second series, XIX, 203–4; W. P. Cutter, "A Pioneer in Agricultural Science," U. S. Dept. of Agr., *Yearbook*, 1895, p. 502. E. G. Swem in his "Bibliography of Edmund Ruffin" (*Bulletin of the Virginia State Library*, XI, 132) lists the second edition published at Richmond in 1853.

62. Va. St. Agr. Soc., *Rep. of the Pres. to the Farmers' Assembly*, 1856, reprinted in *DeBow's Review*, XXII (1857), 495–505.

63. Va. St. Agr. Soc., *Rep. of the Pres. and Ex-Com.*, 1856-1857; *Southern Planter*, XVII (1857), 193–205; T. C. Johnson, *Scientific Interests in the Old South*, 53; Brown, *loc. cit.*, 205–12.

64. W. J. Beal, *History of Mich. Agr. Coll.*, 9–17, 22–28; Mich. St. Agr. Soc., *Trans.*, 1856, pp. 287–328.

65. T. C. Mendenhall, ed., *Hist. of Ohio St. Univ.*, I, 68; *The Plough, The Loom, and The Anvil*, VII (1854), 340; Ky. St. Agr. Soc., *Rep.*, 1857, p. 211.

66. U. S. Agr. Soc., *Monthly Bull.*, I (1858), 11.

67. W. M. Hepburn and L. M. Sears, *Purdue University*, 12–15; W. C. Latta, *Outline Hist. Ind. Agr.*, 278–79, 312–14.

68. The chief organ of the agitation for industrial education in this state was the *Iowa Farmer and Horticulturist* founded by James W. Grimes at Burlington in 1853. When Grimes became governor in 1855 Wilson took over the editorship. The earliest proposal was to use the university fund for a technical college. Grimes recommended this in his inaugural address. B. F. Shambaugh, ed., *Messages and Proclamations of the Governors of Iowa*, II, 8–9. The inadequacy of the university income in the early years and the desire of the agricultural leaders for a college in the open country away from the distracting influences of town life led

to the movement for a new, separate college. For the establishment and early legislative history of the college, see B. F. Gue in Johnson Brigham, *Iowa: Its History and Foremost Citizens,* II, 456–58; Ia. Agr. Coll., *Rep.,* 1866–67, pp. 5–10.

69. Wis. St. Agr. Soc., *Trans.,* 1852, pp. 441–45, 1858–59, p. 136; *Country Gentleman,* XI (1858), 193, 228.

70. D. S. Hall and R. I. Holcombe, *Minn. Agr. Soc.,* 54, 65–67; W. W. Folwell, *Hist. of Minn.,* IV, 80–85.

71. W. W. Ferrier, *Univ. of Cal.,* 32–41; E. J. Wickson, *Rural Cal.,* 349–51.

72. B. E. Powell, *Univ. of Ill.,* I, 10–101; A. C. Cole, *Era of the Civil War,* 239–45.

73. M. T. Carriel, *Jonathan Baldwin Turner.*

74. *Ibid.,* Chs. X–XII; Powell, *op. cit.,* 14–24, 377–400; Commissioner of Patents, *Rep.,* 1851, II, 37–44; F. H. Turner, "Misconceptions Concerning the Early History of the University of Illinois," Ill. St. Hist. Soc., *Trans.,* 1932, pp. 66–68.

75. Carriel, *op. cit.,* Chs. XIII–XV; Ill. St. Agr. Soc., *Trans.,* 1861–64, pp. 971–87; Powell, *op. cit.,* 24–91, 400–411. For Turner's educational ideas and prejudices, in addition to the "Plan," see his letter to Jonathan Blanchard in 1848, Powell, *op. cit.,* 357–62; "Industrial Universities for the People" (pamphlet of the Industrial league, 1853), *ibid.,* 365–77; "Sketch of Articles" for the University charter, Carriel, *op. cit.,* 175–76; digest and review of his pamphlet on "Industrial University Education," prepared at the request of the Commissioner of Agriculture but not published in his report. *Cultivator,* XII (1864), 229.

76. Carriel, *op. cit.,* 140–41. Turner also contributed to Cary's paper. *Cincinnatus,* III (1858), 78–79.

77. Carriel, *op. cit.,* 141–43; C. A. Harper, *Development of the Teachers College,* 9–20.

78. *H. R. Doc.* No. 334, 26 Cong., 2 Sess.; *Cultivator,* VI (1839), 24; W. J. Rhees, ed., *Smithsonian Institution,* I, 146, 155–63.

79. H. A. Kellar, *Solon Robinson,* I, 99–100, 209, 212; True, *op. cit.,* 89; Rhees, *op. cit.,* I, 238–39.

80. N. H. St. Agr. Soc., *Trans.,* 1850, p. 47.

81. U. S. Agr. Soc., *Journal,* 1854, p. 47.

82. *Country Gentleman,* IV (1854), 376. Richard Yates suggested to Turner in 1854 that the proposed colleges be not associated with the Smithsonian foundation as its officials were strongly opposed to such connections. Carriel, *op. cit.,* 155.

83. II, 147.

84. *Cincinnatus,* II (1857), 481–89.

85. N. H. St. Agr. Soc., *Trans.,* 1857, pp. 253–54.

86. *Cong. Globe,* 34 Cong., 1 Sess., 530. The resolution was objected to and was not received.

87. See, for typical instances, Kellar, *op. cit.*, II, 32–33, 416; *The Plough, The Loom, and The Anvil,* I (1848), 258–59, 321, 578; N. H. St. Agr. Soc., *Trans.*, 1850, pp. 47–48; Cal. St. Agr. Soc., *Trans.*, 1859, pp. 443–44.

88. Lyman Carrier, "The United States Agricultural Society, 1852–1860," *Agricultural History*, XI, 278–88.

89. *H. R. Doc.* No. 69, 26 Cong., 2 Sess.

90. *The Plough, The Loom, and The Anvil,* I (1848), 321.

91. Carriel, *op. cit.*, 121–28; Powell, *op. cit.*, 49–54, 406–13.

92. Carriel, *op. cit.*, 155–57; Powell, *op. cit.*, 92.

93. U. S. Agr. Soc., *Jour.*, 1856, pp. 24, 78–79.

94. *Ibid.*, 1857, p. 61.

95. *Ibid.*, 63.

96. *Ibid.*, 63–66.

97. *Ibid.*, 66.

98. *North American Review,* CV (1867), 501. For a general classification and survey of such institutions about 1860, see U. S. Agr. Soc., *Monthly Bull.*, I (1858), 11; *DeBow's Review,* XXVI (1859), 250–56; Powell, *op. cit.*, I, 117–20.

99. Me. Bd. of Agr., *Rep.*, 1856 (digest agr. socs.), 57–58; N. H. St. Agr. Soc., *Trans.*, 1857, pp. 172–73; *The Plough, The Loom, The Anvil,* IX (1857), 516–18.

100. Ia. Agr. Soc., *Rep.*, 1863, p. 260.

101. Carriel, *op. cit.*, 158.

Chapter III. The Federal Solution

1. A. C. True, *Hist. Agr. Education,* 99–101.

2. Morrill Papers, Library of Congress; W. B. Parker, *Life and Public Services of Justin Smith Morrill.*

3. Parker, *op. cit.*, 23–25.

4. Ira Davis to Morrill, Nov. 9, Dec. 22, 1848; Morrill to Davis, Dec. 8, 1848, Morrill Papers.

5. The question of disputed authorship is considered in some detail in the writer's article, "The 'Father' of the Land-Grant College," *Agricultural History*, XII, 151–86. The discussion that follows is largely a summary of the evidence there presented.

6. Memorandum made about 1874. Parker, *op. cit.*, 262–63.

7. *Ibid.*, 262.

8. G. W. Atherton, *Legislative Career of Justin S. Morrill,* 67.

9. Dec. 8, 1885, Howard Papers.

10. Feb. 6, 1894. Morrill Papers.
11. Vt. commencement address, 1893, *The Land-Grant Colleges,* 26.
12. True, *op. cit.,* 82–83.
13. Morrill to Charles Cook, July 23, 1863, Morrill Papers.
14. D. C. Linsley to Morrill, Jan. 9, 1857, *ibid.,* U. S. Agr. Soc., *Journal,* 1856, pp. 7–8, 1857, p. 10.
15. *Op. cit.,* 99.
16. Soc. for the Promotion of Agricultural Science, *Proceedings,* 1907, pp. 50–52. General claims of priority for Illinois had been made from time to time in the past, but had occasioned no particular controversy. Thus at the National Agricultural Convention called by the Commissioner of Agriculture in 1872, Regent Peabody of the Illinois Industrial University asserted that "the earliest movement for the establishment of industrial schools and universities was made in the State of Illinois." *Proceedings,* 23. A dozen years later in a brief summary of the history of agricultural colleges "Father" Clarkson of Iowa observed, with curiously mixed figure: "Illinois, if it did not originate the idea, at least set the ball in motion which finally proved successful." *Iowa State Register* (Weekly Edition), Apr. 18, 1884.
17. D. W. Morton to James S. Morrill, July 20, 1908, Morrill Papers.
18. E. J. James, *The Origin of the Land Grant Act of 1862 (The So-Called Morrill Act) and Some Account of its Author Jonathan B. Turner,* 7, 32.
19. M. T. Carriel, *Turner,* 159; B. E. Powell, *Semi-Centennial Hist. Univ. of Ill.,* I, 95; James, *op. cit.,* 35.
20. Turner to J. P. Reynolds, Nov. 28, 1865, Ill. St. Agr. Soc., *Trans.,* 1861–64, p. 38.
21. Trumbull to Turner, Oct. 19, 1857, Carriel, *op. cit.,* 158.
22. Turner to Trumbull, Jan. 4, 1858, Powell, *op. cit.,* 97–98.
23. *Ibid.,* 97; Carriel, *op. cit.,* 164; Davenport, *loc. cit.,* 51; James, *op cit.,* 36. Neither Turner's letter nor a copy of Morrill's reply are in the Morrill Papers. Three years earlier Cary had called Morrill's attention to Turner's article in the *Cincinnatus.* Cary to Morrill, Feb. 5, 1858, Morrill Papers. When asked about the possible relationship in 1894, Morrill stated: "I do not happen now to know Professor Turner, though I do remember when my bills were before congress a western professor came to see me and heartily espoused the idea. It may have been Professor Turner. It is so long since, I have forgotten his name, as I saw a large number of professors, some who favored my idea and some who did not." James, *op. cit.,* 35–36; Parker, *op. cit.,* 280.
24. June 4, 1872, Morrill Papers.
25. L. H. Bailey, *Cyclop. of Amer. Agr.,* IV, 409; Davenport, *loc. cit.,* 48.
26. Carriel, *op. cit.,* 278.
27. Turner and Kennicott in *Prairie Farmer,* XI (1863), 81; Ill. St. Supt. of Pub. Instruction, *Rep.,* 1865, quoted in Comr. of Ed., *Rep.,* 1867–68, p.

305; Carriel, *op. cit.,* 173; Powell, *op. cit.,* ch. VI. Bronson Murray's descendants have emphasized—largely on the basis of the records compiled by B. E. Powell for his history of the University of Illinois—his contribution to the industrial league and to the entire movement in Illinois. J. M. Seaver, *Murray Family Records* (American Historical-Genealogical Society), 51–55. Ms. letters of J. B. Murray to "C." Jan. 7, 1931, and J. B. Murray to R. M. Hughes, Nov. 21, 1932, inserted in the copy of the foregoing book in the Iowa State College Library.

28. Assoc. of Amer. Agr. Colls. and Exp. Stas., *Proc.,* 1912, p. 157. Cf. F. H. Turner, "Misconceptions Concerning the Early History of the University of Illinois," Ill. St. Hist. Soc., *Trans.,* 1932, pp. 68–72. John B. Bowman, the leading promoter of the land-grant establishment in Kentucky, said in 1868, "Great is the man who conceived this plan, but I do not yet know his name." M. H. Pollitt, *J. K. Patterson,* 116.

29. *North Amer. Rev.,* CV (1867), 501–502.

30. Memorandum of 1874, Parker, *op. cit.,* 264–69; *Proceedings at Unveiling of Portrait,* 14–15; to Howard, Dec. 8, 1885, Howard Papers; to Hewett, Feb. 6, 1894, Morrill Papers and printed in Parker, *op. cit.,* 277, where the letter is incorrectly addressed to Atherton.

31. Copies of these testimonial letters 1862–1866 and J. E. Brown to Hewett, Apr. 2, 1894. Hewett Papers. Wade was characteristically emphatic in his judgment: "Great credit is due to the exertions of the Hon. Mr. Morrill of the House, for his unwearied labors in its behalf. Yet I always believed and still believe, that had it not been for the able, energetic and unwearied exertions of the Rev. Amos Brown, President of the People's College, it would never have become a law. . . . All these difficulties, however, were overcome by the intelligent and persevering labors of Mr. Brown, whom I consider really the father of the measure, and whose advice I believe entitled to more weight, in carrying the law into execution than that of almost any other man." To E. B. Morgan, Dec. 1, 1862; later statement to same effect, quoted by J. E. Brown to Hewett, Apr. 2, 1894. Fessenden, who stated that he wrote at Dr. Brown's request, was no less definite in his judgment: "Mr. Brown, as I believe, was not only father of the bill, but to his persistent, efficient, and untiring efforts, its success was mainly due. I have no hesitation in saying that but for him it would have failed, in my judgment, altogether." To E. B. Morgan, Dec. 6, 1862. See also Charles Cook to Morrill, Apr. 12, 1858, Morrill Papers; Hedrick, *Hist. of Agr. in N. Y.,* 422; C. W. Dabney in N. M. Butler, *Education in the U. S.,* II, 16. Per contra, for the charge of limitations of Brown's contribution and of his personal errancy and instability, see W. H. Brewer to Hewett, Feb. 4, 1894, Hewett Papers. Among the articles deposited in the corner stone of the People's College were "Morrill's Land Bill and Speech on the same." *Public Exercises,* 16.

32. Moses Brown to Hewett, Feb. 20, 1894, Hewett Papers. Morrill felt that Brown was overzealous at times. Brewer memoranda of conversation in 1867. Copy in True Papers.

33. *Report upon a Plan for the Organization of Colleges for Agriculture and the Mechanic Arts,* 32, 34.

34. Williams to Morrill, Apr. 23, Nov. 15, 1858, Morrill Papers; W. J. Beal, *Mich. Agr. Coll.,* 36–39.

35. Cary to Morrill, Feb. 5, 1858, Feb. 15, 19, 1859, Morrill Papers. Editorial comment in *Cincinnatus,* III (1858), 49, 54.

36. W. M. Hepburn and L. M. Sears, *Purdue University,* 15–16.

37. U. S. Agr. Soc., *Monthly Bull.,* I (1858), 3–4.

38. U. S. Agr. Soc., *Journal,* 1859, pp. 18–20, 28.

39. N. S. Young, Batavia, Ia., Feb. 1, 1858, James Thorington, Davenport, Ia., May 17, 1858, J. W. Hoyt, Madison, Wis., June 1, 1858, O. C. Hale, Keokuk, Ia., Oct. 16, 1858, N. P. Banks, Boston, Jan. 11, 1859 (introducing C. L. Flint, secretary of the Mass. state board), Morrill Papers, in addition to the institutional and organization aid already referred to. Clemson's biographers, largely by inference, attribute a very considerable influence to his support of the bills. A. G. Holmes and G. R. Sherrill, *Clemson,* 19, 123, 128–31, 143. Greeley, whose own support Morrill cordially recognized, accorded final honors to Morrill, Wade, and Brown. *N. Y. Tribune,* June 21, 1862.

40. Parker, *op. cit.,* 263–66. In 1885 Morrill had a synopsis of the legislative history of the land-grant bills prepared for Howard by the clerk of the finance committee; it is a model of clarity and conciseness. Howard Papers.

41. Parker, *op. cit.,* 264–65; *Cong. Globe,* 35 Cong., 2 Sess., 855–56.

42. Letters of John Kimball, Dec. 28, 1857, and Samuel Whitcomb, Dec. 16, 1857, Morrill Papers; Parker, *op cit.,* 269–70; *Cong. Globe,* 35 Cong., 2 Sess., 723; resolutions of Vt. St. Agr. Soc., *Country Gentleman,* XI (1858), 81.

43. *Cong. Globe.,* 35 Cong., 1 Sess., 1692–97.

43a. Morrill's tribute to and plea for the mechanics illustrates the prevailing individualism in industrial relations: "There is no class of our community of whom we may be so justly proud as our mechanics. Their genius is patent to all the world. For labor-saving contrivances, their tact seems universal; and when any one of them is detailed to do the breathing of any engine, he speedily furnishes lungs for the engine to do that sort of work for itself. But they snatch their education, such as it is, from the crevices between labor and sleep. They grope in twilight. Our country relies upon them as its right arm to do the handiwork of the nation. Let us, then, furnish the means for that arm to acquire culture, skill, and efficiency." *Ibid.,* 1694.

44. Elisha Whittlesey, Canfield, Ohio, to Morrill, May 14, 1858, Morrill Papers. Cobb admitted that he had been persuaded by Miss Dix's eloquence against his better judgment to vote for the asylum bill, but he had later become convinced that the act was unconstitutional. *Cong. Globe,* 35 Cong., 1 Sess., 1742.

45. *Cong. Globe,* 35 Cong., 1 Sess., 1740–42.

46. *Ibid.,* 2 Sess., 718–24, 851–57.

47. *Ibid.,* 714–15.

48. *Ibid.,* 1 Sess., 1742. Harlan of Iowa, arguing that the bill was opposed by those who were against the uplift of the masses through popular education twitted Virginia of having the largest proportion of white illiteracy of any of the states. *Ibid.,* 2 Sess., 720.

49. *Ibid.,* 1 Sess., 1741; 2 Sess., 715–17, 785, 854.

50. *Ibid.,* 1 Sess., 1742; 2 Sess., 851, 857. For suggestion of partisan motives in the introduction of the bill at this time, see I. L. Kandel, *Federal Aid for Vocational Education,* 85–88; H. C. Taylor, *Educational Significance of the Early Land Ordinances,* 121. For a sectional analysis of the vote, see P. W. Gates, "Western Opposition to the Agricultural College Act," *Indiana Magazine of History,* XXXVII, 121–22.

51. Morrill to Howard, Dec. 8, 1885, Howard Papers; Morrill to Hewett, Feb. 6, 1894, Morrill Papers.

52. *Cong. Globe,* 35 Cong., 2 Sess., 1412–13.

53. Ohio A. and M. Coll., *Rep.,* 1874, p. 14.

54. E. W. Allen in an address at the inauguration of President Kinley of the University of Illinois in 1922 commented on Buchanan's charge that the grant would pass from federal control without power to compel use for the purpose designed, "It must be admitted that subsequent events supplied some measure of justification for his apprehension." *The Relation of the Federal Government to Education,* 48, 54.

55. For instance, Harlan, *Cong. Globe,* 35 Cong., 2 Sess., 719.

56. *Ibid.,* 1414; Parker, *op. cit.,* 268.

57. Powell, *op. cit.,* 442–56.

58. U. S. Agr. Soc., *Journal,* 1860, pp. 39–40, 52–54.

59. Powell, *op. cit.,* 117–22.

60. Carriel, *op. cit.,* 159–60.

61. In his general discussion of the bill (June 6, 1862) Morrill made these interesting and significant comments on the military provision: "Something of military instruction has been incorporated in the bill in consequence of the new conviction of its necessity forced upon the attention of the loyal States by the history of the past year. A total unpreparedness presents too many temptations even to a foe otherwise weak. The national school at West Point may suffice for the regular Army in ordinary years of peace, but it is wholly inadequate when a large army is to be suddenly put into service. If we ever expect to reduce the Army to its old dimensions, and again rely upon the volunteer system for defense, each State must have the means within itself to organize and officer its own forces. With such a system as that here offered—nurseries in every State—an efficient force would at all times be ready to support the cause of the nation and secure that wholesome respect which belongs to a people whose power is always equal to its pretensions." In the present struggle he felt that many lives might have been saved if there had not been the assumption that, like patriotism, "military discipline was also spontaneous. If ever again our legions are summoned to the field, let us show we are not wholly unprepared." These colleges, he urged, would not only increase the prosperity of agriculture, manufacturing, and commerce but might "to some extent guard against the sheer ignorance of all military art which shrouded the country, and especially the North, at the time when the tocsin of war sounded at Fort Sumter. This latter view becomes more important from the suggestive discovery that in any

grave controversy the Old Governments of the world are not our friends. They would see us humbled. . . . In peace they would buy and sell with us, but in war they would sell us and buy our enemies. Commercially they find us, when docile, at least useful; but politically they would shun us as a pestilence that walketh at noonday: We can only be secure at home and abroad by being ready at all times to 'ask nothing but what is clearly right, and submit to nothing wrong'; and with Jacksonian nerve accept any responsibility of our position. The true way to nurse patriotism, after having institutions really worth a struggle, is to inspire our people with confidence, by giving them proper training, that they are equal to their mission and that failure is impossible." *Cong. Globe,* 37 Cong., 2 Sess., Appendix, 256, 259. In his conference with the Sheffield professors in 1867, Morrill stated that he had been impressed by the superior preparedness of the South due to her military schools and that he felt that this feature of land-grant college training should be maintained as a measure of national preparedness. W. H. Brewer memoranda, copy in True Papers. For a summary of Morrill's later comments on military training in the debates on grant bills, Kandel, *op. cit.,* 88–89. There was no discussion of the provision in the Senate debate on the bill. In the spring of 1862, the New York board of regents in response to a legislative resolution reported a plan for militia drill at state expense in six colleges and one academy. N. Y. Assembly, *Report* No. 135 (March, 1862) . For a discussion of the claim that the military clause was an incidental addition, W. L. Nash, *Aims and Purposes of Dept. of Mil. Sci. in Land-Grant Colls.,* 17–19. Explanations and interpretations of the provision, with opposing interpretations, are in S. Johnson, "Military Training in the Land-Grant Colleges," *Ill. Law Rev.,* XXIV, 274–81; Mass. Agr. Coll., *Rep.,* 1891, p. 74; A. D. White, *Autobiography,* I, 387; C. W. Dabney in Butler, *op. cit.,* II, 36. Paul Chadbourne, president of the Massachusetts Agricultural College, in his last address, before the New England Agricultural Society, February 7, 1883, said that the purpose of the land-grant act was "to raise up a generation of men who shall understand all the principles of agriculture, all the principles of the mechanic arts, and at the same time shall be perfectly trained for service in time of invasion or rebellion to organize armies, and lead them on the battle-field. That is, it was to educate the man plus the American citizen." Quoted *Iowa State Register* (Weekly Edition) , Apr. 6, 1883.

62. *Cong. Globe,* 37 Cong., 2 Sess., 2769–70; Parker, *op. cit.,* 269–71. On June 6, 1862, under parliamentary privilege of general debate, Morrill made an analysis and fervent appeal for the bill in an extended speech entitled "Agricultural Colleges." This address was one of the most interesting and witty of his congressional speeches, though, aside from the discussion of the military provision, it followed the main lines and arguments of his speech in 1858. As it was a lone pronouncement and did not involve debate, the latter speech has received comparatively little attention. It is, however, of importance as an elaboration of Morrill's ideas on industrial education and an indication of the groups of interests to whom he was appealing. *Cong. Globe,* 37 Cong., 2 Sess., Appendix, 256–59.

63. Quotations and citations in E. D. Ross, "Northern Sectionalism in the Civil War Era," *Iowa Journal of History and Politics,* XXX, 463–66.

64. June 21, 1862.

65. *Milwaukee Sentinel,* June 20, 26, 1862; *Wisconsin Daily State Journal,* July 2, 1862; *Cong. Globe,* 37 Cong., 2 Sess., 2275, 2395.

66. *Cong. Globe,* 37 Cong., 2 Sess., 2248, 2275, 2328, 2395, 2626–27.

67. *N. Y. Tribune,* May 27, 1862.

68. *Cong. Globe,* 37 Cong., 2 Sess., 2276.

69. *Ibid.,* 2276; W. O. Thompson in *Hist. Ohio St. Univ.,* III, 174–75; Assoc. of Amer. Land-Grant Colls., *Proc.,* 1912, p. 89.

70. *Cong. Globe.,* 37 Cong., 2 Sess., 2249, 2328–29, 2626, 2632, Appendix, 257.

71. *Ibid.,* 2395.

72. *Ibid.,* 2441.

73. *Ibid.,* 2442.

74. *Ibid.,* 2395.

75. *Ibid.,* 2441.

76. June 20, 1862.

77. *Cong. Globe,* 37 Cong., 2 Sess., 2626.

78. June 20, 1862.

79. *Cong. Globe,* 37 Cong., 2 Sess., 2248–49, 2630, 2633–34; Parker, *op. cit.,* 270. Grimes offered an amendment to include the territories in the restriction that assignees should locate not more than one million acres within any one state. All the states were concerned in the territories, he held, and their interests should be protected. He did not believe that the states would be injured by the scrip selection as that would subject the lands to taxation, but in any case, whether an injury or a benefit, he wanted the territories put on the same basis as the new states. The amendment was defeated 14 to 23 mainly by eastern opposition and for this reason Grimes voted against the final bill in spite of the instruction of his state's legislature.

80. *Ibid.,* 2626–29.

81. *Ibid.,* 2630.

82. *Ibid.,* 2632–33.

83. *Ibid.,* 2634, 2769–70. For sectional analysis, Gates, *loc. cit.,* 124.

84. *Ibid.,* Appendix, 256; Parker, *op. cit.,* 271, 277.

85. Wis. St. Agr. Soc., *Trans.,* 1858–59, pp. 287–99.

86. Hewett to Morrill, Feb. 2, 1894, Morrill Papers; W. C. Langdon to Louise Swan, Jan. 30, 1917, *ibid.;* J. E. Brown to Hewett, Apr. 2, 1894, Hewett Papers.

87. Cf. W. H. Shepardson, *Agr. Education in the U. S.,* 17.

88. July 22, 1862.

89. IX (1858), 157, XIII (1862), 222.

90. XI (1858), 81, 273.

91. XX (1862), 13, 17.

92. XXI (1862), 197.

93. *U. S. Statutes at Large,* XII, 503–505. The date of the act is usually given as July 2, but as F. H. Turner points out (Ill. St. Hist. Soc., *Trans.,* 1932, p. 75) announcement was made to the Senate on that day that the bill had been signed by the President on July 1 when it consequently became a law. *Cong. Globe,* 37 Cong., 2 Sess., 3062.

94. *N. Y. Tribune,* June 21, 1862.

Chapter IV. State Option

1. *Cong. Globe,* 35 Cong., 2 Sess., 1414. See also Morrill's statement in 1862. *Ibid.,* 37 Cong., 2 Sess., Appendix, 256.

2. *U. S. Statutes at Large,* XIII, 47, XIV, 208, XVII, 416–17; B. F. Andrews, *Land Grant Act of 1862,* 9–38, and for special acts under the states involved.

3. *Proceedings Unveiling Portrait of Morrill,* 7–8.

4. Ohio St. Univ., *Rep.,* 1884, pp. 113–14. Cf. C. W. Dabney in N. M. Butler, *Education in U. S.,* II, 25–26.

5. *Op. cit.,* 8.

6. *The American Colleges and the American Public,* 254. Cf. Justice S. F. Miller in *Harper's Magazine,* LXXIX (1889), 173–74. Dr. J. G. Holland, in *Seven Oaks, a Story of To-Day* (1875), represents his hypocritical financial villain as concluding, after pondering the possibilities of popular acclaim and moral buildup through philanthropies, that he is really "pining for a theological seminary." His New York business factor and social mentor assures him that there is nothing at all impracticable in such a scheme: "All these fellows want is your money. They will give you everything you want for it in the way of glory." That this general attitude toward the possibilities of collegiate establishment persisted until comparatively recent times is indicated by the observation of the president of the Carnegie Foundation in 1913 (*Eighth Report,* 77) that, "The privilege of founding a university is as fully accorded in most states as that of opening a grocery store, and the university frequently has the smaller resources."

7. *Report upon a Plan for the Organization of Colleges,* 32–33.

8. White, *op. cit.,* 8–9; Harrison Howard, "Sketch of People's College," Howard Papers.

9. Henry F. French to Morrill, May 24, 1865, Morrill Papers; Calvin Stebbins, *Goodell,* 257.

10. Ohio A. and M. Coll., *Rep.,* 1874, p. 5.

11. Jonas Viles, *Univ. of Mo.,* 118.

12. B. E. Powell, *Univ. of Ill.,* I, 178–95; *Rural New-Yorker,* XIII (1862), 21.

13. A. G. Porter to Morrill, Feb. 8, 1867, Morrill Papers; W. M. Hepburn and L. M. Sears, *Purdue Univ.*, 28.

14. M. C. Fernald, *Maine State Coll.*, 20–21.

15. Pugh to S. W. Johnson, Nov. 18, 1861, True Papers; F. A. Walker, *Discussions in Education,* 10, 50, 71–72.

16. Hepburn and Sears, *op. cit.*, 28.

17. E. A. Bryan, *State Coll. of Wash.*, 36.

18. F. W. Blackmar, *Fed. and St. Aid to Higher Education,* 234.

19. W. W. Ferrier, *Univ. of Cal.*, 60–61.

20. Hepburn and Sears, *op. cit.*, 28; Viles, *op. cit.*, 118. In 1864 Representative Holman offered an amendment to allow Indiana to use her fund for the education of war orphans. The proposal was decisively rejected. *Cong. Globe,* 38 Cong., 1 Sess., 1284–85, 1496, 1499.

21. In 1869 Andrew D. White, evidently impressed with the trend toward centralization, predicted that within ten years Michigan's land-grant fund would go to the university. White to J. B. Angell, Sept. 13, 1869, Angell, *From Vermont to Michigan,* 107. For later alleged competition from the university, see Dept. of Agr. Convention of Delegates, 1885, *Proceedings,* 116.

22. *Report Upon a Plan,* 33–35; E. A. Osborne, *Letter-Files of S. W. Johnson,* 144; John M. Thomas to W. B. Parker, Jan. 6, 1923, Morrill Papers; A. L. Starrett, *Through One Hundred and Fifty Years—Univ. of Pittsburgh,* 149.

23. True, *Agr. Ed.*, 67.

24. C. R. Aurner, *Hist. of Education in Iowa,* IV, 207–209.

25. John W. Hoyt, agricultural journalist and notable educational leader, was especially influential in securing the grant for the university. *Wisconsin Farmer,* XIV (1862), 470–71; Wis. St. Agr. Soc., *Trans.*, 1861–68, pp. 74–79, 102.

26. M. S. Snow, *Higher Education in Missouri* (Bur. of Ed., Circular of Information, 1898), 26–27; Viles, *op. cit.*, 119–26.

27. A. G. Pean to Morrill, Oct. 6, 1865, Crosby Miller to Morrill, Nov. 6, 1865, Morrill Papers; Andrews, *op. cit.*, 50; J. B. Angell, *From Vermont to Mich.*, 244; same, *Reminiscences,* 122–23.

28. R. H. Chittenden, *Sheffield Scientific School,* I, 92; D. C. Gilman, *University Problems,* 130.

29. The selection was due largely to the influence of Professor George H. Cook, a Rensselaer graduate and pioneer agricultural scientist and administrator. C. R. Woodward and I. N. Waller, *N. J. Agr. Exp. Sta.*, 21.

30. M. H. Pollitt, *Patterson,* 79–86.

31. J. B. Horner, *Ore. Hist. Quart.*, XXXI (1930), 42–43.

32. L. B. Richardson, *Dartmouth Coll.*, II, 534–37.

33. Mass. St. Bd. Agr., *Rep.*, 1906, pp. 368–71.

34. Fernald, *op. cit.,* 22–23.

35. Hepburn and Sears, *op. cit.,* 31–33.

36. An act of the Washington territorial legislature in 1865 charted "Washington College" to be located at Vancouver. Trustees and location commissioners were named, but the college was not developed. F. E. Bolton and T. W. Bibb, *Hist. of Education in Wash.* (Office of Education Bulletin, 1934), 256–59.

37. A. D. White, *Proceedings Unveiling Portrait,* 7.

38. Ohio A. and M. Coll., *Rep.,* 1874, pp. 4–5; *Hist. Ohio St. Univ.,* III, 120.

39. Powell, *op. cit.,* Ch. XI, 590–98.

40. Ferrier, *op. cit.,* 272–75.

41. J. H. Reynolds and D. Y. Thomas, *Hist. Univ. of Ark.*

42. General reference for all the states may be made to Andrews, *op. cit.,* and to the collections of state land-grant college laws in Comr. of Education, *Rep.,* 1867–68, pp. 135–214, 1902, I, 1–90, 1903, I, 39–226.

43. Harrison Howard, "Sketch of People's College," Howard Papers; People's College, *Circular* (1863); Regents of the University of the State of N. Y., *Rep. on People's College, Sen. Rep.* No. 45; *Harper's Weekly,* IX (1865), 243.

44. A. D. White, *Autobiography,* I, 295–98; W. T. Hewett, *Cornell Univ.,* I, 81–82, 98–99.

45. *Autobiography,* I, 292–93; White to Gerrit Smith, Sept. 1, 1862, A. W. Smith, *Ezra Cornell,* 145–49.

46. A. D. White, *Autobiography,* I, 298–99.

47. *Ibid.,* I, 299–305; Hewett, *op. cit.,* I, 83–84; White to Hewett, Apr., 1894, Hewett Papers; *Nation,* I (1865), 44.

48. Powell, *op. cit.,* chs. IX–X; F. H. Turner, *Trans. Ill. St. Hist. Soc.,* 1932, pp. 75–85. In Oregon the legislative committee recommended that the fund be conferred on Wilamette University until a state institution was provided, but local influence secured the substitution of Corvallis. Horner, *loc. cit.,* 43. The South Dakota location was secured in exchange for desired patronage (*W. H. Powers, South Dakota St. Coll.,* 1–2), and in the bitter contest in Washington a United States senatorship, among numerous other considerations, was involved. Bryan, *op. cit.,* 32–36, 56. Morrill had predicted an active competition between towns which would relieve the states of the cost of land and buildings. June 6, 1862, *Cong. Globe,* 37 Cong., 2 Sess., Appendix, 256.

49. But even here one sectarian group opposed the otherwise harmonious adjustment. Ferrier, *op. cit.,* 272, 286. Gilman in his inaugural paid tribute to the humble parent: "You have inherited from the College of California a good name, good books, good collections, and good will. Honor to those who founded it, and honor to those who enlarged it!" *University Problems,* 158.

50. Andrews, *op cit.,* under the respective states; and the histories of the colleges involved.

51. Buckham to Morrill, Feb. 14, 1878, Jan. 30, 1888, June 15, 1890, June 15, 1892, Morrill Papers; Jonathan Periam, *Groundswell,* 533–36; T. C. Atkeson, *Hist. Patrons of Husbandry,* 87, 123; same, *Pioneering in Agr.,* 128–29; W. W. Folwell, *Autobiography,* 214–15; Pollitt, *op. cit.,* 143, 263; Viles, *op. cit.,* 236; W. L. Fleming, *La. St. Univ.,* 430.

52. Wis. St. Agr. Soc., *Trans.,* 1882–83, p. 185, 1887, pp. 336–40. For elaborate discussion pro and con on separation, see *ibid.,* 181–230, 304–305.

53. Brown Univ., *Pres. Reps.,* 1873, p. 14, 1874, p. 20, 1890, p. 15, 1891, pp. 16–18.

54. Yale Univ., *Rep. of Pres.,* 1890, p. 40; A. T. Hadley in *Harper's Magazine,* LXXXVIII (1894), 766; Chittenden, *op. cit.,* I. 228–36, 267–73; Walter Stemmons, *Conn. Agr. Coll.,* 56–57, 62, 64–65, 69–77; Osborne, *op. cit.,* 246–47.

55. Richardson, *op. cit.,* II, 541, 598, 627–29.

56. Pollitt, *op. cit.,* 100–14.

57. Ore. St. Agr. Coll., *Rep.,* 1889–90, p. 4; Horner, *loc. cit.,* 46–47.

58. J. M. White, "Origin and Location of the Mississippi A. and M. College," *Pubs. Miss. Hist. Soc.,* III, 345–51.

59. C W. Dabney, *Universal Education in the South,* I, 186–88; D. A. Lockmiller, *Hist. N. C. St. Coll.,* ch. II.

60. Dabney, *op. cit.,* 241; A. G. Holmes and G. R. Sherrill, *Clemson,* 168–76; F. B. Simkins, *Tillman Movement,* 84–86, 99–100, 138.

61. O. W. Firkins, *Cyrus Northrop,* 345–54; Joseph Schafer, *Agr. in Wis.,* 159–60; Ferrier, *op. cit.,* 369–72.

62. Herbert Myrick to Morrill, Oct. 1, 1890; Buckham to Morrill, Oct. 10, Nov. 27, 1890, Oct. 20, 1892, Mar. 11, 1893; Morrill to Buckham, Oct. 26, 1892; A. D. White to Morrill, Oct. 14, 1893, Morrill Papers; Morrill, *State Aid to Land-Grant Colleges* (1888); *The Land-Grant Colleges* (1893).

63. Andrews, *op. cit.,* 55.

64. W. L. Fleming, *op. cit.,* 292–97.

65. F. P. Rand, *Yesterdays at Mass. St. Coll.,* 55–57.

66. "Report of the Corporation of Brown University relative to the lands granted by the United States to the State of Rhode Island for the establishment of an Agricultural College," in S. W. Halliday, *History of the Agricultural College Land Grant,* 20–31.

67. Such, for instance, was the case in Missouri. Viles, *op. cit.,* 158–59.

68. For a general discussion of land and scrip disposal, see P. W. Gates, *Ind. Mag. of Hist.,* XXXVII, 129–36. The most available statistics of the receipts and investments of land-grant funds are in the compilation cited in note 66 above made by Cornell's attorney in connection with a litigation with the state in 1890, and in Andrews, *op. cit.* For alleged mismanagement in certain states, see M. H. Pollitt, *op. cit.,* 269; W. I. Scott to Herbert B. Adams, June 13, 1894, W. S. Holt, ed., *Historical Scholarship . . . in the Correspondence of Herbert B. Adams,* 233.

Chapter V. Trial and Error: Organization and Staff

1. *North Amer. Rev.*, CV, 514.
2. *Morrill Centenary Exercises,* 21.
3. Ohio St. Univ., *Rep.*, 1884, p. 110.
4. *Amer. State University,* 26.
5. E. A. Bryan, *Wash. St. Coll.*, 31.
6. M. C. Fernald, *Me. St. Coll.*, 21–22.
7. Tex. A. and M. Coll., *Semi-Centennial Celebration,* 71; Clarence Ousley, *A. and M. Coll. of Tex.*, 44–45, 50–51.
8. J. D. Walters, *Kan. St. Agr. Coll.*, 16–19; J. T. Willard, *Kan. St. Coll.*, 28–29.
9. Neb. Univ., *Rep.*, 1875–76, p. 7.
10. *Ore. Hist. Quart.*, XXXI, 46.
11. G. G. Bush, *Hist. of Education in Fla.* (Bur. of Education Circular of Information, 1891), 45.
12. A. D. White, *Proceedings Cornell Inauguration,* 7; same, *Proceedings Unveiling Morrill Portrait,* 6; Maryland catalogue, quoted *Country Gentleman,* XVIII (1861), 320; D. C. Gilman, Mass. A. C., *Rep.*, 1872, p. 14; W. W. Folwell, National Agr. Convention, 1872, *Procs.*, 20–21; G. W. Atherton, N. E. A., *Procs.*, 1873, p. 67; Joseph Sullivant, Ohio A. and M. Coll., *Rep.*, 1875, p. 7; A. T. Hadley, *Harper's Magazine,* LXXXVIII (1894), 766.
13. C. W. Eliot, "The New Education," *Atlantic Monthly,* XXIII (1869), 203–20, 358–67; same, *Educational Reform;* D. C. Gilman, *University Problems,* 130–31; same, *Launching of a University,* 146; A. D. White, *Autobiography,* I; F. A. Walker, *Discussions in Education;* F. A. P. Barnard, *Rise of a University,* 66–155; J. B. Angell, *From Vermont to Michigan,* 161, 181, 194, 257.
14. *American Colleges,* 260–69. A quarter of a century later his successor, Arthur T. Hadley, characterized the rival interests as those of "science without tradition" and "tradition without science." *Loc. cit.*, 768.
15. Mass. Bd. of Agr., *Rep.*, 1869 (agr. socs.), 89. Certain classically trained land-grant administrators, characteristically of the ardent proselyte, became most assertive supporters of the narrow-gauge position.
16. B. E. Powell, *University of Ill.*, I, 328.
17. G. W. Knight and J. R. Commons, *Higher Education in Ohio* (Bur. of Education Circular of Information 1891), 40.
18. Ia. Agr. Coll., *Addresses at Opening,* 11, 15, 17, 21. At its first meeting, in 1859, the board had recommended that "in general use the name Iowa Farmer's College be the designation." *Northwestern Farmer,* IV (1859), 49. A few years later Governor C. C. Carpenter scheduled to address the board on "The Relation of Industrial Education to the State," pleaded inadequacy of time for preparation of this highly

pertinent theme and substituted an oration on the boyhood struggles of Henry Clay. *Aurora* (Iowa Agr. Coll.), III (Oct., 1875), 6.

19. Ousley, *op. cit.,* 51–53; H. W. Wiley, *Autobiography,* 130–31.

20. Cal. St. Agr. Soc., *Trans.,* 1870, pp. 98–99, 1871, pp. 419–24; *Patrons of Husbandry on Pacific Coast,* 371.

21. Philadelphia *Rural Advertiser,* quoted in *Country Gentleman,* XXIV (1864), 80. Cf. similar sentiment of Representative Dumont of Ohio, Apr. 8, 1864. *Cong. Globe,* 38 Cong., 1 Sess., 1497.

22. XXVI (1867), 6.

23. Ezra Cornell was reported to have received his ideas regarding the organization and methods of an agricultural college from this institution. *All the Year Round,* Oct. 10, 1868, quoted in A. W. Smith, *Ezra Cornell,* 120–21.

24. Bryan, *op. cit.,* 36. The president of the Carnegie Foundation for the Advancement of Teaching as late as 1913 expressed essentially this view of the main function and scope of agricultural education. *Eighth Report,* 95–98.

25. Comr. of Ed., *Rep.,* 1867–68, pp. ix, 129–309, 354–60, 501–503. A. S. Welch arguing in the Senate for the maintenance of the Bureau a fortnight before his inauguration as president of the Iowa Agricultural College asserted somewhat daringly: "It seems to me that it would be well for this Government to see that the vast amount of land it has donated for the progress of agricultural and industrial science is so appropriated as to secure the great objects for which it is made; and that is one great purpose for which this Department is established." *Cong. Globe,* 40 Cong., 3 Sess., 1797.

26. Comr. of Agr., *Rep.,* 1865, pp. 145–48, 1867, p. 332; Nat. Agr. Con., 1872, *op. cit.,* 18–19. These views were not always consistently maintained. See, for example, editorial in *Rural New-Yorker,* XV (1864), 117.

27. *Legislative Career of Justin S. Morrill,* 66.

28. Annie T. Smith, "The Education of Agriculturists," *Education,* II, (1881), 167.

29. Cf. I. L. Kandel, *Fed. Aid for Vocational Education,* 82–85. It is not to be understood that there was this consciously reasoned progression or alteration in his thinking, but to judge by his somewhat ambiguous and at times seemingly contradictory statements this seems to have been the trend of his interpretation and emphasis. The fullest sources for his changing views after the original act are his speeches on the bills of 1872, 1876, 1890, *Cong. Globe,* 42 Cong., 3 Sess., 36–40; *Cong. Rec.,* 44 Cong., 1 Sess., 2761–67, 51 Cong., 1 Sess., 6084–85; Conference with professors of the Sheffield Scientific School, November, 1867, Wm. H. Brewer's memoranda, copy in True Papers; *Proceedings at the Unveiling of the Portrait;* letter to P. M. Sutton (Iowa State senator) Feb. 11, 1884, *Aurora,* XII, (Mar., 1884), 9; "The Industrial Colleges," *Agricultural Science,* I (1887), 11–12; Mass. Agr. Coll., *Address . . . 25th Anniversary of the Passage of the Morrill Land Grant Act; U. S. Land-Grant Colleges, an Address in Behalf of the Univ. of Vt. and St. Agr. Coll.*

(1888); *The Land-Grant Colleges* (Univ. of Vt. commencement, 1893); letter to a board of regents, quoted in Ia. St. Coll., *Rep.*, 1898–99, p. 16.

30. See especially letters from G. W. Benedict, July 18, 1865, Buckham, continuously from the early seventies, White, Aug. 25, 1873, Nov. 2, 1874, Oct. 14, 1893, Morrill Papers; Brewer, "The Intent of the Morrill Land Grant," a summary, written about 1890, of the conference of the Sheffield faculty with Morrill in 1867, copy in True Papers.

31. Borne out by his correspondence with Buckham, his discussion of the state situation in his address to the legislature in 1888, and his commencement address in 1893.

32. Commissioner of Agr., *Rep.*, 1865, pp. 145–48, 1867, p. 332. Cf. Morrill's statements in his speech in 1862. *Cong. Globe,* 37 Cong., 2 Sess., Appendix, 256, 259.

33. C. S. Lyman to Morrill, Sept. 16, 1867, Morrill Papers; Brewer, *loc. cit.*

34. July 23, 1863, in reply to resolutions of the People's College board expressing gratitude to Congress, the President, Morrill, and Wade for the passage of the bill, Morrill Papers.

35. May 21, 1883, in reply to invitation to attend the Cornell commencement exercises, *ibid.*

36. *Cong. Globe.*, 42 Cong., 3 Sess., 36.

37. J. M. Gregory, N. E. A., *Proc.*, 1880, p. 232.

38. *Diary and Letters,* IV, 385.

39. Mass. A. C., *Rep.*, 1873, p. 10; Ohio A. and M. Coll., *Rep.*, 1874, pp. 14–16. In 1884, during a conflict between the two factions that had led to an administrative reorganization, the Iowa legislature enacted unanimously a measure redefining the scope and purpose of the college in almost the precise terms of the Morrill act. The argument of the author of the bill, Senator P. M. Sutton, a graduate of the Illinois Normal University, for a liberal interpretation of the national act was held by a local paper to be "the most noted plea for colleges of this class that has ever been put forward in any of the states. . ." In the debate Sutton presented a telegram from Morrill himself on the intent of the act. *Ames Intelligencer,* Mar. 15, 1884. The student paper, *The Aurora,* gave almost an entire issue (Mar., 1884) to the speech.

40. Matthew Hale Smith in *Merchants Magazine,* LII (1865), 331.

41. *Educational Reform,* 11–12.

42. *Op. cit.,* 66.

43. *Op. cit.,* 30–31.

44. Assoc. Amer. Agr. Colls. and Exp. Stas., *Proc.,* 1913, pp. 88–89.

45. For typical experiences, Gregory, *op. cit.,* 230; J. B. Angell, *Reminiscences,* 122–23; W. J. Beal and J. B. Angell, *Semi-Centennial Mich. A. C.,* 91, 209; Eugene Davenport in Tex. A. and M., *Semi-Centennial,* 43; T. C. Atkeson, *Pioneering in Agr.,* 71.

46. N. E. A., *Proc.,* 1873, p. 43.

47. N. H. St. Agr. Soc., *Trans.*, 1851–53, p. 28.

48. Gail Hamilton, "Glorying in the Goad," *Atlantic Monthly,* XIV (1864), 21–33.

49. *Prairie Farmer,* XI (1863), 81.

50. *Nation,* II (1866), 772.

51. *Report of a Plan,* 29.

52. Ohio A. and M. Coll., *Rep.*, 1875, pp. 6–7.

53. Fernald, *op. cit.*, 417. An Iowa governor, noted mainly for his economical management of the state's finances, viewed the federal-endowed agricultural college as a sound business investment: "The educational advantages accruing to the youth of the state in this institution, being of an eminently practical character, the results whereof must have a beneficial effect on her development, have not cost the tax-payers of the state a cent aside from the expense of the buildings, and in all probability never will, as the means of the College are ample and constantly increasing." B. F. Shambaugh, *Messages and Proclamations of the Govs. of Ia.*, V, 34.

54. *Ore. Hist. Quart.*, XXXI, 49.

55. Fernald, *op. cit.*, 60; W. M. Hepburn and L. M. Sears, *Purdue Univ.*, 79–80. The Iowa organization committee in 1867, headed by a veteran legislator, observed that reliance upon legislative appropriations constituted "a very uncertain and unpleasant method of procuring an endowment." Ia. Agr. Coll., *Rep.*, 1866–67, p. 30.

56. Fernald, *op. cit.*, 418–22; W. J. Beal, *Mich. Agr. Coll.*, 406; Calvin Stebbins, *Goodell,* 91.

57. Mass. A. C., *Rep.*, 1876, pp. 9–10.

58. W. T. Hewett, *Cornell Univ.*, I, 112; A. D. White, *Autobiography,* I, 309–18; H. S. White, *Willard Fiske,* 407.

59. A. D. White, *Autobiography,* I, 438–39; J. G. Schurman, *A Generation of Cornell,* 19–28; R. T. Ely, *Ground Under Our Feet,* 57 (conversations with White, 1879–80).

60. In the case of the defalcation of a college treasurer it was found that through careless oversight of the board that official's bond had not been renewed. Ia. Gen. Assembly Joint Com., *Invest. of Ia. A. C.* (1874), 544–45.

61. Ex-President Hayes' work on the Ohio board was a notable instance of devoted and enlightened service. See especially memorial tribute in *Diary and Letters,* V, 203. Brief biographies of the Purdue trustees are given in T. R. Johnston and Helen Hand, *The Trustees and the Officers of Purdue University, 1865–1940.*

62. B. F. Andrews, *Land-Grant Colleges,* 17, 26, 29–30, 36–38, 57; A. D. White, *Autobiography,* I, 320–22, 414–21; *American Agriculturist,* XXXI, (1872), 325, XXXII (1873), 206, 246; Ia. Gen. Assembly Joint Com., *op. cit.*, vi.

63. XXII (1863), 238.

64. *Op. cit.,* 32.

65. Mich. St. Agr. Soc., *Trans.,* 1856, p. 300. For the conditions of the Michigan and Kansas campuses in the seventies, see David Fairchild, *The World Was My Garden,* 3, 7–8.

66. Ia. A. C., *Opening Addresses,* 8; *Aurora,* XVIII (1889), 8.

67. A. D. White, *Autobiog.,* I, 344; *Correspondence of Goldwin Smith,* 18.

68. Bryan, *op. cit.,* 8.

69. *Op. cit.,* 152, Cf. W. H. Dunn, *Donald G. Mitchell,* 318. W. S. Munroe's *Bibliography of Education* lists thirty American publications to 1892 on "School Architecture and Equipment."

70. Walters, *op. cit.,* 23; Willard, *op. cit.,* 30–31.

71. Fernald, *op. cit.,* 29–30.

72. Bryan, *op. cit.,* 86–88.

73. Ia. St. Coll. and Farm, *Rep.,* 1859–60, pp. 5–6. The reference to the dome and stairs was a fling at the state university which had been given the "Old Stone Capitol."

74. Hepburn and Sears, *op. cit.,* 39; T. I. Mairs, *Pa. Pioneers,* 46.

75. *Harper's Weekly,* X (1866), 818; *Cultivator and Country Gentleman,* XXVIII (1866), 208; Hewett, *op. cit.,* I, 305; Fernald, *op. cit.,* 28; F. L. Olmsted, *A few things to be thought of before proceeding to plan buildings for the national agricultural colleges* (report to the board of Massachusetts A. C., 1866).

76. Fernald, *op. cit.,* 30–31.

77. Hewett, *op. cit.,* I, 306–307.

78. W. W. Ferrier, *Univ. of Cal.,* 66.

79. *Atlantic Monthly,* XXIII, 365. Cf. James A. Garfield on "the case of *Brains vs. Brick and Mortar*" in his address before the Department of Superintendence, *Proc.,* 1877, in Bur. of Education, *Circular of Information,* 158–59, and reprinted in B. A. Hinsdale, *President Garfield and Education,* 337–39.

80. Garfield is said to have come down to the bare log in an alumni dinner address (*Dict. of Amer. Biog.,* IX, 216), but in the officially recorded statements the equipment, while crude, was several stages more advanced: "Give me a log hut, with only a simple bench, Mark Hopkins on one end and I on the other, and you may have all the buildings, apparatus, and libraries without him."—"If I could be taken back into boyhood to-day, and had all the libraries and apparatus of a university, with ordinary routine professors offered me on the one hand, and on the other a great, luminous, rich-souled man, such as Dr. Hopkins was twenty years ago, in a tent in the woods alone, I should say, 'Give me Dr. Hopkins for my college course, rather than any university with only routine professors.'" Hinsdale, *op. cit.,* 43, 338. President Patterson of Kentucky at his university's "golden jubilee" in 1916 declared, "President Mark Hopkins and his appreciative pupils working together in a log cabin represent the nucleus and contain the germ of university

life." M. H. Pollitt, *Patterson,* 201. The traditions of the "log colleges" may very likely have suggested the log cabin figure. David Starr Jordan, in a teachers' institute address in Indiana in 1885, made the log "rotten" (perhaps with the added advantage of studying insects and fungi) and otherwise modified the sentiment: "Garfield once said that a rotten log, with Mark Hopkins on one end of it, and himself on the other, would be a university." Quoted in J. A. Woodburn, *Hist. of Ind. Univ.,* I, 383. Abraham Flexner (*Universities American, English, German,* 151) adds to the confusion by making Hopkins himself responsible for the sentiment: "The dictum of Mark Hopkins is frequently recalled: the ideal college consists of a log of wood with an instructor at one end and a student at the other." The suggestion for Garfield's statement—whatever it was—was no doubt Cardinal Newman's well known sentiment, "Have a university in shanties, nay in tents, but have great teachers in it."

81. N. E. A., *Proc.,* 1876, p. 251; Texas A. and M., *Semi-Centennial,* 46–47; *Cong. Rec.,* 51 Cong., 1 Sess., 6085.

82. *Educational Reform,* 6. See also on the general backwardness of science teaching in the seventies, Prof. A. A. Bennett in Class of '97, *Hist. and Reminiscences of Ia. Agr. Coll.,* 280–83.

83. Ely, *op. cit.,* 29, 32; N. W. Butler, *Across the Busy Years,* I, 86 (conditions at Dartmouth and Columbia in the seventies and early eighties).

84. *Op. cit.,* 152.

85. *Atlantic Monthly,* XXIII, 365.

86. Ia. Agr. Coll. and Farm, *Rep.,* 1865–67, p. 27; *Aurora,* XVIII (1889), 9.

87. *Atlantic Monthly,* XXIII, 366. On the past prevalence of clerical executives, G. P. Schmidt, *Old Time Coll. Pres.,* 60, 184–85.

88. M. T. Carriel, *Turner,* 143.

89. For instance, the first "regent" of Illinois, three early Michigan presidents, the first three of Kansas, three of the first six of Iowa. State university presidents, especially in the South, were frequently ministers.

90. Stebbins, *op. cit.,* 257.

91. *Ibid.,* 258; J. W. Burgess, *Reminiscences,* 50.

92. Hepburn and Sears, *op. cit.,* chs. V–VIII; Wiley, *op. cit.,* 123–126.

93. To S. W. Johnson, Feb. 22, 1855, True Papers.

94. Mairs, *op. cit.,* 105–106. B. F. Gue of Iowa in editorial correspondence from Philadelphia in 1867 paid this tribute: "Dr. Pugh who died a few years ago was head, front, and life of the College, and was building up a noble Institution for the farmers of Pennsylvania. His sudden death arrested everything and seemed to almost strike a death blow to the College." *Iowa North West,* Nov. 20, 1867.

95. C. R. Aurner, *Hist. of Education in Ia.,* IV, 244–57; Ia. St. Coll., *Historical Sketch,* 11.

96. C. W. Dabney, *Universal Education in the South,* I, 187, 240, 378; M. M. Wilkerson, *Thomas Duckett Boyd,* 59–78, 85–92, ch. VII. Jefferson Davis

was elected as the first president of the Texas college. He finally declined but recommended the man who was secured in his stead. Ousley, *op. cit.*, 42–43.

97. Bryan, *op. cit.*, 83–131. The official historian of the Washington State College thus laconically summarizes the initial fatalities: "The college was already a year and a half old and had had two presidents, a scandal, and a legislative investigation. Now it had its second board of regents and its third faculty." *Ibid.*, 131. Cf. W. H. Powers, *S. Dak. St. Coll.*, 13, 22–23. Quixotic and notional attitudes on executive qualifications were not confined to the new states. In 1884 a preferred candidate for the presidency of Indiana University shocked the university audience by his reference to the various "dam" places that he had visited in Holland and for this inept pun he was immediately dropped from consideration. Woodburn, *op. cit.*, 369. The nominating committee of the Missouri board of curators in 1889 rejected a candidate, otherwise satisfactory, by reason of short stature. H. O. Severance, *R. H. Jesse*, 24. Ohio executives as late as the nineties complained of board dictatorship and executive insecurity. W. S. Holt, *Historical Scholarship*, 224–25, 231–33.

98. W. W. Folwell, *Autobiog.*, 205.

99. *Atlantic Monthly*, XXIII, 305.

100. *North Amer. Rev.*, CV, 517.

101. *American Farm Book*, 17–18.

102. *Op. cit.*, 238–41.

103. U. S. Agr. Soc., *Journal*, 1859, p. 20; *Cong. Globe*, 42 Cong., 3 Sess., 1689; *Cong. Rec.*, 51 Cong., 1 Sess, 6085.

104. Oscar Clute in A. C. McLaughlin, *Higher Education in Mich.* (Bur. of Education Circular of Information, 1891), 111–12. See also La. St. Univ., *Rep.*, 1870, p. 12.

105. Typical representatives of the first group were Evan Pugh, S. W. Johnson, G. H. Cook, W. S. Clark, Ezra Carr, G. C. Caldwell, E. W. Hilgard, James Law, F. W. Prentice, W. H. Brewer, W. O. Atwater, S. W. Babcock, W. J. Beal, C. W. Dabney; of the second, N. S. Townshend, Manly Miles, E. M. Pendleton, A. E. Foote, E. R. Hutchins, R. C. Kedzie, H. W. Wiley, J. T. Rothrock; and of the third, Levi Stockbridge, John Stanton Gould, G. E. Morrow, T. J. Burrill, Jonathan Periam, I. P. Roberts, S. A. Knapp, James Wilson, James Mathews, J. L. Budd, Luther Tucker.

106. Designations of honor for staff members without degrees seem to have been something of a problem; civil titles such as "hon.," "esq.," and military titles from captain to general were frequently used. See, for example, the first Massachusetts faculty in which all but the gardener have some such recognition. Mass. A. C., *Rep.*, 1869, pp. 27–28. A later solution was the granting of honorary professional degrees. I. P. Roberts, *Autobiog.*, 182–83; Ia. A. C., *Rep.*, 1878–79, p. 70; 1886–87, p. 185. In one instance a faculty committee reported adversely on conferring the M. S. on staff members who had graduated in an engineering curriculum on the ground "that neither on the authority of the reformed

usage of the best institutions nor by any construction of the rules the Faculty has adapted to guide them in conferring degrees can the degree of M.S. be given to those who have taken their first degree in Depts. so technical as those of Civil and Mechanical Engineering." The members of the committee were in the diverse fields of botany, veterinary science, and English literature. "After a discussion extending through the entire evening" the committee's recommendation was rejected by one vote. The president, his wife, one of the members involved in the award and his wife voted with the majority. Ia. Agr. Coll., MS. Faculty Minutes, Apr. 1, 8, 1878, pp. 338–42. The Kansas Agricultural College conferred an A. M. on a degreeless instructor "in recognition of his faithful and successful service as a teacher and his high worth as a man." Willard, *op. cit.*, 444.

Professional degrees were sometimes sought directly from the board. In one such case a man resigning after ineffective service made the following modest request: "I wish to submit to your judgment whether I have not earned at your hands the degree of Master of Horticulture." After considerable disagreement this request was given committee interment. Ia. Agr. Coll., MS. Trustees Minute Book, Nov. 17, 1876, p. 324. "Rev." was prefixed at times to clerical members in catalogues and announcements—perhaps as an evidence of spiritual balance. A committee was designated in faculty minutes as "Professor Bennett, Dr. Halstead, Reverend Barrows." Ia. Agr. Coll., MS. Faculty Minutes, Oct. 25, 1887, p. 283. The use of "honorable" as a presidential title, due in a few cases to previous political office holding but in general signifying that the position had a dignity and distinction comparable even to those in the political sphere, was a common practice. Within a dozen years a veteran land-grant administrator announced to a faculty the selection of "the Honorable ————" (a man whose entire career had been academic) as the new president.

Land-grant student bodies and constituencies were often indifferent or insensitive to the gradations and distinctions of academic designations, especially to damarcation of earned and honorary. As late as the turn of the century a student paper in detailing the attainments of their president—who had taken special work at the Yale divinity school and later received the conventional decoration from a denominational college—recorded an achievement that would have startled the Carnegie Foundation as well as the university concerned: "Later he took two years of post graduate work at Yale University, receiving the degree of LL.D." *Iowa Agriculturist,* I (Jan., 1902), 5. More recently a leading agricultural paper made light of the lack of any degree by an A. and M. president. *Iowa Homestead,* LXVIII (1923), 1058.

A verified story, too good to need documentation, is of a degreeless modern language teacher—whose peculiar methods were appreciated by no one but the president—who one day appended an A. M. (a degree never conferred by the institution) to the card on her classroom door. Upon insistent inquiry of colleagues as to the source of this advanced degree she explained with hysterical petulance that the president had told her that she might have it. With a change of administration the next year the degree was dropped as precipitately as it had been acquired. The fact that the executive's degrees had been secured apparently in somewhat the same off-hand way no doubt suggested this original procedure of conferring.

107. Ill. Indus. Univ., *Rep.*, 1878–80, p. 14; A. T. Steinel and D. W. Working, *Agr. in Col.*, 589; Bryan, *op. cit.*, 94.

108. W. L. Fleming, *La. St. Univ.*, 191–92, 355; Wilkerson, *op. cit.*

109. L. B. Richardson, *Dartmouth*, II, 537.

110. Stebbins, *op. cit.*, 86–87.

111. M. S. Kirshman, *Life of E. W. Stanton*, 27.

112. *I. S. C. Alumnus*, I, 162–66.

113. Ore. St. Agr. Coll., *Rep.*, 1889–90, pp. 10, 14.

114. Powers, *op. cit.*, 18–19. See also Mairs, *op. cit.*, 43, 45, 48.

115. At Iowa President Welch in addition to his regular chair of psychology, political economy, and sociology, taught, at various times, rhetoric, English literature, German, philosophy of science, normal instruction, geology, landscape gardening, and stock breeding. President Chamberlain of the same institution had the official title of "professor of ethics and civics and lecturer on practical agriculture." A notable case of presidential teaching was that of James K. Patterson of Kentucky who in addition to directing the administration and business, large and small, and maintaining paternalistic supervision of the student body conducted his teaching in metaphysics and history for forty-five years. Pollitt, *op. cit.*, 188–89. See also on presidents' teaching Mairs, *op. cit.*, 44; Fernald, *op. cit.*, 56–57.

116. Mich. St. Bd. Agr., *Rep.*, 1878, p. 68.

117. La. St. Univ., *Rep.*, 1871, p. 13.

118. Ia. Gen. Assem. Joint Com., *op. cit.*, 212, 252–53, 507–509.

119. S. P. E. E., *Proc.*, 1894, p. 288.

120. S. B. Doten, *Univ. of Nev.*, 59.

121. Ill. Indus. Univ., *Rep.*, 1882–84, p. 171.

122. Mass. A. C., *Rep.*, 1876, p. 8. Cf. Beal, *op. cit.*, 311. President Moss of Indiana University in his report for 1876 made a still more startling comparison: "If rumor be true, head cooks in our city hotels are better paid than the best teachers." Quoted in Woodburn, *op. cit.*, I, 322.

123. Hepburn and Sears, *op. cit.*, 71, 177; Mairs, *op. cit.*, 53.

124. Powell, *op. cit.*, I, xx.

125. Peter Collier to Morrill, Dec. 31, 1876, Oct. 18, 1877, H. B. Anthony to same, Apr. 6, 1883, Morrill Papers; Dept. of Agr. Con. of Delegates 1885, *Proc.*, 108–109; Folwell, *Autobiog.*, 218; Holt, *op. cit.*, 231–33; Hepburn and Sears, *op. cit.*, 58; Roberts, *op. cit.*, 169–72; Ousley, *op. cit.*, 48–51; Bryan, *op. cit.*, 86, 94–100, 121–25; Powers, *op. cit.*, 19–23; *Aurora*, XIX (1890), 141; L. H. Pammel, "Dr. H. J. Detmers," *Prominent Men I Have Met*, Part II, 38, 41. Willard, *op. cit.*, 37–38. A university board member who had shortly before been a land-grant president was of the opinion that tenure was "too stable sometimes for the good of the University." W. I. Chamberlain to H. B. Adams, June 5, 1894. Holt, *op. cit.*, 228. In a legislative investigation in 1874

a board member in denouncing a young professor, who was later to have a long and distinguished career in a leading university, gave this rare and original test of character analysis: "I have expressed myself emphatically the last 4 or 5 years to the members of the Board . . . that whenever I looked at him, I thought of Uriah Heap [sic] and David Copperfield. . . . I go more on the countenance of a man, than anything else about him. Also in a horse. Give me a good countenance in a horse and I will show you a good horse and the reverse holds true." Ia. Gen. Assem. Joint Com., *op. cit.,* 370.

126. For example, H. E. Starr, *Sumner,* ch. XV; Holt, *op. cit.,* 227, 232, 234.

127. For the growing alumni influence, Porter, *op. cit.,* 244–47, an influence he was about to have a disturbing demonstration of in the "Young Yale" movement, Starr, *op. cit.,* 79–95; J. P. Munroe, *Walker,* 239–41; Ely, *op. cit.,* 29–30; *Aurora,* VI (Nov., 1878), 7, VII (Oct., 1879), 4. In the early seventies a new president whose innovations were meeting with strong opposition was reported to have refused to allow an alumni meeting on the campus unless the leaders would agree that no reflections would be cast on his policies. The meeting was held in a church. Willard, *op. cit.,* 515.

128. Bryan, *op. cit.,* 97–98; *Rural New-Yorker,* XLVI (1887), 769; Powers, *op. cit.,* 21–22; F. P. Rand, *Yesterdays at Mass. St. Coll.,* 75–81; *Aurora,* XV (1886), 153, XVI (1887), 43; Laur. Larsen's impressions at the Univ. of Wis. in 1866, *Norwegian-American Studies and Records,* X, 113; Jonas Viles, *Univ. of Mo.,* 196, 199; Class of '97 Ia. Agr. Coll., *op. cit.,* 120.

The unfortunate effects of direct dealing of students with the board was illustrated by a year's record at one institution. In May the members of the junior class in agriculture petitioned the board to be relieved from the course in horticulture because (1) a part of the instruction was given in agriculture by another professor; (2) they considered "the instructive labor as pursued under him utterly valueless to us by reason of the disagreeableness of his manners," and (3) a part of the teaching was in direct opposition to those in botany and he gave no authority for his departures "utterly ignoring that of Gray and other standards!" The petition was granted. In November following, a student petitioned for a re-examination in a subject as he had been "unfairly treated" and a few days later 31 upper classmen sent a communication expressing "our *dissatisfaction* with our present instructor in Physics and Geology," while another group of 20 certified that they had confidence in said professor and hoped the board would "act considerately in his case." In neither of these later cases was the relief sought granted and the board no doubt was brought to see the desirability of leaving instructional concerns to the faculty. Ia. Agr. Coll., MS. Trustee Minute Book, May 3, Nov. 13–17, 1876, pp. 222–24, 297, 307–308, 321.

129. The beginnings of professional defensive consciousness may be noted in protests against political interference with scientists in government bureaus. A notable case was the action regarding the dismissal of Dr. C. C. Parry as botanist of the Department of Agriculture in 1871. Professor Asa Gray's presentation of the case for the botanists might serve as a model for committee A of the A. A. U. P. *American Naturalist,* VI (1872), 39–45; *American Journal of Science and Arts,* 3rd Series, III (1872), 315–18.

Chapter VI. Trial and Error: Curriculum and Students

1. Eugene Davenport in Texas A. and M., *Semi-Centennial*, 49; H. W. Wiley, *Autobiography*, 127.

2. W. H. Powers, *S. Dak. St. Coll.*, 26; N.E.A., *Proc.*, 1890, pp. 220–25.

3. Mass. A. C., *Rep.*, 1873, p. 13.

4. Ohio A. and M., *Rep.*, 1875, p. 45.

5. N.E.A., *Proc.*, 1875, p. 73.

6. Comr. of Agr., *Rep.*, 1874, p. 330.

7. S. P. E. E., *Proc.*, 1893, pp. 168–72, 175–76, 1897, pp. 281, 286, 290, 293–94, 1900, pp. 81–88; M.I.T., *Rep.*, 1876, pp. 124–47; M. C. Fernald, *Me. State Coll.*, 53; W. M. Hepburn and L. M. Sears, *Purdue*, 67; A. D. White, *Autobiog.*, I, 373–74; Arthur MacArthur, *Education in Relation to Manual Industry*, 29–32, 35, 71–76.

8. R. H. Chittenden, *Sheffield Scientific School*, I, 144; A. T. Hadley in *Harper's Magazine*, LXXXVIII (1894), 766.

9. White, *op. cit.*, I, 369.

10. Brown Univ., *Rep.*, 1873, p. 31.

11. W. W. Folwell, *Autobiog.*, 206.

12. Univ. of Tenn., *Rep.*, 1879–80, p. 18.

13. White, *op. cit.*, I, 367–70; H. S. White, *Willard Fiske*, 411; I. P. Roberts, *Autobiog.*, 177–86. To meet popular and legislative dissatisfaction at the neglect of agriculture in the eighties a Missouri president, on his own initiative, rechristened the institution, "Missouri Agricultural College and University." The protest of students and alumni was immediate and overwhelming, and the board hastened to restore the old balance of subjects and emphasis. Jonas Viles, *Univ. of Mo.*, 190–91.

14. Roberts, *op. cit.*, 160; U. S. Dept. of Agr., *Yearbook*, 1899, pp. 498–500: annual reports of the commissioner of education on land-grant college equipment. In some colleges the collections of the literary societies were the main resource. *Delaware Notes*, VIII, 111. For an exceptional attention to library development, C. Stebbins, *Goodell*, 103. Wisconsin felt that her library needs were fully met in the seventies although no special mention was made of scientific books: "The university has a library of its own, numbering 4,600 volumes, and the students also have access, free of charge, to the library of the State Historical Society, which contains 50,000 volumes, embracing almost every subject concerning which information might be desired." Comr. of Agr., *Rep.*, 1872, p. 393.

15. Roberts, *op. cit.*, 160–63. See also on land-grant pioneers in general science teaching, Herbert Osborn, *Fragments of Entomological Hist.*, 97–98; L. H. Pammel, "Charles Edwin Bessey," *Prominent Men I Have Met*, Part VI, 17–22.

16. For summary and references, see E. D. Ross, "Manual Labor Experiment in the Land-Grant College," *Miss. Vall. Hist. Rev.*, XXI, 513–28.

17. Henry Wallace, *Uncle Henry's Own Story,* III, 48–51; D. S. Fairchild, *Early History of the Veterinary Department of Iowa State College,* manuscript, Iowa State College history collection; J. R. Commons and J. B. Andrews, *Doc. Hist.,* X, 120–22; R. B. Hayes, *Diary and Letters,* IV, 325; Comr. Colman at Con. of Delegates, 1885, *Proc.,* 6. Wm. Duane Wilson, the first secretary of the Iowa Agricultural College, as leader of the state Grange led the attack on the college administration that culminated in the notorious legislative investigation of 1874.
18. *Rural New-Yorker,* XLII (1883) , 3, 285; William Crozier and Peter Henderson, *How the Farm Pays,* 11–12.
19. Rodney Cline, *Seaman Knapp,* 25.
20. N. Y. St. Agr. Soc., *Rep.,* 1891, pp. 267–69. A scant generation ago a plea for "barnyard agricultural education" received respectful attention and qualified endorsement from an influential farm paper. *Iowa Homestead.* LIV (1909) , 1846.
21. Quoted in *American Agriculturist,* XXXIV (1875) , 8.
22. XLVI (1887) , 368.
23. XXXV (Dec. 26, 1890) , 5. See also attacks of the same purport in issues of Nov. 28, Dec. 5, 12, 1890.
24. L (1881) , 864.
25. *Discussions in Education,* 97. Cf. G. C. Caldwell in *Rural New-Yorker,* LI (1882) , 795–96.
26. N. H. Bd. of Agr., *Rep.,* 1883–84, pp. 88–90; *Cultivator and Country Gentleman,* L (1885) , 126–27.
27. A. D. White, *op. cit.,* I, 387–89; B. E. Powell, *Univ. of Ill.,* I, 289–90; W. J. Beal, *Mich. Agr. Coll.,* 483; L. S. Merriam, *Higher Education in Tenn.* (Bureau of Education, Circular, 1893) , 74; M. M. Wilkerson, *T. D. Boyd,* 67–69. Both Secretary Stanton and General Sherman held that military science rather than the drill should be emphasized. Brewer memoranda, True Papers.
28. Confer. Presidents of St. Univs. and Colls., 1877, *Proc.,* 186; *Southern Planter and Farmer,* XXXVIII (1877) , 563–64. The Japanese minister in viewing the Massachusetts cadets observed, "Ah, that will teach the people to feed themselves and defend themselves." Nat. Agr. Con., 1872, *Proc.,* 74.
29. Mass. A. C., *Rep.,* 1891, pp. 76–77.
30. Confer. of Presidents, *op. cit.,* 187.
31. M.I.T., *Rep.,* 1874, pp. 26–27. By reason of his own military record Governor Ben Butler's personal testimony to the disciplinary efficacy of military training would have been taken by many with as great reservation as would his assurance that the college-trained soldier if "attentive and apt" would be as well fitted for a commission as a graduate of West Point. Mass. A. C., *Rep.,* 1882, p. 4.
32. Mass. A. C., *Rep.,* 1891, p. 79.
33. *Ibid.,* 1882, p. 31, 1887, p. 34, 1890, pp. 77–78; M.I.T., *Rep.,* 1874, pp.

25–26; N.E.A., *Proc.*, 1875, pp. 130–31; Confer. of Presidents, *op. cit.*, 186–87; *Southern Planter*, LV (1884), 397; Ia. Agr. Coll., *Rep.*, 1885, p. 46.

34. Confer. of Presidents, *op. cit.*, 187.

35. M.I.T., *Rep.*, 1883, p. 25.

36. Mass. A. C., *Rep.*, 1875, p. 9. In a number of cases in the early years the drill was elective. A few colleges specified that in the case of conscientious objection of a student or his parents, exemption would be made. Pa. St. Coll., *Rep.*, 1874, p. 27; Nev. St. Univ., *Rep.*, 1889, p. 11. There is one report of a mother who objected that her son's uniform was not sufficiently warm. *Delaware Notes*, VIII, 110.

37. Convention of Delegates, 1885, *op. cit.*, p. 145.

38. For instance, Fairchild of Kansas. David Fairchild, *The World Was My Garden*, 13.

39. Proceedings in Mich. St. Bd. of Agr., *Rep.*, 1871, pp. 352, 357, 363, 374.

40. National Agr. Con., 1872, *Proc.*, 69–75, 79.

41. Confer. of Presidents, *op. cit.*, 185–90.

42. Convention of Delegates, 1885, *op. cit.*, 54–55, 145–46. President Patterson of Kentucky observed retrospectively, "The subject was never a popular one . . . in the national meetings." M. H. Pollitt, *J. K. Patterson*, 142–43.

43. Ill. Indus. Univ., *Rep.*, 1882–83, p. 57.

44. Sec. of War, *Rep.*, 1881–90 (secretary, adjutant general, and inspector general).

45. *Ibid.*, 1890, p. 278; Buckham to Morrill, Dec. 29, 1873, May 28, 1877, Sec. Lincoln to Morrill, Sept. 1, 1884, Morrill Papers; Univ. of Neb., *Rep.*, 1875–76, p. 6; Ill. Indus. Univ., *Rep.*, 1876–78, p. 78; M. C. Fernald, *Me. St. Coll.*, 66–69; *S. B. Doten, Univ. of Nev.*, 56.

46. M. I. T., *Rep.*, 1874, pp. 18–21, 1875, p. 26; Mass. A. C., *Rep.*, 1875, p. 69; *Aurora*, VI (Aug. 1878), 8, (Sept. 1878), 8, VIII (Sept. 1880), 120. In his final report one officer even offered suggestions for the more effective placement of graduates through alumni organization. M. I. T., *Rep.*, 1876, pp. 163–64. A Massachusetts visiting committee found the drill "apparently viewed by the students more as a recreation than a task." Mass. A. C., *Rep.*, 1872, p. 111.

47. Nat. Agr. Con., 1872, *op. cit.*, 74.

48. M. I. T., *Rep.*, 1876, pp. 154–63.

49. *I. A. C. Student*, Sept. 30, 1893.

50. M. I. T., *Rep.*, 1875, pp. 24–25; Viles, *op. cit.*, 217.

51. Mass. A. C., *Rep.*, 1875, p. 74, 1876, pp. 32–33.

52. Ia. St. A. C., *Rep.*, 1886–87, p. 81; Nev. St. Univ., *Rep*, 1889, p. 12; Viles, *op. cit.*, 216–17. The Iowa women's companies gave exhibition drills at the Columbian Exposition.

53. Iowa St. Agr. Coll., *Addresses at Opening*, 12–13, 29–40, 42–47. In his

brief senatorial service, Welch had advocated equal pay for women in federal bureaus. *Cong. Globe,* 40 Cong., 3 Sess., 1775.

54. At Chicago conference in 1871, Mich. St. Bd. of Agr., *Rep.,* 1871, pp. 357–58.

55. Fernald, *op. cit.,* 48–49.

56. Comr. Agr., *Rep.,* 1874, p. 318.

57. Reprinted in Allan Nevins, *Amer. Soc. Hist. by British Travellers,* 429. For an intimate and pleasing view of coeducation at Cornell in 1881, see *Letters of John Fiske,* 462–65. See also A. D. White, *op. cit.,* I, 398–402; *Cong. Rec.,* 46 Cong., 3 Sess., 188–91 (coeducational statistics) ; N. Hamp. Bd. of Agr., *Rep.,* 1883–84, p. 85. In the Iowa legislative investigation of 1874 a professor was charged by a hostile colleague with misogyny—a term that had to be defined for the committee. Ia. Gen. Assem. Joint Com., *Investigation of Ia. Agr. Coll.,* 499–500. Laur. Larsen's observations in 1866 were very unsympathetic. *Norwegian-American Studies and Records,* X, 117–22. For a reasoned estimate of the contribution of the state university to the education of women, J. B. Angell's Johns Hopkins' address in *State Aid to Higher Education,* 39.

58. H. D. Sheldon, *Student Life and Customs,* 256–59. Elaborate lists of rules, regulations, and procedures are to be found in the early announcements and catalogues. A vivid, sympathetic description of a regimented college day is in Roberts, *op. cit.,* 165–66. Student recollections seem unanimous that the faculty-controlled student government had no developmental possibilities. Opinion in the Iowa investigation differed widely as to the justice and effectiveness of the college governing system. W. T. Hornaday remarked of his college experience: "At Ames everything was to the good except the Bolshevik plan of student self government; which is a world-beater system for the payment of personal grudges against students who do not sufficiently kow-tow." *Ia. St. Coll. Alumnus,* XXIV (1929) , 239.

59. *Aurora* (Ia. A. C.) , XVII (July, 1888) , 8–9. The antifraternity movement was mainly in the West. Sheldon, *op. cit.,* 222–24; Fernald, *op. cit.,* 363–64.

60. Records and reminiscences in the various college histories; student papers of which the *Aurora* and the first volumes of the *Student* of the Iowa A. C. are typical.

61. Before a legislative committee a clerical professor denounced a colleague as profane and a bad moral influence on the ground that under the provocation of being asked to show special leniency to the son of a "man of prominence" he had uttered the "substantive damn" and on another occasion the "adjective damned" and a former student reported similar profane utterance made in the midst of surveying difficulties. The censorious professor further indicted the culprit for deliberately absenting himself from chapel. Ia. Gen. Assem. Joint Com., *op. cit.,* 474, 500–505, 513. At the seventy-fifth anniversary celebration, it is interesting to note, this same "profane professor" was named among the great moral leaders in the making of the college. Harvey W. Wiley scandalized the college community at Purdue by playing baseball in uniform and even more by riding a high-wheeled bicycle. For the latter offense he was reprimanded by the board. Wiley, *op. cit.,* 156–58.

62. Pa. St. Coll., *Rep.,* 1875, p. 5. Religious activities, however, were not allowed to interfere wtih college regulations. At the Iowa Agricultural College a company of students came before the discipline committee for attending a camp meeting, and the president reported to the faculty that 30 of the group had promised "not to be guilty of a like offense in the future." MS. Faculty Minutes, Aug. 29, 1870, p. 49. At the same institu tion in 1882 two students were penalized for attending a church social and securing entrance on their return by the chapel window. Ia. Agr. Coll., MS. Judicial Committee, p. 73.

63. A major objective of the Massachusetts Agricultural College was held to be the inculcation of correct ethical and religious principles and the formation of good habits. "For this purpose, the Bible is adapted as an invaluable textbook, and its teachings regarded as constituting the best rules for the conduct of life." In addition to daily chapel, Bible classes, and a student union, "moral science" was studied daily for one term. *Rep.,* 1869, p. 16. A lay president gave the following hortative catalogue statement of his course in ethics: "Hickok's Moral Science, revised by President Seelye, is used as the principal textbook (1886) because on the whole it seems to present the correct theory of moral obligation. The textbook is supplemented by lectures, the main object of the whole being to impress upon the mind of the student the belief that man has a moral nature; that this world is, for man, a moral world, created and ruled by a Moral Being for moral ends. That, in no narrow sense, 'honesty is the best policy', this is, *right conduct* morally is the wisest *settled principle of action.* That our spiritual environment favors right conduct. That there is 'a Power not ourselves that makes for righteousness,' and that it is, in the highest sense, wise to work with, and not against that Power. And, finally, that the Christian Scriptures, apprehended by our reason, are on the whole our best means of learning what is the mind and will of that Power. Principles are sought; mere questions of casuistry are avoided." W. I. Chamberlain, Ia. St. Coll., *Catalogue,* 1886, pp. 63–64. The clerical president of the Kansas Agricultural College "frequently deplored the undercurrent of caricature in Dickens' books, which he believed was not Christlike." David Fairchild, *op. cit.,* 15.

64. A clerical professor of literature issued a series of pamphlets to combat the "materialistic trend in science." Naturally he invited and got vigorous response from scientific associates. *Aurora,* VI, Apr.–Sept., 1878, VII, Mar., 1879. For the desire for nonsectarian religious leadership in a state university, see W. I. Chamberlain and W. Q. Scott in W. S. Holt, *Historical Scholarship,* 228, 233–34; T. C. Mendenhall, ed., *Hist. Ohio St. Univ.,* I, 76–77. When H. W. Wiley was elected president of Purdue is 1900, Trustee Benjamin Harrison secured a reversal of the decision on the plea that Wiley was a bachelor and that he was not regular in his church attendance. Wiley, *op. cit.,* 161–62.

65. The rule of the Iowa Agricultural College on "Public Worship" explicated: "The object of those sermons is to emphasize the principles of the Christian religion, but in a State institution like this, it would be manifestly improper to teach or controvert the tenets of sectarianism." MS. Faculty Minutes, May 28, 1883, p. 379. One state university president had the theory that the only way to keep his institution nonsectarian was to have all the leading denominations represented on the faculty. Viles, *op. cit.,* 180–81.

66. A. D. White, *op. cit.,* I, 279, 315, 403–407, 422–26; J. B. Angell, *From Vt. to Mich.,* 17, 55–80, 128; same, *State Aid to Higher Education,* 34–35; D. C. Gilman, *Univ. Probs.,* 177–79; C. W. Eliot, *Educational Reform,* 42–43; A. C. Flick, *Hist. St. of N. Y.,* IX, 121. Some institutions had special sectarian complications. A Louisiana president recommended a triple chaplaincy to represent the leading faiths. La. St. Univ., *Rep.,* 1877–78, p. 43; W. L. Fleming, *La. St. Univ.,* 81, 175–76, 245–46.
67. *Aurora,* VIII (Aug., 1880) , 97, XVI (May, 1887) , 72–73.
68. *Cong. Rec.,* 44 Cong., 1 Sess., 2766.
69. Walker, *op. cit.,* 96.

Chapter VII. Reconciling Science and Practice

1. T. I. Mairs, *Pa. Pioneers in Sci. Agr.,* 21, 108; W. J. Beal, *Mich. Agr. Coll.,* 135. The Iowa legislative investigation committee in 1874 repeatedly sought evidence on the meaning of the term "model farm," specified in the original state act, but received only indefinite and conflicting opinions. Some institutions, however, claimed to provide both in the same farm. E. g. Univ. of Tenn., *Rep.,* 1879–80, pp. 32–33.
2. An early domestic science teacher contributed a witty article to the student magazine on the subject, "A Plea for Pie." The essay, appropriately enough, was printed in the literary department but a correction note at the end advised that it should have been included in the scientific. *Aurora* (Ia. A. C.) , XII (June, 1884) , 81–82.
3. Ill. Indus. Univ., *Rep.,* 1880–82, pp. 56–57.
4. For convenient summary of early agricultural research, see A. C. True, *Agr. Research in U. S.*
5. A. C. True and V. A. Clark, *Agr. Exp. Stas.,* 32–33; R. H. Chittenden, *Sheffeld Sci. School,* I, 200–203; E. A. Osborne, *Letter–Files of S. W. Johnson,* 192–256.
6. True and Clark, *op. cit.,* 31–32; Univ. of Cal., *Rep.,* 1881–82, pp. 15, 25–27. For Hilgard's own views on the experimental function, see his articles in the *Atlantic Monthly,* XLIX (1882) , 540–41, 653–54.
7. True and Clark, *op. cit.,* 34; True, *Agr. Research,* 82–117.
8. Mich. St. Bd. of Agr., *Rep.,* 1883, pp. 32–33; C. R. Woodward and I. N. Wallar, *N. J. Exp. Sta.,* 29–30, 40–48; Mairs, *op. cit.,* 80; M. C. Fernald, *Me. St. Coll.,* 272–73; M. H. Pollitt, *J. K. Patterson,* 144; I. P. Roberts, *Autobiog.,* 205–207, 218–20; Successful Farming, *Master Minds of Dairying,* 11, 66–69; Neb. Univ., *Rep.,* 1883–84, p. 36; *Cong. Rec.,* 46 Cong., 3 Sess., 189.
9. True and Clark, *op. cit.,* 30–31.
10. *Ibid.,* 34–35.
11. Mich. St. Bd. of Agr., *Rep.,* 1883, pp. 30–32; Nat. Agr. Con., 1872, *Proc.,*

25, 61–68; Con. of Agriculturists, 1882, *Proc.*, 13–42, 1883, pp. 109–10; True, *Agr. Ed.*, 204–205; True, *Agr. Res.*, 123.

12. Con. of Delegates, 1885, *Proc.*, 27–42, 104–105; True, *Agr. Res.*, 124–28; *Cong. Rec.*, 49 Cong., I Sess., 154, 530, 2 Sess., 631, 721–25, 1039, 1083, 1155, 1300, 2282–84. The bill was passed in the House under suspension of rules, by a vote of 152 to 12. On Colman's relation to the bill, see Eugene Davenport in Soc. for Prom. Agr. Sci., *Proc.*, 1907, p. 51; *Dict. Am. Biog.*, IV, 314.

13. S. B. Doten, *Univ. of Nev.*, 59, 75.

14. *Agricultural Science*, I (1887), 244; Mairs, *op. cit.*, 11; Beal, *op. cit.*, 300–301; C. W. Dabney, *Universal Education in the South*, II, 178; *Iowa Homestead*, XXXV (Nov. 21, 1890), 8–9, (Dec. 19), 9; Jonas Viles, *Univ. of Mo.*, 193. Peter Collier, director of the New York Experiment Station at Geneva, wrote to S. W. Johnson, Feb. 2, 1890: "I wish you would consult with Brewer and tell me of any good available men in any branch of agricultural science." Osborne, *op. cit.*, 238.

15. True and Clark, *op. cit.*, 54, 68–75.

16. *Ibid.*, 76–78; Con. of Agrs., 1883, *op. cit.*, 52; Eugene Davenport in Univ. of Ill., *Rel. of Fed. Gov't. to Ed.*, 14–17; same, Texas A. & M., *Semi-Centennial*, 46, 56; P. P. Claxton, Rutgers College, *Anniversary*, 217–18; Neb. Univ., *Rep.*, 1887–88, pp. 48–49; *Cong. Rec.*, 51 Cong., 1 Sess., 6088 (statement of committee of Assoc. of Agr. Colls.).

17. Dept. of Agr., *Yearbook*, 1899, pp. 180–81; Osborne, *op. cit.*, 232. At the national gathering in 1872 a universtiy president had moved "that this convention recommend all the colleges and universities of the country to introduce a suitable text-book on agriculture. Such a work as Morrison's Manual, it seems to me, should be studied as well as chemistry or botany or any other subject." Whether feeling that such general recommendation was beyond its jurisdiction or that there was no text that could be safely endorsed, the meeting took no recorded action. Nat. Agr. Con., 1872, *op. cit.*, 25.

18. S. P. E. E., *Proc.*, 1894, pp. 30, 168.

19. *Cong. Rec.*, 46 Cong., 3 Sess. (1880), 188–91 (report on equipment of different colleges); N. H. Bd. of Agr., *Rep.*, 1883–84, p. 88; Con. of Dels., 1885, *op. cit.*, 80, 127; Assoc. of Agr. Colls. and Exp. Stas., *Proc.*, V (1891), 106–108; Beal, *op. cit.*, 201; Fernald, *op. cit.*, 227, 253–55; Roberts, *op. cit.*, 195, 232–34, 253; Calvin Stebbins, *H. H. Goodell*, 260.

20. S. P. E. E., *Proc.*, 1893, pp. 96–98, 152–53, 160–61, 312, 1894, pp. 149, 280–83, 1896, p. 40, 1900, pp. 337–40; J. S. Peck, *Functions of the Laboratory in Engr. Ed.*, 6–10. Even history professors in technical colleges were beginning to talk of their "laboratories." W. S. Holt, *Historical Scholarship*, 63.

21. S. P. E. E., *Proc.*, 1893, pp. 244–46, 292.

22. Dept. of Agr., *Yearbook*, 1899, p. 182. In the seventies Charles Kendall Adams, then of the Univ. of Mich., in advising that Cornell should follow Johns Hopkins and develop work on a graduate level, gave the deprecatory estimate of applied science study: "The industrial and agricultural

departments cannot, of course, be improved; but they ought not to be allowed to keep the others down." C. F. Smith, *C. K. Adams,* 45.

23. Assoc. of Agr. Colls. and Exp. Stas., *Proc.,* III (1889), 23, 126–30; Sec. of War, *Rep.,* 1890, pp. 17, 278–81. In the debate on the grant bill of 1890, Morrill made the exaggerated claim that land-grant graduates would provide a reserve force of "a value hardly less than that confidently relied upon from our renowned national institution at West Point." *Cong. Rec.,* 51 Cong., 1 Sess, 6084.

24. C. M. Fuess, *Amherst,* 197; Merle Curti, *Soc. Ideas of Amer. Educators,* 246; Mass. A. C., *Rep.,* 1869, p. 14; Brown Univ., *Rep.,* 1870, p. 11, 1874, p. 10, 1876, pp. 9–10; M. I. T., *Rep.,* 1874, pp. xiii–xiv, 1875, pp. 27–33; Univ. of Cal., *Rep.,* 1889–90, p. 98.

25. *American Colleges,* 187. Eliot did not mention the subject in his inaugural in 1869.

26. J. A. Krout, *Annals of Sport,* 79–84, 145, 188; Stephen Epler, *Six-Man Football,* 1–4; C. H. Patten and W. T. Field, *Eight o'Clock Chapel,* 277–83; Fuess, *op. cit.,* 197–201; R. T. Ely, *Ground Under Our Feet,* 30–31; H. D. Sheldon, *Student Life and Customs,* 230–34; H. W. Wiley, *Autobiog.,* 111.

27. Brown Univ., *Rep.,* 1870, pp. 11–12, 1884, pp. 9–13; F. A. P. Barnard, *Rise of a University,* 205–206; A. T. Steinel and D. W. Working, *Agr. in Col.,* 590–91; Beal, *op. cit.,* 220. Hadley felt that athletics unified the various divisions of the student body at Yale. *Harper's Magazine,* LXXXVIII (1894), 767–68.

28. *Rise of a Univ.,* 207.

29. F. P. Rand, *Yesterdays at Mass. St. Coll.,* 29–31; Mass. A. C., *Rep.,* 1871, p. 16.

30. *Autobiog.,* I, 352. Dr. Harvey W. Wiley, while professor of chemistry, organized the first baseball team at Purdue. W. M. Hepburn and L. M. Sears, *Purdue,* 78. For the evolution of athletics at the pioneer agricultural college, Beal, *op. cit.,* 219–21. President Smart of Purdue took the initiative in the organization of the Big Ten Conference in 1895. Hepburn and Sears, *op. cit.,* 166.

31. For instance, Brown Univ., *Rep.,* 1870, p. 12; J. B. Horner, *Ore. Hist. Quart.,* XXXI, 48. At the college excursions held by the Iowa State Coll. at the beginning of the new century, intercollegiate athletic contests were among the most popular features of the exhibitions and entertainments provided to enable the citizens to know their college.

32. *Cong. Rec.* 44 Cong., I Sess., 2766; see also his statement in 1880, *ibid.,* 44 Cong., 3 Sess., 149–51.

33. N. Y. St. Agr. Soc., *Trans.,* 1868, p. 66; White, *op. cit.,* I, 378–83.

34. *University Problems,* 171–73.

35. *Aurora,* XII (Mar., 1884), 15–16. Eliot recognized the neglect of the social as well as of the physical and natural sciences. See his article of 1884, reprinted in *Educational Reform,* 105–109. On the contemporary problem of citizenship teaching in the schools, S. W. Mendum, "How to Teach Citizenship," *North Am. Rev.,* CLII (1891), 120–23.

36. N. H. A. and M. Coll., *Rep.*, 1891–92, pp. 42–43.

37. I. L. Kandel, *Fed. Aid for Voc. Ed.*, 110–15; Con. of Dels., 1885, *op. cit.*, 167; Fernald, *op. cit.*, 57; Ia. A. C., *Rep.*, 1876–77, p. 114; same, *Catalogue*, 1886, pp. 50, 62–63; A. S. Welch, *Syllabus of Short Histories of the Various Civilizing Forces* (1887).

38. Dept. of Agr., *Yearbook*, 1899, p. 175. The Univ. of Ill., 1867–90, listed a course in "the history and literature of agriculture" (Kandel, *op. cit.*, 115) but in line with current emphasis it was doubtless technical rather than social and institutional.

39. *Atlantic Monthly*, LV (1885), 444–50. See also on the increasing need for this study, Eliot, *Century*, XXVIII (1884), 208–209. But as late as the nineties economics was not regarded in popular estimation as a practicable life work, and like the other social sciences had difficulty in gaining established academic recognition. Ely, *op. cit.*, 124; Holt, *op. cit.*, 65–66, 213–14.

40. N. H. A. and M. Coll., *Rep.*, 1890, p. 17.

41. Buckham to Morrill, Nov. 23, 1894, Morrill Papers.

42. Morrill to Greeley, Jan. 15, 1870, *Forum*, XXIV (1897), 404. "All our college-educated men," he concluded, "are educated as Free-Traders. This ought not to be so."

43. For such attitudes, reports of literary societies in Hepburn and Sears, *op. cit.*, 179–80, and of literary societies, junior exhibitions, and commencements in *Aurora* (Ia. A. C.). Robert M. LaFollette won an interstate oratorical contest in 1879, not on a question of public utilities or international relations but on the subject "Iago," and a student paper that printed the oration commented, "He seems to revel in Shakespeare's characters." *Ibid.*, VII (May, 1879), 1–4.

44. See, for instance, a recognition and appreciation of the changed policy in *Aurora*, XVI (Apr., 1887), 45–46. A rather remarkable expedient in the transition from the old paternalism was the use of a contractual agreement between entering students and the faculty, the president signing for the latter. Ia. A. C., *Rep.*, 1878–79, p. 146. This institution after passing through the officially designated types of "student government" (faculty-directed), "executive government" proclaimed under a dictatorial president, and "faculty government" under a more temporizing one, gradually and without benefit of special decrees came around to this modernized adjustment. *Ibid.*, 1884–85, p. 151; 1888–89, p. 157.

45. The *Aurora* (IX, 107) of Sept., 1881, reported the case of two students against whom an unfavorable decision had been rendered on the question of right to vote when not dependent on parents, even though their residence was maintained only for educational purposes. The student opinion was that this case was different from previous ones cited as precedents and a defense fund of $150 was raised and an appeal planned. See also the arguments for student voting in *ibid.*, XVII (Nov., 1888), 7, and XXI (Oct., 1892), 1.

46. The literary societies at one college adopted a most thorough plan "to eradicate our ignorance of and lack of interest in current topics." The world's happenings were grouped into five classes which suggest the

inclusiveness of a modern news weekly—(1) politics and governmental affairs; (2) foreign news; (3) science and useful arts; (4) social events; and (5) religion, art, and literature. The subjects were to be taken up in rotation by each society, so that the entire list would be presented each week, and supposedly the information disseminated through the student body. *Aurora,* XIX (Sept., 1890), 99–100.

47. The colleges' participations in regional and national programs, while belonging to a later period, were the natural consequence of the progression of this social control.

Chapter VIII. Any Person in Any Study

1. It has been suggested that Cornell's original phrasing of the celebrated motto was even more forceful, if less elegant, than the official version. *Scribner's Magazine* XCIX, 317; D. S. Jordan, *Trend of Amer. Univ.,* 90. In 1869 Daniel Read of the University of Missouri and formerly of Ohio University and the state universities of Indiana and Wisconsin apparently expressed a similar sentiment. J. A. Woodburn, *Hist. of Ind. Univ.,* I, 190.

2. J. G. Schurman, in Univ. of Mo., *Exercises at Inauguration of A. R. Hill,* 61; Amer. Soc. of Mech. Engineers, *Trans.* XIV, 875. Cf. David Starr Jordan, "The man who knows the steam engine has an equal place in the university and an equal share in the honors of scholarship." *Op. cit.,* 60.

3. Mass. A. C., *Rep.,* 1882, p. 3.

4. Ill. Indus. Univ., *Rep.,* 1880–82, p. 63.

5. N. H. Bd. of Agr., *Rep.,* 1883–84, p. 86.

6. H. H. Goodell in *New England Magazine* (1890), Calvin Stebbins, *Goodell,* 265. Cf. *Cultivator and Country Gentleman,* LI (1886), 549; Oscar Clute in A. C. McLaughlin, *Higher Ed. in Mich.* (Bureau of Education, Circular of Information, 1891), 112.

7. Dept. of Agr., *Yearbook,* 1899, p. 174.

8. A. F. A. Liautard in *American Veterinary Review,* I, 8–10.

9. W. T. Hewett, *Cornell Univ.,* II, 350–53; Con. of Agriculturists, 1882, *Proc.,* 67–77, 133–34.

10. C. H. Stange, *History of Vet. Med., Ia. St. Coll.,* 6; A. Rosenberger, *Millikan Stalker,* 18; A. J. Klein, *Survey of Land-Grant Colls.,* II, 327.

11. Robert Fletcher in S. P. E. E., *Proc.,* 1896, p. 38.

12. *Ibid.,* 1893, p. 167.

13. *Ibid.,* 1900, p. 37, Ill. Indus. Univ., *Rep.,* 1880–82, pp. 60–61; La. St. Univ. and A. and M. Coll., *Rep.,* 1880–82, p. 21; N. H. Bd. of Agr., *Rep.,* 1883–84, pp. 69, 82; W. M. Hepburn and L. M. Sears, *Purdue,* 89–91; Rutgers Coll., *Anniversary,* 277–78.

14. S. P. E. E., *Investigation of Engr. Ed.,* 545–47.

15. W. E. Stone in *Hist. Ohio St. Univ.*, III, 151.

16. C. R. Mann., *Study of Engr. Ed.*, 6–7.

17. R. H. Chittenden, *Sheffield Scientific School*, I, 150–52.

18. A. D. White, *Autobiog.*, I, 372–78.

19. Me. Bd. of Agr. (dig. agr. socs.), *Rep.*, 1856, pp. 128–29; Ill. Agr. Soc., *Trans.*, 1861–64, pp. 587–88; Cal. St. Agr. Soc., *Trans.*, 1871, p. 425; Jonathan Periam, *Groundswell*, 537–38.

20. Willystine Goodsell, *Pioneers of Women's Education*, 197–207.

21. To S. W. Johnson, Mar. 16, 1855, True Papers. A western agricultural paper, the following year, was no less facetious about this sort of training: "It is proposed to establish in some of our cities an institution in which the science of Spinology, Weaveology, and Cookology may be taught to young ladies, and where, after obtaining these accomplishments, they may receive a regular diploma, with the honorary degree of F.F.W.—Fit for Wives." *Northwestern Farmer* (Dubuque, Iowa), I (1856), 342.

22. Ia. St. A. C., *Rep.*, 1878–79, pp. 13, 91–95, 177–79; H. V. Keefer, *Develop. of Home Econ. Curricula of Ia. St. Coll.*, 1869–1913 (manuscript thesis Iowa State College); Bur. of Ed., *Training Schools of Cookery* (Circular of Information, 1879), 35–36.

23. Bur. of Ed., *op. cit.*, 34–35; Kan. St. A. C., *Rep.*, 1885–86, p. 5; Isabel Bevier, *Home Econ. in Ed.*, 123.

24. Bur. of Ed., *op. cit.*, 33–34; Ill. Indus. Univ., *Rep.*, 1874–76, p. 67, 1878–80, p. 16.

25. Bevier, *op. cit.*, 128. A course with a special degree was planned at Missouri in 1880, but it did not prove popular and was soon abandoned. Jonas Viles, *Univ. of Mo.*, 203.

26. Bevier, *op. cit.*, 114, 147, 195–96; C. L. Hunt, *Ellen H. Richards*, 177–93, 280–81. B. R. Andrews terms Catherine Beecher's *Treatise on Domestic Economy* (1841) "the first text-book in Home Economics." *Journal of Home Economics*, IV, 211–22.

27. See, for example, the general science course established by Walker at M. I. T., J. P. Munroe, *Walker*, 218–19.

28. The pioneer Rensselaer Institue at first conferred the degrees bachelor of arts in Rensselaer School and master of arts in Rensselaer School—abbreviated A.B. (r.s.) and M.A. (r.s.). The inclusion of the qualifying letters was held to be essential to the legal use of the degrees. Ten years later the degrees bachelor of natural science (B.N.S.) and civil engineer (C.E.) were awarded. P. C. Ricketts, *Hist. of Rensselaer Poly. Inst.*, 40, 81.

29. Ill. Indus. Univ., *Rep.*, 1876–78, p. 62.

30. Confer. Pres's. and Dels. St. Univs. and Colls., 1877, *Proc.*, 180–83, 192. Illinois followed, in form at least, these recommendations. Ill. Indus. Univ., *Rep.*, 1878–80, pp. 42–43.

31. *University Problems*, 135.

32. W. L. Fleming, *La. St. Univ.*, 208, 397. Delaware College in the pre-

land-grant period designed a normal course for pupils from the district schools leading to the award, for those "found qualified to act as teachers and worthy of the degree," of "master of school keeping." *Delaware Notes,* VIII, 59. Such a use, it might be noted, marked a return, in a most elemental manner, to the original significance of a degree.

33. Engineering organizations gave much consideration to degrees. *Engineering News,* XXVIII (1892), 232, 256; S. P. E. E., *Proc.,* 1894, pp. 59–94, 288, 1895, pp. 152–56, 1897, pp. 308–309. The *Engineering News* (XXIX (1893), 109) in commenting on the abuses of degrees in general science courses, made the caustic observation that if it were necessary to keep the M.S. degree for such students, "let us at least turn the lie into Latin and make it S.M.! It seems less offensive to tell lies in Latin; it seems medieval and fitting; but lies told in modern English and solemnly attested seem—well, rather bad form to say the least, and rather bad morals, as well, according to modern ideas."

34. W. J. Beal, *Mich. Agr. Coll.,* 440.

35. The Ia. A. C. in 1886 conferred the graduate degree, master of domestic economy (M. D. E.) upon two candidates. *Rep.,* 1886–87, p. 185. In 1899 the home economics conference at Lake Placid under the leadership of Ellen H. Richards secured the change of classification of their subject under the Dewey library system from useful arts to the economics of consumption. Hunt, *op. cit.,* 266.

36. Clarence Ousley, *A. and M. Coll. of Texas,* 88–89.

37. W. H. Powers, *S. Dak. St. Coll.,* 8; E. A. Bryan, *Wash. St. Coll.,* 189. The Kansas Agricultural College conferred the honorary master of arts degree upon the entire first class (of five members) four years after their graduation. J. T. Willard, *Kan. St. Coll.,* 64.

38. At the beginning of Cornell, President White secured the adoption of a rule that no honorary degrees should be conferred. The rule was not broken during his administration and only twice afterward, under a mistaken notion as to the desire of the alumni. White, *op. cit.,* I, 389. Trustee Hayes reported a division of opinion among the Ohio board in 1890 over the conferring of four honorary degrees. He was "opposed to the practice" and concluded, no doubt with relief, "Our honorary degrees probably illegal. Referred to attorney–general." *Diary and Letters,* IV, 582. A few years ago a popular magazine writer in a satirical article on honorary degrees referred to the granting of a D. D. to a prominent evangelist by a leading land-grant college. It was promptly pointed out that the college, thus uncomplimentarily characterized, conferred no degrees honoris causa and would in any case from its particular interest and status not presume to enter the theological field. *Harper's Magazine,* CLXXV, 43, and the correspondence pages of the following issue.

At least one separate land-grant college early in its career (1868) did confer a D. D. degree upon a clergyman who was chaplain of an army post and a member of their board of regents, apparently with no sense of impropriety or incongruity. Willard, *op. cit.,* 444. This is the only case of such an award by a land-grant college that has been noted although the degree was sought from some of them as late as the first decade of the present century.

39. Univ. of Tenn., *Rep.*, 1879–80, p. 14.

40. N. H. Bd. of Agr., *Rep.*, 1883–84, pp. 82–85; Successful Farming, *Master Minds of Dairying,* 67–68; W. W. Folwell, *Autobiog.*, 189–90; O. W. Firkins, *Cyrus Northrop,* 350–52; N.E.A., *Proc.*, 1890, pp. 215–18; Eugene Davenport in Texas A. and M., *Semi-Centennial,* 53–56.

41. Dept. of Agr., *Yearbook,* 1899, p. 175; Wis. St. Agr. Soc., *Trans.*, 1888, p. 86.

42. XXXIV, 249.

43. N. E. A., *Proc.*, 1888, p. 291.

44. Quoted in H. S. Olcott, *Yale Agr. Lectures,* 8.

45. Olcott, *op. cit.;* John Hamilton, *Farmers' Institutes,* 23; Chittenden, *op. cit.*, I, 112.

46. Hamilton, *op. cit.*, 20–94; Beal, *op. cit.*, 158–59; M. C. Fernald, *Me. St. Coll.*, 262; C. R. Woodward and I. N. Waller, *N. J. Exp. Sta.*, 18–19; I. P. Roberts, *Autobiog.*, 166; Barton Morgan, *Exten. Serv. Ia. St. Coll.*, 13–16; Hepburn and Sears, *op. cit.*, 90, 114; Successful Farming, *op. cit.*, 69–70; A. T. Steinel and D. W. Working, *Agr. in Col.*, 593, 611; Ore. St. Agr. Coll., *Rep.*, 1889–90, p. 9.

47. A. C. True, *Hist. Agr. Exten.*, 14–25; C. B. Smith and M. C. Wilson, *Agr. Exten. Sys.*, 29; F. J. Turner to H. B. Adams, Sept. 27, Dec. 8, 1890, W. S. Holt, *Historical Scholarship,* 136, 144–45.

48. Roberts, *op. cit.*, 247–60; T. C. Atkeson, *Pioneering in Agr.*, 135–39; Successful Farming, *op. cit.*, 67–69; W. W. Ferrier, *Univ. of Cal.*, 371–72; Con. of Dels., 1885, *Proc.*, 116; Hamilton, *op. cit.*, 18, 94–96; N. H. A. and M. Coll., *Rep.*, 1890, p. 7.

49. Editorial in *American Agriculturist,* LI (1892), 8; Con. of Delegates, 1885, *op. cit.*, 114–15.

50. Beal, *op. cit.*, 173–74; True, *op. cit.*, 13; A. C. True and V. A. Clark, *Exp. Stas.*, 66; Woodward and Waller, *op. cit.*, 492–95; *Southern Planter,* XLVI, Oct., 1885 ff. (a series of "Virginia Agricultural and Mechanical College Papers").

Chapter IX. Union and Strength

1. A. C. True, *Agr. Ed.*, 144; Ia. Agr. Coll., *Rep.*, 1866–67, pp. 25–58; Ohio A. and M. Coll., *Rep.*, 1874, p. 5; W. M. Hepburn and L. M. Sears, *Purdue,* 38, 43; Jonas Viles, *Univ. of Mo.*, 138–52.

2. L. S. Merriam, *Higher Ed. in Tenn.* (Bureau of Education, Circular of Information, 1893), 71–72; *Rural New-Yorker,* XL (1881), 37–38; A. G. Holmes and G. R. Sherrill, *Clemson,* 159–60, 193. General Stephen A. Lee soon after his election to the presidency of Mississippi Agricultural College paid a visit to the Iowa Agricultural College and made extended observations of agricultural organization and methods in that state. *Aurora,* VIII (June, 1880), 68–69; *Iowa City Republican,* June 9, 1880.

3. *University Problems,* 169.

4. "We shall constantly look towards Cornell for light," Folwell assured White in 1869. W. W. Folwell, *Autobiog.,* 199. Walker wrote to Mayo-Smith in 1890: "Indeed, and indeed, if I were President of Columbia, I should say to my Professors, Get thee forth; go and see the schools of technology and the other Colleges of the land and participate in the festivities thereof. Especially go to Boston and learn of it." J. P. Munroe, *Walker,* 341. Mass. A. C. had for some years an arrangement with Boston University for interchanging courses and degrees. Mass. A. C., *Rep.,* 1876, pp. 14–15; Calvin Stebbins, *Goodell,* 259. At the establishment of the separate land-grant college in Kentucky in 1879, President Patterson circularized the other land-grant institutions on amount and administration of endowment, annual appropriations, and extent and value of property. Full and frank replies were promptly made. M. H. Pollitt, *Patterson,* 115–19.
5. True, *op. cit.,* 201.
6. This "convention of friends of agricultural education" was reported in the Ill. Indus. Univ., *Rep.,* 1870–71, pp. 215–35, and the Mich. St. Bd. of Agr., *Rep.,* 1871, pp. 291–389.
7. Nat. Agr. Con., 1872, *Proc.;* True, *op. cit.,* 195.
8. Conference of Presidents and Other Delegates of St. Univs. and Colls., 1877, *Proc.*
9. Dept. of Agr., Con. of Agriculturists, 1882, *Proc.*
10. *Ibid.,* 1883.
11. Dept. of Agr., Con. of Dels., from Agr. Colls. and Exp. Stas., 1885, *Proc.*
12. *Ibid.,* 138–40, 159; True, *op. cit.,* 208–11; A. C. True and V. A. Clark, *Agr. Exp. Stas.,* 83–85; E. A. Osborne, *Letter–Files of S. W. Johnson,* 233; Pollitt, *op. cit.,* 142; Stebbins, *op. cit.,* 104–109; Milton Conover, *Office of Experiment Stations.*
13. Confer. of Presidents and Delegates, *op. cit.,* 190; Eaton to Morrill, May 1, 1880, Morrill Papers.
14. *Atlantic Monthly,* XLIX (1882), 660–61; see also, for more specific charges, Con. of Agriculturists, 1882, *op. cit.,* 49–50, 108–10, 144–47. In the commissioners' annual reports from 1865 to 1876, inclusive, there were reports from various colleges and general discussions of problems of industrial education. Pictures of college buildings were sometimes included. In 1877 with the administration of W. G. LeDuc, whose relations with the colleges were not cordial, this feature of the report was dropped.
15. Comr. of Agr., *Rep.,* 1868, pp. 1–2, 1871, p. 3, 1872, p. 4; Nat. Agr. Con., 1872, *op. cit.,* 53–54, 58–59, 76, 82; Con. of Agriculturists, 1882, *op. cit.,* 19; Con. of Delegates, 1885, *op. cit.,* 15.
16. Nat. Agr. Con., 1872, *op. cit.,* 66–68; Comr. Colman to S. W. Johnson, Feb. 2, 1888, Dept. of Agr. Letter File; Osborne, *op. cit.,* 235–36.
17. Osborne, *op. cit.,* 237.
18. Folwell to White, Aug. 30, 1869, Folwell, *op. cit.,* 196; Nat. Agr. Con., 1872, *op. cit.,* 20, 23–24; *Cong. Globe,* 42 Cong., 3 Sess., 39–40; A. D. Smith to Morrill, May 13, 1872, Morrill Papers.

19. *Cong. Globe,* 42 Cong., 3 Sess., 524–26.

20. *Ibid.,* 40, 1688.

21. N. E. A., *Proc.,* 1873, pp. 32–35.

22. *Ibid.,* 44.

23. *Ibid.,* 40–43, 47, 70–73, 1874, pp. 58–76, 204–12, 1880, pp. 230–34; Mass. A. C., *Rep.,* 1873, pp. 8–9; Ohio A. and M. Coll., *Rep.,* 1874, p. 13; A. D. White, *The Relations of the National and State Governments to Advanced Education* (reprint from *Old and New,* 1874); White to Morrill, Aug. 25, 1873, Nov. 2, 1874, Morrill Papers; G. H. Cook to Morrill, Oct. 6, 1873, *ibid.;* Pollitt, op. cit., 102.

24. N. E. A., *Proc.,* 1873, p. 33.

25. *Ibid.,* 44.

26. Mass. A. C., *Rep.,* 1873, pp. 8–9.

27. Ohio A. and M. Coll., *Rep.,* 1874, p. 13.

28. N. E. A., *Proc.,* 1873, p. 42.

29. *Cong. Rec.,* 43 Cong., 1 Sess., 1131.

30. Atherton to Morrill, Jan. 10, 1874, Morrill Papers. President Grant's speech at a gathering of veterans in Des Moines, September 29, 1875, was misquoted, intentionally or accidentally, in a way to indicate the General's opposition to state and federal aid to education beyond the common schools. Sectarian opponents of publicly supported colleges sought to capitalize the speech for their ends. L. F. Parker, *Higher Education in Iowa* (Bur. of Education, Circular of Information, 1893), 105–108.

31. *House Rep.,* 43 Cong., 2 Sess., No. 57, p. 10. White had written to Monroe with the purpose of persuading him of the great service that he could render by "breaking away from his Oberlin college notions" and becoming a leader of the new education. White to Morrill, Nov. 2, 1874, Morrill Papers.

32. P. R. V. Curoe, *Educational Attitudes of Labor,* 80–81.

33. Cf. G. W. Knight, "Land Grants for Education," *Papers of Amer. Hist. Assoc.,* I, No. 3, pp. 26–27.

34. Comr. of Ed., *Rep.,* 1870, pp. 418–21; N. E. A., *Proc.,* 1873, pp. 107–20 (Eliot's opposing report), 1874, pp. 173–87 (Hoyt's reply); L. C. Helderman, *George Washington, Patron of Learning,* 70–71; E. B. Wesley, *Univ. of the U. S.,* 14–17.

35. A convenient summary of proposed land-grant legislation, 1871–1890, with chronological outline and references to the documents was made by the bibliographer of the Association of Land-Grant Colleges, Dr. A. C. True, and published in their *Proceedings,* 1925, pp. 90–98. For a concise account see True, *Agr. Ed.,* 196–200.

36. Nat. Agr. Con., 1872, *op. cit.,* 22–23, 34–52, 57.

37. *Autobiography,* I, 265; Hoar to J. B. Bowman, Nov. 15, 1874, maintaining that common schools should have a portion of the fund, but expressing uncertainty as to whether Morrill would make such a concession. A copy

of this letter was sent by Bowman to Morrill (Nov. 18, 1874), with the hope that Morrill and Hoar could combine their interests. Morrill Papers.

38. E. P. Cubberley and E. C. Elliott, *State and County School Admin.,* II, 104–107. (Blair's account of his education bills before the Department of Superintendence, 1887.)

39. *Cong. Globe,* 42 Cong., 3 Sess., 36, 39–40, 526.

40. *Ibid.,* 524–26, 566–67, 1706–1708. Senator Thurman charged that the protectionist interests were seeking to deplete the treasury of land receipts. *Ibid.,* 529.

41. *Ibid.,* 40–41, 525, 1690; 44 Cong., 1 Sess., 2761, 2766; 46 Cong., 3 Sess., 225.

42. *Ibid.,* 44 Cong., 1 Sess., 2762, 2765. More fully Morrill's argument was that the increasing pressure of immigrant competition was necessitating a superior training of native workers. The longer experience and better system of apprenticeship of the European trained workers were being seriously felt in many crafts. "This, with the imported barbarous despotism reiging over our 'trades unions,' restricting the number of apprentices among the masters, not unlike the tyranny of wild horses, which kill off male colts, is tending to cripple the progressive growth of native mechanics, and the number of young men now seeking to learn trades is unnaturally circumscribed." The only hope of maintaining the position of the American laborer, as he viewed the matter, was in the greater productive efficiency of the native worker in both quantity and quality of output. This is an admirable statement of the conservative view of the breaking up of the old apprenticeship system, the substitution for which was to be not in collegiate but in secondary vocational training.

43. Con. of Agriculturists, 1882, *op. cit.,* 102–103.

44. Cf. True, *Agr. Ed.,* 199.

45. *Ibid.,* 211–12; letters to Morrill, Mar.–Aug., 1890, from Buckham (Vt.), Battle (N. C.), Scott (Ohio), Patterson (Ky.), White (Cornell), Goodell (Mass.), Morrill Papers; Pollitt, *op. cit.,* 144–45; Stebbins, *op. cit.,* 111; *Cong. Rec.,* 51 Cong., 1 Sess., 6088–89 (information given to Senate committee by the land-grant association). Representatives of the leading colleges had corresponded with Morrill in connection with each bill presented, and a number of them had come to Washington usually at their institutions' expense, to lobby for the measure, but these efforts heretofore had lacked unity.

46. *Cong. Rec.,* 51 Cong., 1 Sess., 6088, 6337–38, 8828–29, 8834–35, 8839; *Cultivator and Country Gentleman,* LV (1890), 736; W. J. Beal, *Mich. Agr. Coll.,* 410–11.

47. *Cong. Rec.,* 51 Cong., 1 Sess., 6369–72.

48. *Ibid.,* 6345, 6348, 6350; Morrill to Goodell, June 16, 1890, Stebbins, *op. cit.,* 110.

49. *Cong. Rec.,* 51 Cong., 1 Sess., 6086, 6333, 8832–33, 8836.

50. *Ibid.,* 8835–38.

51. *Ibid.*, 8836–39.

52. *Ibid.*, 6372, 8839, 8874.

53. *U. S. Stat. at Large,* XXVI, 417–19.

54. *Cong. Rec.,* 51 Cong., 1 Sess., 8829.

55. A. F. Macdonald, *Federal Aid,* 23–24; P. R. Mort, *Fed. Support for Pub. Ed.,* 50.

56. *The American Agriculturist* (L (1891), 100) compiled a report from the leading colleges on their plans for the utilization of the new fund. Contemporary official reports and college histories alike emphasize the act as the turning point for the particular institution. Naturally there was at times disagreement and rivalry over the expenditure. After a meeting of the Ohio board to consider the matter, Hayes reported, "We divided between equipment and new instruction." *Diary and Letters,* IV, 615.

57. A generation ago one of the most distinguished governors of an eastern state in observing the cultures of a dairy exhibit at the state fair was led to lament, "If we could only bottle up our politics that way!"

58. To Willard Fiske, Jan. 11, 1898, H. S. White, *Fiske,* 457.

59. A. S. Draper, *American Education,* 191. In a survey of the development of national scientific and educational institutions in 1890, G. Brown Goode of the Smithsonian Institution made this significant comment: "The movement was at first unpopular among American educators, but after a quarter of a century of trial the land-grant college system has not only demonstrated its right to exist, but is by many regarded as forming one of the chief strongholds of our national scientific prosperity." "The Origin of the National Scientific and Educational Institutions of the United States," *Papers of the Amer. Hist. Assoc.,* IV, Pt. 2, p. 70.

60. A survey as late as 1897 indicated the persistence of the older names in spite of long agitation for change:

agricultural and mechanical colleges	2
colleges of agriculture and mechanic arts	8
agricultural colleges	13
polytechnic institutes (Ala. and Va.)	2
institute of technology (M. I. T.)	1
state colleges	4
state universities	16
special name from donor (Clemson, Cornell, Purdue)	3

S. P. E. E., *Proc.,* 1897, p. 306.

INTRODUCTORY AND SELECTIVE BIBLIOGRAPHY

By the nature of this study and the conditions under which it was conducted, any approach to completeness in determining and exploiting the sources was impossible. The papers of certain outstanding leaders in the movement were not available; state and college archives and periodicals, utilized rather intensively for a single institution, might be multiplied for most of the land-grant colleges. It is believed, however, that the materials drawn upon have been reasonably representative and typical. They are listed here to indicate the bounds and bases of the findings and conclusions of the present exploratory essay and to suggest the main classes of determined and potential sources as an aid to more intensive studies of particular institutions and regions.

Bibliographical Guides

Association of Land-Grant Colleges. *Reports,* 1924–28. Burlington, Vt., 1924-28. Articles, with detailed specific references, by the bibliographer, A. C. True, on the history of agricultural education, research, and organization, including the legislative history of the Morrill Act of 1890 (1925, pp. 90–98) and of the Hatch Act of 1887 (1926, pp. 93–107).

Bidwell, P. W., and Falconer, J. I. *History of Agriculture in the Northern United States 1620–1860.* Washington, 1925. Contains a "classified and critical bibliography."

Bowker, R. R. *State Publications.* New York, 1908.

Edwards, E. E. *A Bibliography of the History of Agriculture in the United States.* U. S. Dept. of Agr., Misc. Pub. No. 84. Washington, 1930. The most complete and serviceable guide for students of American agricultural history in its different phases.

Gray, L. C. *History of Agriculture in the Southern United States to 1860.* Washington, 1933. Contains an elaborate carefully classified bibliography.

Hasse, A. R. *Index of Economic Material in Documents of the States of the United States.* Carnegie Institution of Washington, 1907. A convenient guide to the publications of the thirteen states indexed.

Monroe, Will S. *Bibliography of Education* (International Education Series, edited by W. T. Harris). New York, 1903. Issued in 1897 and hence lists works contemporary to this study. In general the selections and classifications are carefully and helpfully made.

Monroe, Walter S., and Shores, Louis. *Bibliographies and Summaries in Education.* New York, 1936.

Schlesinger, A. M., and Fox, D. R. *A History of American Life.* New York, 1927 ———. The "Critical Essay on Authorities" in each volume gives unusual attention to education and research.

Schmidt, L. B. *Topical Studies and References on the History of American Agriculture.* Iowa State College, 1937. A wide range of carefully selected references on special topics organized within chronological limits.

Swem, E. G. *A Contribution to the Bibliography of Agriculture in Virginia.* Richmond, 1918.

——— *Analysis of Ruffin's Farmer's Register with a Bibliography of Edmund Ruffin.* Richmond, 1918.

True, A. C. *A History of Agricultural Education in the United States, 1785–1925.* U. S. Dept. of Agr., Misc. Pub. No. 36. Washington, 1929. Citations of a wide and extended number of federal and state publications.

United States Bureau of Education. *An Index to the Bureau's Publications, 1867–1890.* U. S. Comr. of Ed., *Rep.*, 1888–89, II, 1453–1551. Washington, 1889.

——— *Analytical Index to Barnard's American Journal of Education.* Washington, 1892.

——— *List of Publications of the United States Bureau of Education, 1867–1907. Bulletin* 1908, No. 2. Washington, 1908.

——— *Bibliography of Education in Agriculture and Home Economics. Bulletin* 1912, No. 10. Washington, 1912.

Manuscript Sources

Brewer, William H. "The Intent of the Morrill Land Grant." A memorandum, written about 1890, of the conference of the Sheffield School faculty with Morrill. Copy in True Papers, U. S. Dept. of Agr. Library. Gives some sidelights on Morrill's views and even more on those of Brewer and his colleagues.

Capron, Horace. Memoirs of Horace Capron. Volume I, Autobiography; Volume II, Expedition to Japan, 1871–75. Conclusion dated 1884. Copy in the U. S. Dept. of Agr. Library. Discusses briefly his relations as commissioner with the agricultural colleges.

Hewett, W. T. Manuscripts on land-grant college history—correspondence, original and copies, and memoranda collected in preparation for his history of Cornell. Cornell University Library. Includes important correspondence with Morrill, White, and other prominent land-grant leaders.

Howard, Harrison. People's College Collection. Cornell University Library. Manuscript letters, addresses, and memoranda, as well as printed circulars, pamphlets, and clippings. Indispensable for the history of People's College.

Iowa State Agricultural College. "College History Collection." Correspondence, recollections, and interviews dealing with the period to 1890.

——— Faculty Judiciary Committee Record, 1879–84.

——— Faculty Minutes, 1869–90.

———Trustee Minute Books, 1865–90.

LeDuc, William Gates. Papers. Minnesota Historical Society.

——— Recollections of a Quartermaster; Autobiography of General Wm. G. LeDuc, 1890. A copy of the original manuscript in the possession of H. M. LeDuc. U. S. Dept. of Agr. Library. Both sources indicate the Commissioner's attitude toward the colleges.

Morrill, Justin S. Papers, 1825–1923. 50 vols. Library of Congress. In the main letters received with only an occasional penciled reply or memorandum. The fullest collection of letters on all phases of the movement from the forties to the end of the century.

Pugh, Evan. Letters to Samuel W. Johnson, Feb. 22, 1855, to Dec. 8, 1863. Copies in A. C. True Papers, U. S. Dept. of Agr. Library. Pugh's plan for an agricultural college and the attitude of the two young scientists toward existing education and research in applied science are well brought out.

United States Patent Office, Agricultural Department. Letters, reports, essays, memoranda, 1839–1860. 21 vols. U. S. Dept. of Agr. Library.

United States Department of Agriculture. Letter Files: letters sent July 7, 1879—Jan. 29, 1880. 2 vols. (LeDuc); "Congressional Letters." Feb. 1, 1886—Feb. 11, 1889. 4 vols. (Colman); general correspondence, Oct. 16, 1885—Feb. 11, 1889. 19 vols. (Colman); beginning of secretaryship, Feb. 1889—Feb. 1890 (Colman and Rusk). U. S. Dept. of Agr. Library. No other files could be found in 1935. Some of the letters deal with problems of education and research.

Laws and Legislative Records

State legislative journals, reports, and session laws. Convenient compilations of land-grant college enactments by the various states are in U. S. Commissioner of Education, *Report,* 1867–68, pp. 135–214, 1902, I, 1–90, 1903, I, 39–226.

United States *Congressional Debates.* Washington, 1825–37.

——— *Congressional Globe.* Washington, 1834–73.

——— *Congressional Record.* Washington, 1873 ———.

——— *Congressional Documents.* Washington, 1789 ———.

——— *Statutes at Large,* 1789–1895. Boston and Washington, 1850–95.

Correspondence, Diaries, and Recollections

Adams, Herbert Baxter. *Historical Scholarship in the United States, 1876-1901: as revealed in the correspondence of Herbert B. Adams.* Edited by

W. Stull Holt. Johns Hopkins *Studies in Historical and Political Science*, Series LVI, No. 4. Baltimore, 1938. Adams' correspondence regarding the presidency of the University of Ohio throws light on land-grant conditions. Valuable also for general college and university background.

Angell, James Burrill. *From Vermont to Michigan, Correspondence, 1869–1871*. With a foreword by his son James Rowland Angell. Edited by Wilfred B. Shaw. Ann Arbor, 1936.

——— *Reminiscences*. New York, 1912. Science and the classics; religious influences in state institutions; beginnings of land-grant education in Vermont.

Atkeson, Thomas Clark and Mary M. *Pioneering in Agriculture, One Hundred Years of American Farming and Farm Leadership*. New York, 1937. Of value for the relations of agricultural organizations to the colleges.

Brown, Rev. Charles E. *Personal Recollections, 1813–1893*. n. p., n. d. For manual labor school experience.

Brown, William Adams. *A Teacher and His Times; a Story of Two Worlds*. New York, 1940. Intimate view of Yale in the eighties, including the relations of the College with the Sheffield School.

Butler, Nicholas Murray. *Across Crowded Years, Recollections and Reflections*. Vol I. New York, 1939. General collegiate conditions from the seventies to the nineties.

Ely, Richard Theodore. *Ground Under Our Feet, An Autobiography*. New York, 1938. General background and references to land-grant leaders.

Fairchild, David. *The World Was My Garden, Travels of a Plant Explorer*. New York, 1938. Brief views of early days at the agricultural colleges of Michigan, Kansas, Iowa, and New Jersey.

Fiske, John. *Letters of John Fiske*. Edited by Ethel F. Fisk. New York, 1940. Supplements J. S. Clark's biography, listed below.

Folwell, W. W. *The Autobiography and Letters of a Pioneer of Culture*. Edited by Solon J. Buck. Minneapolis, 1933. A major source. Correspondence with White and Eliot especially significant.

Hanus, Paul H. *Adventuring in Education*. Cambridge, 1937. General educational background.

Hayes, Rutherford Birchard. *Diary and Letters*. Edited by Charles R. Williams. Columbus, 1922–26. The intimate record of a diligent and highly conscientious trustee of a state university.

Hoar, George Frisbie. *Autobiography of Seventy Years*. New York, 1903. Deals briefly with the public school-college congressional contest for public land aid.

Hone, Philip. *Diary, 1828–1851*. Edited by Allan Nevins. New York, 1936.

Howard, L. O. *A History of Applied Entomology (Somewhat Anecdotal)*. Smithsonian Miscellaneous Collections, vol. 84. Washington, 1930.

Iowa Agricultural College Class of '97. *History and Reminiscences of I. A. C.* n. p., n. d. Valuable recollections and records of events.

Johnson, Samuel William. *From the Letter-Files of S. W. Johnson, Professor of Agricultural Chemistry in Yale University, 1856–1896. Director of the Connecticut Agricultural Experiment Station, 1877–1900.* Edited by Elizabeth A. Osborne. New Haven, 1913. The best source for the early experiment station movement.

Jordan, David Starr. *The Days of a Man; Being Memoirs of a Naturalist, Teacher, and Minor Prophet of Democracy.* Yonkers, N. Y., 1922. Early days of Cornell and general background.

Kegley, Charles Hill. *Personal Memoirs.* Los Angeles, California, 1936. Intimate views of Iowa Agricultural College in the seventies and early eighties.

Larsen, Laur. "A Newcomer Looks at American Colleges" [May, 1866]. Translated and edited by Karen Larsen. *Norwegian-American Studies and Records,* X, 107–26, Norwegian-American Historical Association. Northfield, Minnesota, 1938. Conditions at the University of Wisconsin and various denominational colleges. Reflects the attitude of the sectarian classicist toward the state university and the new science.

Lyon, Mary. *Mary Lyon Through Her Letters.* Edited by Marion F. Lansing. Boston, 1937.

Naismith, James. *Basketball, Its Origin and Development.* New York, 1941. By "the inventor of the game." Revealing sidelights on early college athletics.

Osborn, Herbert. *Fragments of Entomological History Including Some Personal Recollections of Men and Events.* Columbus, Ohio, 1937.

Roberts, Isaac Phillips. *Autobiography of a Farm Boy.* Albany, 1916. The frank, charming life story of a pioneer agricultural teacher and administrator.

Smith, Goldwin. *The Early Days of Cornell.* Ithaca, New York, 1904.

——— *A selection from Goldwin Smith's Correspondence, 1846–1910.* Edited by Arnold Haultain. New York, 1913.

Wallace, Henry. *Uncle Henry's Own Story of His Life, Personal Reminiscences.* Des Moines, 1917–19.

Wattles, Gurdon Wallace. *Autobiography.* Privately printed, 1922. Iowa Agricultural College in the seventies.

White, Andrew Dickson. *Autobiography.* New York, 1907. The best source for the origin and early development of Cornell University.

Wiley, Harvey W. *An Autobiography.* Indianapolis, 1930. Pioneer experiences at Purdue.

Reports and Contemporary Writings

Allen, R. L. *The American Farm Book,* 3rd ed. New York, 1879 (c. 1869). An agricultural editor actively interested in agricultural colleges.

Association of American Agricultural Colleges and Experiment Stations. Proceedings 1889 ———. Burlington, Vt., 1889 ———. Name changed to

Association of Land-Grant Colleges in 1919. Many papers and addresses dealing with the earlier history of the colleges.

Barnard, Frederick A. P. *The Rise of a University, the Later Days of Old Columbia College From the Annual Reports of Frederick A. P. Barnard, President of Columbia College, 1864–1889.* Edited by William F. Russell, with an introduction by Nicholas Murray Butler. New York, 1937. Valuable for general collegiate problems of the period.

Atkeson, T. C. *Semi-Centennial History of the Patrons of Husbandry.* New York, 1916. Largely a digest of the proceedings of the national conventions including action on agricultural education.

Buel, Jesse. *The Farmer's Companion or Essays on the Principles and Practice of American Husbandry.* 3rd edition. Boston, 1842. Contains a suggestive and well-reasoned discussion of agricultural education in an address prepared shortly before his death in 1839. The volume was originally published in 1839 as a number of the "School Library" sponsored by the Massachusetts Board of Education.

Bureau of Education. "Training Schools of Cookery," *Circulars of Information.* No. 4. Washington, 1879. The earliest survey of this branch of land-grant instruction.

Carr, Ezra S., M.D., LL.D. *The Patrons of Husbandry on the Pacific Coast, etc.* San Francisco, 1875. The views of a narrow-gauge champion.

Commons, John R., *et al.* eds. *Documentary History of American Industrial Society,* Vols. V–X, Cleveland, Ohio, 1910. The most convenient collection of materials dealing with the labor agitation for industrial education.

Crozier, William, and Henderson, Peter. *How the Farm Pays, the Experiences of Forty Years of Successful Farming and Gardening by the Authors.* New York, 1902 (c. 1884). Practical horticulturists' attack on agricultural colleges.

Downing, A. J. *Rural Essays.* Edited with memoir by George William Curtis. New York, 1869. Includes an interesting essay on agricultural schools, first published in 1849.

Eliot, Charles William. "The New Education," *Atlantic Monthly,* XXIII (1869), 203–20, 358–67. Boston, 1869. An epochal paper for Eliot himself and for technological education.

——— *Educational Reform, Essays and Addresses.* New York, 1909.

[Gilman, Daniel Coit] "Our National Schools of Science," *North American Review,* CV (1867), 495–520. A liberal, understanding contemporary appraisal.

——— "Report on the National Schools of Science," *Rep., Comr. of Education,* 1871, pp. 427–44. Washington, 1872.

——— *University Problems in the United States.* New York, 1898.

——— *The Launching of a University, and Other Papers.* New York, 1906.

Goodsell, Willystine, ed. *Pioneers of Women's Education in the United States:* Emma Willard, Catherine Beecher, Mary Lyon. New York, 1931.

Hadley, Arthur T. "Yale University," *Harper's Magazine,* LXXXVIII (1894), 764–72.

Halliday, Samuel D. *History of the Agricultural College Land Grant of July 2, 1862, Together With a Statement of the Condition of the Fund Derived Therefrom as It Now Exists in Each State of the Union.* Ithaca, N. Y., 1890. By the attorney of Cornell University. A convenient compilation of statistics of the various colleges.

Hamilton, Gail. "Glorying in the Goad," *Atlantic Monthly,* XIV (1864), 21–33. Expresses somewhat satirically the dirt farmer's indifference to book learning for his occupation.

Hilgard, Eugene W. "Progress in Agriculture by Education and Government Aid," *Atlantic Monthly,* XLIX (1882), 531–41, 651–61. A thoughtful analysis by an outstanding representaive of the broad-gauge group.

James, Edmund J. *The Origin of the Land Grant Act of 1862 (The so-called Morrill Act) and Some Account of Its Author, Jonathan B. Turner. The University Studies,* University of Illinois. Urbana, Illinois, 1910. The official statement of the "Turner Thesis."

Jordan, David Starr. *The Trend of the American University.* Stanford University, California, 1929. Contains a significant address on "The Evolution of the College Curriculum," delivered in 1887.

Kinley, David. *Government Control of Economic Life and Other Addresses.* New York, 1936.

Klein, A. J., ed. *Survey of Land-Grant Colleges and Universities.* Office ot Education, Bulletin 1930, No. 9. Washington, D. C., 1930. Contains brief historical summaries.

Knight, E. W., ed. *Reports on European Education by John Griscom, Victor Cousin, Calvin E. Stowe.* New York, 1930.

Land-Grant Colleges and Universities. *Reports.* Of the reports of the two dozen institutions consulted, those of Michigan (printed in the Agricultural Reports), Illinois, Iowa, Massachusetts (Agricultural College and Institute of Technology), and Ohio have proved to be the most representative. Some of the colleges did not print their annual reports in the early years.

Liautard, A. F. A. "History and Progress of Veterinary Medicine in the United States," *American Veterinary Review,* I (1877), 5–19. A convenient summary by a pioneer veterinary educator.

Lowell, A. Lawrence. *What a University President Has Learned.* New York, 1938.

MacArthur, Arthur. *Education in Its Relation to Manual Industry.* New York, 1884.

Magoun, George F. *The West: Its Culture and Its Colleges.* An oration delivered at the annual commencement of Iowa College, Davenport, Iowa, July 18, 1855. Davenport, 1855. An early and able attempt at a reconciliation of the "old" and the "new" in content and of the sectarian and the public in control.

Robinson, Solon. *Pioneer and Agriculturist, Selected Writings,* 1825–51. Edited by Herbert A. Kellar. Indianapolis, 1936.

Scott, C. W. *Agricultural Education Historically Considered.* Reprint from New Hampshire Board of Agriculture, *Transactions,* 1883–84. Concord, N. H., 1884. A thoughtful, fair-minded view.

Smith, Annie Tolman. "The Education of Agriculturists," *Education,* II (1882), 166–72. Unsympathetic.

Society for the Promotion of Agricultural Science. *Proceedings,* 1880–1920. Syracuse, N. Y., 1883–1921.

Society for the Promotion of Engineering Education. *Report of the Investigation of Engineering Education,* 1923–29. Vol. I. Pittsburg, Pa., 1930.

——— *A Study of Technical Institutes.* n. p., 1931. Contains a valuable historical summary.

State Agricultural Societies and Boards. *Reports and Transactions.* For the period of this study most of the northern states and, for brief periods, Virginia, Kentucky, Tennessee, and North Carolina have such publications. The dates for the various states may be checked in R. R. Bowker, *State Publications,* and for the 13 states covered, a partial analysis of the contents may be found in A. R. Hasse, *Index of Economic Material in Documents of the States of the United States.*

Sumner, William Graham. *War and Other Essays.* New Haven, 1919. "Our Colleges Before the Country," 355–73, reprinted from *Princeton Review,* March, 1884.

Thurston, Robert H. "Technical Education in the United States, Its Social, Industrial, and Economic Relations to Our Progress." A paper presented at the meeting of the American Society of Mechanical Engineers at the Worlds Columbian Exposition, Chicago, July, 1893. *Transactions of the American Society of Mechanical Engineers,* XIV, 855–1013. New York, 1893. The views of a pioneer and an enthusiast.

Tocqueville, Alexis de. *Democracy in America* (1835–40). New York, 1898.

True, A. C., and Clark, V. A. *The Agricultural Experiment Stations in the United States.* Paris Exposition, 1900, U. S. Department of Agriculture, Office of Experiment Stations, Bulletin No. 80. Washington, 1900. A convenient compilation and summary.

National Educational Association. *Addresses* and *Proceedings.* Various places, 1858 ———. The National Teachers Association to 1870. Much attention was given to land-grant education in the seventies and eighties.

New York State Agricultural College at Ovid, Seneca County. *Charter, Ordinances, Regulations and Course of Studies, 1859.* Albany, 1859.

Olcott, Henry S. *Outlines of the First Course of Yale Agricultural Lectures.* With an introduction by John A. Porter. New York, 1860.

Olmsted, Fred. Law of Olmsted, Vaux and Co., Landscape Architects. *A few things to be thought of before proceeding to plan buildings for the national agricultural colleges.* (A report to the board of trustees of Massachusetts Agricultural College.) New York, 1866.

Patterson, James Kennedy. *Selections from Speeches and Articles* in M. H. Pollitt's *Biography of J. K. Patterson.* Louisville, Ky., 1925.

Porter, Noah. *The American Colleges and the American Public.* New Haven, Conn., 1870. The best statement of the neo-classical position.

Pugh, Dr. E., President of the Faculty. *A report upon a plan for the organization of colleges for agriculture and the mechanic arts with especial reference to the organization of the Agricultural College of Pennsylvania in view of the endowment of this institution by the land scrip fund, donated by Congress to the State of Pennsylvania, addressed to the Board of Trustees of the Agricultural College of Pennsylvania, convened at Harrisburg, January 6, 1864.* Harrisburg, 1864. The most thorough and understanding early analysis, both informing and interpretative.

Rhees, William Jones, ed. *The Smithsonian Institution, Documents Relative to its Origin and History.* House of Representatives Document No. 732, 56 Congress, 1 Session. Washington, 1901.

Schurman, Jacob Gould. "The Ideal of a University in its Historical Development and Modern Significance," University of Missouri, *Exercises at the Inauguration of Albert Ross Hill, LL.D., as President of the University, December 10, 1908.* Columbia, Missouri, 1909.

Slater, C. P., ed. *History of the Land Grant Endowment of the University of Illinois.* Urbana, 1940. A documentary and statistical compilation.

Turner, Jonathan Baldwin. *A Plan for an Industrial University for the State of Illinois, submitted to the Farmers' Convention at Granville held November 18, 1851. By Prof. J. B. Turner, Published at the request of the Convention under the supervision of the committee of publication.* n. p., 1851. The original publication of the famous "plan."

United States Agricultural Society. *Journal.* Washington and Boston, 1852–58.

——— *Transactions and Monthly Bulletin for 1858.* Washington, 1859.

——— *Quarterly Journal of Agriculture.* Washington, 1860–62.

United States Bureau of Education. *Report of the Commissioner of Education,* 1867 ———. Washington, 1868 ———.

——— *Circulars of Information.* Washington, 1870 ———.

——— *Miscellaneous Publications.* Washington, 1870 ———.

——— *Annual Statement of the Commissioner of Education.* Washington, 1887 ———.

United States Department of Agriculture. *Report of the Commissioner of Agriculture.* Washington, 1862–89.

——— *Report of the Secretary of Agriculture.* Washington, 1889 ———.

——— *Bulletins, Circulars, and Miscellaneous Publications.* Washington, 1862 ———.

——— *Yearbook.* Washington, 1894 ———.

United States Patent Office. *Annual Reports of the Commissioner of Patents.* Washington, 1839–62.

Virginia State Agricultural Society. *Report of the President made to the Farmers' Assembly at the first annual meeting held in the city of Richmond, October 28, 1856.* Richmond, Va., 1856. Philip St. George Cocke's plan for agricultural education.

Walker, Francis A. *Discussions in Education.* Edited by James Phinney Munroe. New York, 1899.

Watts, Frederick, Hiester, A. D., Pugh, Evan. *The Agricultural College of Pennsylvania,* embracing a succinct history of agricultural education in Europe and America, together with the circumstances of the origin, rise, and progress of the Agricultural College of Pennsylvania; as also a statement of the present condition, aims and prospects of this institution, its course of instruction, facilities for study, terms of admission, and C & C. Drawn up by a committee appointed for this purpose by the board of trustees. September, 1862. Philadelphia, 1862. A pamphlet of 63 pages prepared mainly by Dr. Pugh.

White, Andrew D. "The Relations of the National and State Governments to Advanced Education." A paper read before the National Educational Association at Detroit, Aug. 5, 1874. Offprint from *Old and New*. Boston, 1874. A reply to the attacks of Eliot and McCosh.

——— "Scientific and Industrial Education in the United States" in *Popular Science Monthly*, V (1874), 170–91. A revision of an address delivered before the New York Agricultural Society.

Youmans, Edward L. *Hand-Book of Household Science*. New York, 1883. [c. 1857.] A pioneer treatise of great influence.

ANNIVERSARIES, CONVENTIONS, AND CONVOCATIONS

Antioch College. *Educating for Democracy, a Symposium*. Horace Mann Centennial. Yellow Springs, Ohio, 1937.

Connecticut Agricultural College. *Fiftieth Anniversary and Inauguration of Charles Chester McCracken as President of the College*. n. p., 1931.

Cornell University. *Account of the Proceedings at the Inauguration, October 7, 1868*. Ithaca, 1869.

Duke University. *A Century of Social Thought*. Lectures delivered at Duke University during Centennial Celebration. Durham, North Carolina, 1939.

Illinois, University of. *The Relation of the Federal Government to Education, Installation of David Kinley as President of the University of Illinois, December 1 and 2, 1921*. *Bulletin*, Vol. XIX, February 6, 1922. Urbana, 1922.

Iowa State Agricultural College. *Addresses Delivered at the Opening March 17, 1869*. Davenport, Iowa, 1869.

——— *Addresses Delivered at the Inauguration of W. I. Chamberlain, LL.D., to the Presidency, November 9, 1886*. Ames, Iowa, 1886.

Iowa State College. *Inauguration of Charles Edwin Friley as President of The Iowa State College of Agriculture and Mechanic Arts, October 7, 1936*. Ames, Iowa, 1936.

——— *The Outlook for Graduate Study. Papers Presented on the Twenty-fifth Anniversary of the Establishment of the Graduate Faculty of The Iowa State College*. Ames, Iowa, 1941.

Iowa, State University of. *Trends in Graduate Work—a Program Commemorating the Thirtieth Anniversary of the Founding of the Graduate College of the University of Iowa*. Edited by John W. Ashton. Iowa City, 1931.

——— *The Ninetieth Anniversary*. Iowa City, Iowa, 1937.

Johns Hopkins University. *State Aid to Higher Education*. A series of addresses delivered at the Johns Hopkins University. *Johns Hopkins Studies in Historical and Political Science*. Baltimore, 1898.

University of Louisville. *A Century of Municipal Higher Education.* A collection of addresses delivered during the centennial observance of the University of Louisville, America's oldest municipal university. Chicago, [1937].

Massachusetts Agricultural College. *Addresses Delivered June 21, 1887, on the Twenty-fifth Anniversary of the Passage of the Morrill Land Grant Act.* Amherst, Mass., 1887. Includes one of Morrill's most significant statements of the intent and scope of the act.

Michigan State Agricultural College. *Semi-Centennial Celebration of Michigan State Agricultural College.* Edited by Thomas C. Blaisdell. Chicago, 1908.

University of Michigan. *A University Between Two Centuries, the Proceedings of the 1937 celebration of the University of Michigan.* Edited by Wilfred B. Shaw. Ann Arbor, 1937.

University of Missouri. *Exercises at the Inauguration of Albert Ross Hill, LL.D., as President of the University, December 10, 1908.* Columbia, Missouri, 1909.

Morrill, Justin S. *Proceedings at the Unveiling of the Portrait of the Honorable Justin S. Morrill, Senator of the United States from Vermont, at the Annual Commencement of Cornell University,* June 20, 1883. Ithaca, New York, 1884.

——— *State Aid to the U. S. Land-Grant Colleges. An address in behalf of the University of Vermont and State Agricultural College delivered in the Hall of the House of Representatives at Montpelier, October 10, 1888.* Burlington, Vt., 1888.

——— *The Land-Grant Colleges, an address delivered at the eighty-ninth commencement of the University of Vermont and State Agricultural College, June 28, 1893.* Burlington, 1893.

——— *Centenary Exercises Celebrated by the State of Vermont at Montpelier, April 14, 1910, in honor of the birth of Justin Smith Morrill.* Fulton, New York, [1910].

Ohio State University. *Addresses and Proceedings of the Semicentennial Celebration, October 13–16, 1920, History of Ohio State University,* Volume III. Edited by T. C. Mendenhall. Columbus, 1922.

People's College. *Address delivered by William Stuart before the People's College Association at its annual meeting on Aug. 12, 1857.* Binghamton, n. d.

——— *Public Exercises at the Laying of the Corner Stone of the People's College at Havana, N. Y., Thursday, September 2, 1858.* New York, 1858.

Rensselaer Polytechnic Institute. *The Centennial Celebration of Rensselaer Polytechnic Institute, October 3–4, 1924.* Edited by Palmer C. Ricketts. Troy, New York, 1925.

Rutgers College. *The Celebration of the One Hundred and Fiftieth Anniversary of its Founding as Queen's College, 1766–1916.* Published by the College [New Brunswick], 1917.

State Universities and Colleges. *Proceedings of the Conference of the Presidents and Other Delegates of the State Universities and State Colleges, held at Columbus, Ohio, December 27 and 28, 1877.* Bureau of Education, *Circulars of Information,* 1879, No. 2, Appendix B. Washington, 1879.

Agricultural and Mechanical College of Texas. *The Semi-Centennial Celebration, 1876–1926, and the Inauguration of Thomas Otto Walton, LL.D., as President.* College Station, Texas, 1926.

United States Department of Agriculture. *National Agricultural Convention held at Washington, D. C., February 15, 16, and 17, 1872.* 42 Congress, 2 Session, Senate Miscellaneous Document No. 164. Washington, 1872.

——— *Convention of Agriculturists held at the Department of Agriculture January 10th to 18th, 1882. Proceedings.* Washington, 1882.

——— *Convention of Agriculturists Held at the Department of Agriculture January 23, 24, 25, 26, 27, and 29, 1883.* (Second Convention) , *Proceedings.* Department of Agriculture, Miscellaneous Special Report No. 2. Washington, 1883.

——— *Convention of Delegates from Agricultural Colleges and Experiment Stations Held at the Department of Agriculture, July 8 and 9, 1885. Proceedings.* Washington, 1885.

University of Wisconsin. *Jubilee in Celebration of Fiftieth Anniversary, 1904.* Madison, 1905.

Contemporary Periodicals

Agricultural Science. Geneva, N. Y., 1887; Knoxville, Tenn., 1887–90; Lafayette, Ind., 1890–91; State College, Pa., 1892–94. Editors: Charles S. Plumb, 1887–91, William Frear, 1892–94. Gave much attention to the activities of the Society for Promoting Agricultural Science. Some significant discussions of agricultural education.

The American Agriculturist. New York, 1842 ———. Both the Allens and Orange Judd were strong advocates and generally discriminating critics of agricultural education and research.

American Journal of Education. Hartford, 1856–82. Under the able direction of Henry Barnard the outstanding journal of educational discussion at all levels and in all phases for the period.

The Aurora, Ames, Ia., 1873–91. The first student paper of the Iowa Agricultural College. Land-grant college periodicals for the early years—rarely preserved in complete files—have a unique value in reflecting attitudes and points of view of students, faculty, and alumni and, to a much less degree in this period, as a record of events.

The College Quarterly. Edited by the faculty of Iowa Agricultural College. Ames, Ia., 1878–80. A medium of information for the college's constituency.

The Cincinnatus. Cincinnati, 1856–61. The organ of F. G. Cary and his Farmers' College.

The Cultivator. Albany, 1834–64.

Country Gentleman. Albany, N. Y., 1853 ———.

De Bow's Review. New Orleans, La., 1846–80. Contains significant articles and reports on industrial education.

Education. Boston, 1880 ——.

Educational Review. New York, 1891–1928.

Engineering News and American Railway Journal. New York, 1874 ——.

New Genesee Farmer. Rochester, N. Y., 1840–65.

Iowa Farmer and Horticulturist. Burlington and Mount Pleasant, Iowa, 1853–57. The first regular agricultural paper published in the state and an organ of industrial education agitation.

Iowa Homestead. Des Moines, Iowa, 1862–90.

Iowa State Register (weekly edition). Des Moines, Iowa, 1870–90. The years in which the agricultural department was under the notable editorship of "Father" Coker F. Clarkson.

New England Farmer. Boston, 1848–63.

Northwestern Farmer and Horticultural Journal. Dubuque, Iowa, 1856–61.

The Plough, the Loom, and the Anvil. Philadelphia and New York, 1848–57. Reflects John S. Stuart's varied and changing interests including those on education.

Prairie Farmer. Chicago, Ill., 1841 ——.

The Progressive Farmer; A Journal of Practical Agriculture, Horticulture, Mechanic Arts, Livestock, and Literature. Cedar Rapids, Ia., 1875–76. Edited as a college organ by the faculty of Iowa Agricultural College.

Students' Farm Journal. Edited by the Agricultural and Horticultural Association of Iowa Agricultural College. Ames, Ia., 1884–87.

Rural New-Yorker. Rochester and New York, 1850 ——.

Southern Planter. Richmond, Va., 1841 ——.

Working Farmer. New York, 1846–60. James J. Mapes' personal organ.

From the seventies general periodicals like the *Nation, Harper's Weekly, Harper's Magazine,* the *Atlantic Monthly,* the *North American Review,* the *Century,* and the *Forum* published thoughtful articles on higher education with increasing attention to the "new education." Greeley's *New York Tribune* was the only newspaper to give serious attention to the industrial movement in American education. Local papers by turn lauded and berated their colleges with equal lack of understanding and discrimination.

BIOGRAPHIES

Atherton, G. W. *The Legislative Career of Justin S. Morrill.* Washington, 1901. A memorial address delivered before the Association of Agricultural Colleges.

Brigham, Johnson. *James Harlan.* Iowa City, Iowa, 1913.

Carriel, M. T. *The Life of Jonathan Baldwin Turner.* [Jacksonville, Illinois], 1911. Valuable for documentary material.

Clark, J. S. *Life and Letters of John Fiske.* Boston, 1917. An intimate biography, with numerous selections from correspondence, of the most influential expounder of the "new science" and of phases of the "new education."

Cline, Rodney. *The Life and Work of Seaman A. Knapp.* Contributions to Education. George Peabody College. Nashville, Tennessee, 1936.

Coulter, John G. *The Dean [Stanley Coulter], An Account of His Career and His Convictions.* Lafayette, Indiana, 1940. Based mainly on the subject's reminiscences and reflections. Intimate views of the sectarian college of the Middle West in the sixties and seventies and of the formative days of Purdue University.

Dunn, W. H. *The Life of Donald G. Mitchell, Ik Marvel.* New York, 1922. A gentleman horticulturist, critical of the professionals.

Firkins, O. W. *Cyrus Northrop, A Memoir.* Minneapolis, 1925.

Gilman, D. C. *Life of James Dwight Dana, Scientific Explorer, Mineralogist, Geologist, Zoologist, Professor in Yale University.* New York, 1899.

Holmes, A. G., and Sherrill, G. R. *Thomas Green Clemson, His Life and Work.* Richmond, 1937.

Hunt, C. L. *The Life of Ellen H. Richards.* Boston, 1912. Indispensable for the early home economics movement.

Hylander, C. J. *American Scientists.* New York, 1935.

James, Henry. *Charles W. Eliot, President of Harvard University.* Boston, 1930.

Kirshman, M. S. *Edgar Williams Stanton, In Memoriam.* n. p., n. d. An appreciation of a veteran land-grant teacher and administrator.

Leopold, R. W. *Robert Dale Owen, A Biography.* Cambridge, 1940. The labor educational agitation of the thirties; the disposal of the Smithson bequest.

McAllister, Ethel M. *Amos Eaton, Scientist and Educator, 1776–1842.* Philadelphia, 1941. A very complete record of the man and his educational work, including much source material.

Mairs, T. I. *Some Pennsylvania Pioneers in Agricultural Science.* State College, Pa., 1928.

Munroe, J. P. *A Life of Francis Amasa Walker.* New York, 1923.

Murray, J. O. *Francis Wayland. American Religious Leaders.* Boston, 1891.

Nevins, Allan. *John D. Rockefeller, the Heroic Age of American Enterprise.* New York, 1940. Background of industrial education. The national education boards and their relations with public and private colleges.

Ogilvie, W. E. *Pioneer Agricultural Journalists.* Chicago, 1927.

Palmer, G. H. *The Life of Alice Freeman Palmer.* Boston, 1908.

Parker, W. B. *The Life and Public Service of Justin Smith Morrill.* Boston, 1924. Eulogistic but informing, includes much documentary material.

Perry, C. M. *Henry Philip Tappan, Philosopher and University President.* Ann Arbor, 1933.

Pollitt, M. H. *A Biography of James Kennedy Patterson, President of the University of Kentucky from 1869 to 1910.* Louisville, Ky., 1925.

Rosenberger, A. *Dr. Millikan Stalker, In Memoriam.* n. p., n. d.

Schuchert, Charles, and LeVene, Clara M. *O. C. Marsh, Pioneer in Paleontology.* New Haven, 1940. Early days of the Sheffield School.

Severance, H. O. *Richard Henry Jesse, President of the University of Missouri, 1891–1908.* Columbia, Missouri, 1937.

Smith, A. W. *Ezra Cornell, a Character Study.* Ithaca, N. Y., 1934. Eulogistic and anecdotal. No adequate biography exists.

Smith, C. F. *Charles Kendall Adams, a Life Sketch.* University of Wisconsin. Madison, 1924.

Starr, H. E. *William Graham Sumner.* New York, 1925.

Stebbins, Calvin. *Henry Hill Goodell, the Story of His Life with Letters and a few of his Addresses.* Cambridge, 1911. Essential for the history of the Massachusetts Agricultural College.

Successful Farming. *The Ten Master Minds of Dairying.* Des Moines, Iowa, 1930. Valuable for the development of the experiment station.

Sydnor, C. S. *A Gentleman of the Old Natchez Region, Benjamin L. C. Wailes.* Durham, North Carolina, 1938. Illustrates the beginnings of science teaching in the colleges.

Warfel, H. R. *Noah Webster, Schoolmaster to America.* New York, 1936.

White, H. S. *Willard Fiske, Life and Correspondence, a Biographical Study.* New York, 1925. Revealing for early Cornell days.

Wilcox, E. V., with the collaboration of Flora H. Wilson. *Tama Jim.* Boston, 1930. A wholly inadequate, uncritical, poorly arranged eulogy of James Wilson. His educational work is given no understanding attention.

Wilkerson, M. M. *Thomas Duckett Boyd, the Story of a Southern Educator.* Baton Rouge, 1935. The beginnings of the University of Louisiana.

College Histories

Arey, H. W. *Girard College and Its Founder.* Philadelphia, 1857.

Aurner, C. R. *History of Education in Iowa.* Vol. IV. Iowa City, Iowa, 1916.

Baker, R. P. *A Chapter in American Education, Rensselaer Polytechnic Institute, 1824–1924.* New York, 1924.

Beal, W. J. *History of the Michigan Agricultural College.* East Lansing, 1915. By a distinguished pioneer botanist.

Bronson, W. C. *The History of Brown University, 1764–1914.* Providence, 1914.

Bryan, E. A. *Historical Sketch of the State College of Washington,* Pullman, Washington, 1928. By a former president who served during the critical formative years.

Caswell, L. B. *Brief History of the Massachusetts Agricultural College.* Springfield, Mass., 1917. Too brief.

Chittenden, R. H. *History of the Sheffield Scientific School of Yale University, 1846–1922.* New Haven, 1928.

Cole, Arthur C. *A Hundred Years of Mount Holyoke College, the Evolution of an Educational Ideal.* New Haven, 1940. Background and collateral interests.

Coulter, E. M. *College Life in the Old South.* New York, 1928. The early days of the University of Georgia.

Crawford, R. P. *These Fifty Years, a History of the College of Agriculture of the University of Nebraska.* Lincoln, 1925.

Crooks, E. B., ed. *Delaware Notes, Eighth Series.* Newark, Delaware, 1934. Sketches of the early history of the College.

Demarest, W. H. S. *A History of Rutgers College, 1766–1924.* New Brunswick, New Jersey, 1924.

Dodge, G. M. *How We Built the Union Pacific Railway, and Other Railway Papers and Addresses.* New York, 1910. Includes addresses on the early history of Norwich University.

Doten, S. B. *An Illustrated History of the University of Nevada.* University of Nevada, 1924.

Elliott, O. L. *Stanford University, the First Twenty-five Years, 1891–1925.* Stanford University, California, 1937. Shows the influence of land-grant universities upon this new venture.

Fernald, M. C. *History of the Maine State College and the University of Maine.* Orono, Maine, 1916. By an ex-president.

Ferrier, W. W. *Origin and Development of the University of California.* Berkeley, California, 1930.

Fleming, W. L. *Louisiana State University, 1860–1896.* Baton Rouge, 1936.

Ford, G. S. *The Making of the University, An Unorthodox Report.* Minneapolis, 1940. Penetrating interpretation and appraisal of men and measures in the development of a state university.

Fuess, C. M. *Amherst, the Story of a New England College.* Boston, 1935.

Harper, C. A. *Development of the Teachers College in the United States with special reference to the Illinois State Normal University.* Bloomington, Illinois, 1935. Deals with the contest over the disposal of the state university grant.

Hepburn, W. M., and Sears, L. M. *Purdue University, Fifty Years of Progress.* Indianapolis, 1925.

Hewett, W. T. *Cornell University: A History.* New York, 1905. Inadequate, in part a cooperative work though not so designated.

Horner, J. B. "History of Oregon State College 1865–1907." *Oregon Historical Quarterly,* XXXI (1930), 42–50. Salem, Oregon, 1930.

Iowa State College, Semi-Centennial Celebration Committee. *An Historical Sketch of The Iowa State College of Agriculture and Mechanic Arts.* Ames, Iowa, 1920.

Johnson, E. B. *Forty Years of the University of Minnesota.* Minneapolis, 1910.

Johnston, T. R., and Hand, Helen. *The Trustees and the Officers of Purdue University. The Archives of Purdue,* No. 1. Lafayette, Indiana, 1940.

Leffman, Henry. *Centenary of the Franklin Institute of Pennsylvania, 1824–1924.* Philadelphia, 1924.

Lockmiller, D. A. *History of the North Carolina State College of Agriculture and Engineering of the University of North Carolina, 1889–1939.* Raleigh, 1939.

Mendenhall, T. C., ed. *History of the Ohio State University.* Columbus, 1920–26.

Morgan, Barton. *A History of the Extension Service of Iowa State College.* Ames, Iowa, 1934.

Morison, S. E. *Three Centuries of Harvard, 1636–1936.* Cambridge, Massachusetts, 1936.

Nevins, Allan. *Illinois.* New York, 1917. An admirable concise university history.

Ousley, Clarence. *History of the Agricultural and Mechanical College of Texas.* Bulletin of the Agricultural and Mechanical College of Texas, December 1, 1935. College Station, Texas, 1935.

Powell, B. E. *Semi-Centennial History of the University of Illinois.* Volume I, *The Movement for Industrial Education and the Establishment of the University, 1840–1870.* Urbana, 1918. Largely a collection of the sources which are of great value not only for the movement in Illinois but for the country generally.

Powers, W. H., ed. *A History of South Dakota State College.* Brookings, 1931. Remarkably frank for an official history.

Rammelkamp, C. H. *Illinois College, a Centennial History, 1829–1929.* Yale University Press, 1928. Presents the background of the industrial movement in Illinois.

Rand, F. P. *Yesterdays at Massachusetts State College, 1863-1933.* Massachusetts State College, 1933. Vivid but somewhat impressionistic.

Reynolds, J. H., and Thomas, D. Y. *History of the University of Arkansas.* Fayetteville, 1910.

Richardson, L. B. *History of Dartmouth College.* Hanover, N. H., 1932. Well organized and highly informing.

Ricketts, P. C. *History of Rensselaer Polytechnic Institute, 1824–1934.* New York, 3rd ed., 1934.

Rosenberger, J. L. *Rochester the Making of a University.* Rochester, 1927. Shows influence of the industrial movement upon a sectarian institution.

Ross, E. D. *Graduate Study at the Iowa State College: An Historical Survey.* Preprint from the Iowa State College *Bulletin,* Ames, Iowa, 1941. Prepared for the twenty-fifth anniversary of the organization of the graduate faculty.

Schurman, J. G. *A Generation of Cornell, 1868–1898.* [30th Annual commencement address, June 16, 1898.] New York, 1898.

Sheldon, H. D. *History of the University of Oregon.* Portland, Oregon, 1940. Relations of a state university with a land-grant college.

Stange, C. H. *History of Veterinary Medicine at Iowa State College.* Ames, Iowa, 1929.

Starrett, A. L. *Through One Hundred and Fifty Years, the University of Pittsburgh.* Pittsburgh, 1937.

Stemmons, Walter. *Connecticut Agricultural College—A History*. Storrs, Connecticut, 1931.

Viles, Jonas, with the collaboration of several of his colleagues. *The University of Missouri, a Centennial History*. University of Missouri, Columbia, 1939.

Walters, J. D. *Columbian History of the Kansas State Agricultural College* Topeka, Kansas, 1893.

Walters, Raymond. *Historical Sketch of the University of Cincinnati*. Cincinnati, Ohio, 1940. A university bulletin by the president.

White, J. M. "Origin and Location of the Mississippi A. and M. College." *Publications of the Mississippi Historical Society*, III, 34–51. Edited by Franklin L. Riley. Oxford, Mississippi, 1900.

Willard, J. T. *History of the Kansas State College of Agriculture and Applied Science*. Manhattan, Kansas, 1940. An official history written by a former science professor and administrator. Factual and repetitious.

Woodburn, J. A. *History of Indiana University, 1820–1902*. Indiana University, 1940. A reminiscent and documentary record compiled by a professor of American history emeritus.

Woodward, C. R., and Waller, I. N. *New Jersey's Agricultural Experiment Station, 1880–1930*. New Brunswick, New Jersey, 1932. A thorough study, a model for the history of experiment stations.

General Works and Monographs

Anderson, L. F. *History of Manual and Industrial School Education*. New York, 1926.

Andrews, B. F. *The Land-Grant Act of 1862 and the Land-Grant Colleges*. Department of the Interior, Bureau of Education, Bulletin, 1918, No. 13. Washington, 1918. A convenient statistical analysis and summary.

Andrews, B. R. *"Miss Catherine E. Beecher, the Pioneer in Home Economics," Journal of Home Economics*, IV (1912), 211–22.

Bailey, L. H. "Development of the Text-Book of Agriculture in North America," U. S. Department of Agriculture, Office of Experiment Stations, *Report*, 1903, pp. 689–712. Washington, 1904.

Bennett, C. A. *History of Manual and Industrial Education up to 1870*. Peoria, Ill., 1926.

Bevier, Isabel, and Usher, Susannah. *The Home Economics Movement*. Boston, 1918.

Bevier, Isabel. *Home Economics in Education*. Philadelphia, 1924.

Blackmar, F. W. *The History of Federal and State Aid to Higher Education in the United States*. Bureau of Education, *Circular of Information*, No. 1. Washington, 1890.

Boas, L. S. *Woman's Education Begins, the Rise of Women's Colleges*. Norton, Massachusetts, 1935.

Boyd, M. C. *Alabama in the Fifties, a Social Study*. Columbia University *Studies*. New York, 1931.

Brown, R. M. "Agricultural Science and Education in Virginia Before 1860," *William and Mary College Quarterly,* 2nd Series, XIX (1939), 197–213.

Brown, S. W. *The Secularization of American Education.* Teachers' College, Columbia University, *Contributions to Education,* No. 49. New York, 1912.

Buck, S. J. *The Granger Movement, A Study of Agricultural Organization and Its Political, Economic, and Social Manifestations, 1870–1880. Harvard Historical Studies,* XIX. Cambridge, 1913. Shows the attitude of the Grange toward agricultural education in the formative years.

Burkett, C. W. *History of Ohio Agriculture.* Concord, N. H., 1900. Inadequate, brief, and sketchy.

Butler, Nicholas Murray, ed. *Monographs on Education in the United States.* Albany, N. Y., 1900. Prepared for the Paris Exposition. The best collection of studies on all phases of the American system of education.

Butler, V. M. *Education as Revealed by New England Newspapers.* (Temple University Dissertation) n. p., 1935. Includes accounts of manual labor schools.

Butts, R. F. *The College Charts Its Course, Historical Conceptions and Current Proposals.* New York, 1939.

Carlton, F. T. *Economic Influences upon Educational Progress in the United States, 1820–1850.* Bulletin of the University of Wisconsin. Madison, Wis., 1908.

Cubberley, E. P. *Public Education in the United States, a study and interpretation of American educational history.* Revised and enlarged edition. Boston, 1934.

Curoe, P. R. V. *Educational Attitudes and Policies of Organized Labor in the United States.* Teachers' College, Columbia University, *Contributions to Education,* No. 201. New York, 1926.

Curti, Merle. *The Social Ideas of American Educators. Report of Commission on the Social Studies.* New York, 1935.

Dabney, C. W. *Universal Education in the South.* Chapel Hill, 1936. Understanding survey by a veteran scientist and administrator.

Dana, E. S., and others. *A Century of Science in America with special reference to the American Journal of Science, 1818–1918.* New Haven, 1918.

Davenport, Eugene. "History of Collegiate Education in Agriculture," *Proceedings of the Society for the Promotion of Agricultural Science,* 1907. pp. 43–53. Lansing, Michigan, 1907.

Davis, J. W. *Land-Grant Colleges for Negroes.* (West Virginia State College Bulletin.) Institute, W. Va., 1934.

Demaree, A. L. *The American Agricultural Press, 1819–1860.* Columbia University *Studies in the History of American Agriculture,* No. 8. New York, 1941. Summarizes and quotes early discussion of industrial education in agricultural papers.

Draper, A. S. *American Education.* Boston, 1909.

Duvall, S. M. *The Methodist Episcopal Church and Education up to 1869.*

Teachers' College, Columbia University, *Contributions to Education*, No. 284. New York, 1928.

Eckelberry, R. H. "An Early Proposal for a State Polytechnic School," *Ohio Archaeological and Historical Quarterly*, XXXIX (1930), 400–410.

Engineering News and American Railway Journal. "The Engineering Schools of the United States." 41 articles in vols. XXVII–XXIX (March 19, 1892—Feb. 9, 1893). A very helpful compilation though the editors called attention to inaccuracies and inconsistencies in the current statistical reports.

Epler, Stephen. *Six-Man Football*. New York, 1938. Includes a concise history of the evolution of college football.

Foerster, Norman. *The American State University and its Relation to Democracy*. Chapel Hill, 1937. A humanistic interpretation.

Fox, D. R. "Rise of Scientific Interests in New York," in A. C. Flick, *History of the State of N. Y.*, IX, 95–123. New York, 1937.

Fuess, C. M. *Creed of a Schoolmaster*. Boston, 1939. "The Development of the New England Academy," 81–115.

Gates, P. W. "Western Opposition to the Agricultural College Act," *Indiana Magazine of History*, XXXVII (1941), 103–136. Deals mainly with the land interests and motives involved—based upon extended and careful research.

Goode, G. B. "The Origin of the National Scientific and Educational Institutions of the United States," *Papers of the American Historical Association*, IV. New York, 1890.

———. ed. *The Smithsonian Institution, 1846–1896—the History of Its First Half Century*. Washington, 1897.

Goodsell, Willystine. *The Education of Women, Its Social Background and Its Problems*. New York, 1923.

Greathouse, C. H. *Historical Sketch of the U. S. Department of Agriculture*. Washington, 1898.

Hansen, A. O. *Liberalism and American Education in the Eighteenth Century*. New York, 1926.

Hamilton, John. *History of Farmers' Institutes in the United States*. U. S. Department of Agriculture, Office of Experiment Stations, Bulletin No. 174. Washington, 1906.

Hedrick, U. P. *A History of Agriculture in the State of New York*. New York State Agricultural Society, 1933.

Helderman, L. C. *George Washington, Patron of Learning*. New York, 1932.

Hicks, J. D. *The Populist Revolt*. Minneapolis, Minn., 1931.

Hill, D. S. *Control of Tax-Supported Higher Education in the United States*. Carnegie Foundation for the Advancement of Teaching. New York, 1934.

Holmes, D. O. W. *The Evolution of the Negro College*. Teachers' College, Columbia University, *Contributions to Education*, No. 609. New York, 1934.

Honeywell, R. J. *The Educational Work of Thomas Jefferson. Harvard Studies in Education,* XVI. Cambridge, 1931.

Hunt, R. L. *A History of Farmer Movements in the Southwest, 1873–1925.* n. p., n. d.

Jernegan, M. W. *Laboring and Dependent Classes in Colonial America, 1607–1783.* Chicago, 1931.

Johnson, P. O. *Aspects of Land Grant College Education, with Special Reference to the University of Minnesota.* Minneapolis, 1934.

Johnson, Sveinbjorn. "Military Training in the Land Grant Colleges; Is It Optional or Mandatory?" *Illinois Law Review,* XXIV (1929), 271–98.

Jameson, J. F. *The American Revolution Considered as a Social Movement.* Princeton, 1926.

Johnson, T. C. *Scientific Interests in the Old South.* University of Virginia Institute for Research in the Social Sciences. New York, 1936.

Kandel, I. L. *Federal Aid for Vocational Education.* Carnegie Foundation Bulletin No. 10. New York, 1917. Critical and competent appraisal.

Keith, J. A. H., and Bagley, W. C. *The Nation and the Schools, a Study in the Application of the Principle of Federal Aid to Education in the United States.* New York, 1920. A brief for nationalizing education, with an historical summary.

Kilpatrick, W. H. *The Teacher and Society.* First Yearbook of the John Dewey Society. New York, 1937.

Knight, E. W. *Education in the United States.* Boston, 1934.

——— *What College Presidents Say.* Chapel Hill, 1940. A convenient classified collection of extracts from presidential addresses, 1842–1940.

Knight, G. W. "History and Management of Land Grants for Education in the Northwest Territory," *Papers of the American Historical Association,* I. New York, 1885.

Latta, W. C. *Outline History of Indiana Agriculture.* [Lafayette, Ind.], 1938. Provides a few stray facts.

Leonard, F. E. *Pioneers of Modern Physical Training.* New York, 1922.

Macdonald, A. F. *Federal Aid, a Study of the American Subsidy System.* New York, 1928.

Mann, C. R. *A Study of Engineering Education.* Carnegie Foundation for the Advancement of Teaching, Bulletin No. 11. New York, 1918.

Matzen, J. M. *State Constitutional Provisions for Education.* Teachers' College, Columbia University, *Contributions to Education* No. 462. New York, 1931.

Monroe, Paul. "Historic Foundations of American Education," in *Essays in Comparative Education,* II. New York, 1932. Thoughtful and suggestive.

Mort, P. R. *Federal Support for Public Education.* New York, 1936.

Mumford, F. B. *The Land Grant College Movement.* Missouri Agricultural Experiment Station Bulletin 419. Columbia, 1940. The former animal husbandryman and dean undertakes, in brief compass, to set forth "the underlying philosophy of the colleges of agriculture and their influence upon the social, intellectual, and economic life of rural people and the public generally."

Nash, W. L. *A Study of the Stated Aims and Purposes of the Departments of Military Science and Tactics and Physical Education in the Land-Grant Colleges of the United States.* Teachers' College, Columbia University, *Contributions to Education,* No. 614. New York, 1934.

Neely, W. C. *The Agricultural Fair.* New York, 1935. Sociological in emphasis and interpretation.

Orton, Edward, Jr. *The Land-Grant Colleges and Their Part in the National Defense*—a paper read before the Association of American Agricultural Colleges and Experiment Stations, 30th meeting, November 19, 1916, Washington, D. C. Burlington, 1917.

Patten, C. H., and Field, W. T. *Eight O'clock Chapel, a Study of New England College Life in the Eighties.* Boston, 1927.

Peck, J. S. *The Functions of the Laboratory in Engineering Education.* New York, 1936.

Price, R. R. *The Financial Support of State Universities, a Study of the Financial Resources of State Universities in the Light of the Experience of the Universities of the Old Northwest Territory, With a Suggested Policy for the Future. Harvard Studies in Education,* VI. Cambridge, 1924.

Reisner, E. H. *Nationalism and Education since 1789, a Social and Political History of Modern Education.* New York, 1922.

Ross, E. D. "The Evolution of the Agricultural Fair in the Northwest," *Iowa Journal of History and Politics,* XXIV (1926), 445–80.

——— "Lincoln and Agriculture," *Agricultural History,* III (1929), 51–66.

——— "Northern Sectionalism in the Civil War Era," *Iowa Journal of History and Politics,* XXX (1932), 455–512.

——— "The Manual Labor Experiment in the Land-Grant College," *Mississippi Valley Historical Review,* XXI (1935), 513–28.

——— "The Civil War Agricultural New Deal," *Social Forces,* XV (1936), 97–104.

——— "The 'Father' of the Land-Grant College," *Agricultural History,* XII (1938), 151–86.

——— "The Land-Grant College: a Democratic Adaptation," *ibid.,* XV (1941), 26–36.

Ryan, W. C. *Studies in Early Graduate Education.* Carnegie Foundation Bulletin, No. 30. New York, 1939.

Schafer, Joseph. *A History of Agriculture in Wisconsin.* Madison, Wis., 1922. Excellent for formative influences and leaders.

——— *The Social History of American Agriculture.* New York, 1936.

Schmidt, G. P. *The Old Time College President.* Columbia University *Studies.* New York, 1930.

Shafer, H. B. *The American Medical Profession, 1783–1850.* Columbia University *Studies.* New York, 1936.

Sharman, J. R. *Introduction to Physical Education.* New York, 1934.

Sheldon, A. E. *Land Systems and Land Policies in Nebraska. Publications of the Nebraska State Historical Society,* XXII. Lincoln, Nebraska, 1936.

Sheldon, H. D. *Student Life and Customs.* New York, 1901.

Shepardson, W. H. *Agricultural Education in the United States.* New York, 1929. A report for the General Education Board. Lacks appreciation of problems and achievements of the formative period.

Slosson, E. E. *The American Spirit in Education, a Chronicle of Great Teachers. Chronicles of America Series,* XXXIII. New Haven, 1921.

Smith, C. B., and Wilson, M. C. *The Agricultural Extension System of the United States.* New York, 1930.

Snow, L. F. *The College Curriculum in the United States.* Teachers' College, Columbia University, *Contributions to Education,* No. 10. New York, 1907.

Steinel, A. T., and Working, D. W. *History of Agriculture in Colorado.* Fort Collins, 1926.

Taylor, H. C. *The Educational Significance of the Early Federal Land Ordinances.* Teachers' College, Columbia University, *Contributions to Education,* No. 118. New York, 1922.

Taylor, J. M. *Before Vassar Opened, a Contribution to the History of the Higher Education of Women in America.* Boston, 1914.

Tewksbury, D. G. *The Founding of American Colleges and Universities Before the Civil War, with Particular Reference to the Religious Influences Bearing Upon the College Movement.* Teachers' College, Columbia University, *Contributions to Education,* No. 543. New York, 1932.

Thwing, C. F. *A History of Higher Education in America.* New York, 1906.

——— *The American and the German University, One Hundred Years of History.* New York, 1928. Suggestive for the beginnings of scientific research.

Tilden, Arnold. *The Legislation of the Civil War Period Considered as a Basis of the Agricultural Revolution in the United States.* The University of Southern California, *Social Science Series,* No. 18. Los Angeles, 1937.

Treat, P. J. *The National Land System, 1785–1820.* New York, 1910.

True, A. C. *A History of Agricultural Extension Work in the United States, 1785–1923.* U. S. Department of Agriculture, *Miscellaneous Publication,* No. 15. Washington, 1928.

——— *A History of Agricultural Education in the United States, 1785–1925.* United States Department of Agriculture, *Miscellaneous Publication,* No. 36. Washington, 1929.

——— *A History of Agricultural Experimentation and Research in the United States 1607–1925, Including a History of the United States Department of Agriculture.* United States Department of Agriculture, *Miscellaneous*

Publication, No. 251. Washington, 1937. Dr. True's long service with the U. S. Department of Agriculture and his close contact with state agricultural colleges and experiment stations make his writings in part original sources.

Tucker, G. M. *American Agricultural Periodicals.* Albany, 1909. Inadequate and in places inaccurate.

Turner, F. H. "Misconceptions Concerning the Early History of the University of Illinois," Illinois State Historical Society, *Transactions*, 1932. Illinois State Historical Library, Pub., No. 39. Makes some needed corrections and some that hardly need making.

Weiss, H. B. *The Pioneer Century of American Entomology.* New Brunswick, New Jersey, 1936.

Wesley, E. B. *Proposed: The University of the United States.* Minneapolis, Minnesota, 1936.

Wills, E. V. *The Growth of American Higher Education, Liberal, Professional and Technical.* Philadelphia, 1936.

Woodward, C. R. *The Development of Agriculture in New Jersey 1640–1880, a Monograph Study in Agricultural History.* New Brunswick, New Jersey, 1927. One of the most critical and informing of state agricultural histories.

Woody, Thomas. *A History of Women's Education in the United States.* New York, 1929.

NOTE OF ACKNOWLEDGMENTS

The preparation of this study has been facilitated by the courteous aid of the staffs of the libraries at which the research was mainly carried on: the Iowa State College, the Iowa State Department of History and Archives, Cornell University, the United States Department of Agriculture, and the Library of Congress. The manuscript, at various stages, has been read carefully and critically by Mr. Everett E. Edwards, editor of *Agricultural History,* and by the writer's colleagues, Professors Louis B. Schmidt, John A. Vieg, and Charles H. Norby. Professor Charles E. Rogers, chairman of the Board of the Iowa State College Press, and Professor Joseph C. Gilman, editor of the *Iowa State College Journal of Science,* have made helpful suggestions on the form of presentation. A grant from the *Journal* made possible the publication at this time.

INDEX